REYNOLDS

W9-AGC-455

Emerging Literacy:
Young Children Learn to Read and Write

Dorothy S. Strickland
Teachers College
Columbia University

Lesley Mandel Morrow
Rutgers University

Editors

 International Reading Association
Newark, Delaware

INTERNATIONAL READING ASSOCIATION

OFFICERS
1988-1989

President Patricia S. Koppman, PSK Associates, San Diego, California

Vice President Dale D. Johnson, Instructional Research and Development Institute, Brookline, Massachusetts

Vice President Elect Carl Braun, University of Calgary, Calgary, Alberta, Canada

Executive Director Ronald W. Mitchell, International Reading Association, Newark, Delaware

DIRECTORS

Term Expiring Spring 1989

Marie C. DiBiasio, Rhode Island Department of Education, Providence, Rhode Island

Hans U. Grundin, Language and Literacy Consultant, London, England

Nancy W. Seminoff, Central Connecticut State University, New Britain, Connecticut

Term Expiring Spring 1990

Jerome C. Harste, Indiana University, Bloomington, Indiana

Jane M. Hornburger, Brooklyn College, CUNY, Brooklyn, New York

Merrillyn Brooks Kloefkorn, Jefferson County Public Schools, Golden, Colorado

Term Expiring Spring 1991

Vincent Greaney, St. Patrick's College, Dublin, Ireland

Dolores B. Malcolm, St. Louis Public Schools, St. Louis, Missouri

Ann McCallum, Fairfax County Public Schools, Annandale, Virginia

Copyright 1989 by the
International Reading Association, Inc.

Library of Congress Cataloging in Publication Data

Emerging literacy: young children learn to read and write / Dorothy S. Strickland,
Lesley Mandel Morrow, editors.

   p.   cm.
   Includes bibliographies.
   1. Reading (Preschool) 2. Reading (Kindergarten)
I. Strickland, Dorothy S. II. Morrow, Lesley Mandel.
LB1140.5.R4E44 1989   89-2034
372.4-dc19   CIP
ISBN 0-87207-351-3

CONTENTS

Graphic design by Larry Husfelt

Cover photograph by Mary Loewenstein-Anderson
Photo credits: Carole Alborn page 18; Mary Loewenstein-Anderson pages 6, 8;
    Linda Lungren pages 81, 82, 83, 84, 85, 86, 87, 88; Lesley Mandel Morrow
    pages 126, 153; Nancy Roser pages 89, 90, 92, 93, 94; Denny Taylor page 29.

It is not unusual for the parents of a child about to enter school to wonder, "Is my child ready for the experiences of school? Will my child be able to engage with the program? Have I done all I can to prepare my child for what is ahead?" In the past, educators thought about these issues, too, because their thinking was guided by a concept of readiness. Readiness for school and readiness for reading or writing implied that there was some point in development when it was time to begin to learn to read. Some children were ready for a particular series of lessons in a school program and some were not. For those who were not ready, we used to think it was necessary to spend time on other kinds of activities until the ripening of readiness occurred.

Since the 1960s, there has been a gradual discrediting of this view, and children have been the main agents of the change. Among those parents, teachers, and researchers who began to observe and report the literacy activities of preschool children were the authors of this book. They found that children listened to stories, discussed them, and even made up stories of their own. Children scribbled "letters" to family members, wrote their names time and time again, and invented print-like signs. Some children invented ways of writing their own speech before anyone had thought about teaching them to write, and as a result they could "read" it back. Other children taught themselves to read before they came to school, often helped by young siblings who were themselves novice readers. Once we began to look at what little children were doing

in literate homes and societies, we found that literacy was an emerging set of knowledge and skills having its beginnings in very young children who accumulated a little here and a little there as they moved about their preschool settings.

I was surprised when I tried to record what five year old school entrants did in their first year at school. I found that they came to school with literacy knowledge but that it varied greatly from child to child. One child knew a great deal about books; another had explored writing. One was proud of being able to recognize all the family names; another could write most of the letters of the alphabet. Some had clusters of skills, and some had no experience in some of these areas. It was rare to find a child who did not have some literacy knowledge on entry to school.

Such observations led to a different picture of progress in literacy learning. Children were not reaching a point in time when they suddenly took aboard reading and writing; each child was slowly and gradually adding on to what he or she brought to school. What they could already do was the springboard from which they dived into the schools' instruction. Emerging literacy kept emerging.

Gathered in this book are the ideas of educators and researchers who have been able to capture examples of the ways in which literacy knowledge changes from infancy through the preschool years and in the early years of school. Each author provides ideas that can be used in day care centres and classrooms to encourage and support emerging literacy. Each has a somewhat different message about how children change or how they think about literacy activities.

These new views on literacy are helpful both to parents and teachers. While sharing the excitement of watching children puzzle over the peculiarities of the codes we use for reading and writing, an observant adult becomes aware that little children can do wonderful things with codes. They work out how to use the complexities of the language they speak, and they apply equal ingenuity to their work with print. Observant adults begin to interact with children at their growing points. Then the continuing shifts made by children are met by adults who are more supportive and contribute to the changes in skill.

There is a more critical message for teachers who read this book. If they watch the children in their classes, and if they understand the newer viewpoints on the ways in which emerging literacy shows itself in early childhood, they ought to feel somewhat uneasy with some instructional programs. Teachers will realise that in many classrooms the concept of readiness has not disappeared and that some children are kept waiting for a sudden transformation that does not occur. The ideas about different ways to approach and support emerging literacy should encourage teachers to discuss the things that children can do for which there previously has been no room in their programs. So, "Emerging Literacy," which has a way of changing children, also could start a process of change in teachers and schools.

Marie Clay
University of Auckland
New Zealand

INTRODUCTION

As we looked back on this book's beginnings, we realized that the idea had been lingering inside each of us for a very long time—long before we ever talked about it with anyone or shared it with one another. Over the years, we worked with the contributors on a variety of projects related to early literacy, many sponsored by the International Reading Association. They included convention institutes, symposia, and a policy statement on early literacy development (see appendix). In our work, we shared ideas and learned from one another.

There has been much to learn. Interest in young children's reading and writing has received a large measure of attention in recent years. Contemporary researchers have broken new ground to create new paradigms for the way we view children's literacy development and the way we help them learn. Old notions that separate prereading and prewriting from formal instruction have given way to theories that do not demarcate development, but view it as one long continuum of growth. Learning literacy is now seen as a continuous process, which begins in infancy with exposure to oral language, written language, books, and stories. It is a process that has its roots in the home, with branches extending to other environments.

Beyond the home, the school is the major environment for learning to communicate. With a growing number of children attending school at earlier and earlier ages, it seemed critical to us to get this information to the caregivers and teachers who work closely with children every day. Our goal was to provide a book that would be scholarly in its content and grounded in the research. At the same time, it must be practical and usable in a variety of early childhood settings.

The contributors to this volume are well known for their work in children's literacy development. They have written and talked about their work in scholarly journals and research forums throughout the United States and beyond. In this book, we have asked them to share their ideas in a manner that makes the ideas accessible and usable for day care workers, classroom teachers, and curriculum specialists. We focused on theory and practice appropriate for children ages two through eight years and on classrooms ranging from those found in day care and other prekindergarten settings through grade two.

We realized that, although practitioners are vitally interested in keeping current with new research and practice, they rarely have the time or the resources to conduct the literature search required to gather significant material in one place. Attendance at national conferences and institutes may not always be possible, yet the need to keep up is always present. We wanted to appeal to both the practical and the scholarly sides of practitioners. It is our hope that many practitioners will find this material exciting and will use it as a springboard to their own personal exploration into the supporting research. Thus, the book fulfills a dual purpose: It acts as a resource to the research and theoretical perspectives, and it serves as a guide to improve classroom practice.

William Teale and Elizabeth Sulzby open the book with an overview of current understandings of how young children learn about reading and writing and the implications of an emergent literacy paradigm. This is followed by Susan Glazer's discussion of the relationship between oral language and literacy development. The next three chapters center on shared book experiences. Dorothy Strickland and Denny Taylor describe the nature and value of shared book experiences in the home, Bernice Cullinan helps teachers connect literature to young children's language and literacy development in the classroom, and Jana Mason, Carol Peterman, and Bonnie Kerr provide specific techniques for making storybook reading more interactive. Next, Elizabeth Sulzby, William Teale, and George Kamberelis share guidelines and suggestions for parents and teachers who wish to encourage young children to write. A photo essay by Nancy Roser, James Flood, and Diane Lapp illustrates many of the ideas set forth in the book.

More on the development of print awareness and concepts about print is explored by Judith Schickedanz, who extends the discussion to how children learn skills as they are involved in meaningful real life experiences using charts, signs, and symbols. Edward Chittenden and Rosalea Courtney present some innovative solutions to the complex and controversial topic of assessment. They describe the use of frequent documentation of children's progress as an alternative to testing.

Recognizing the school literacy environment as key to a successful program, Lesley Morrow shares ideas on preparing the physical design of the classroom. Dorothy Strickland draws on the content of all the previous chapters to provide a curriculum framework that may be modified to suit the developmental levels of children and the various educational settings of early childhood. The final chapter, by Jerome Harste and Virginia Woodward, pulls together our continuing theme of research to practice by focusing on the various groups that must be tapped in order to create positive change in early childhood literacy programs. This chapter stresses the need for new policy directions and the role of the teacher as an agent for change.

It is important to note that many of the understandings presented here were central to Progressive Education in the early part of this century and have been of core importance in early childhood education theory and expert practice from the 1920s to the present. Early childhood educators have long operated on the premise that children's language and literacy development is interwoven and continuous from infancy onward. They emphasize the fact that language, literacy, and love of literature are largely learned at home, and that parents and schools should work closely together in these, as in other areas. It is very exciting that researchers in various disciplines have recently confirmed the integrated "birth on" approach long intuitively known by many fine educators.

The year 1989 is the "Year of the Young Reader." It is our hope that this yearlong celebration will stimulate a decade of special attention to the youngest readers and writers among us. With this book, we celebrate young children and all those who nurture them.

DSS
LMM

CONTRIBUTORS

Edward Chittenden
Educational Testing Service
Princeton, New Jersey

Rosalea Courtney
Educational Testing Service
Princeton, New Jersey

Bernice E. Cullinan
New York University
New York, New York

James Flood
San Diego State University
San Diego, California

Susan Mandel Glazer
Rider College
Lawrenceville, New Jersey

Jerome C. Harste
Indiana University
Bloomington, Indiana

George Kamberelis
University of Michigan
Ann Arbor, Michigan

Bonnie M. Kerr
University of Illinois
Champaign, Illinois

Diane Lapp
San Diego State University
San Diego, California

Jana M. Mason
University of Illinois
Champaign, Illinois

Lesley Mandel Morrow
Rutgers University
New Brunswick, New Jersey

Carol L. Peterman
Portland State University
Portland, Oregon

Nancy L. Roser
University of Texas
Austin, Texas

Judith A. Schickedanz
Boston University
Boston, Massachusetts

Dorothy S. Strickland
Teachers College
Columbia University
New York, New York

Elizabeth Sulzby
University of Michigan
Ann Arbor, Michigan

Denny Taylor
Teachers College
Columbia University
New York, New York

William H. Teale
University of Texas
San Antonio, Texas

Virginia A. Woodward
Indiana University
Bloomington, Indiana

IRA DIRECTOR OF PUBLICATIONS   Jennifer A. Stevenson

IRA PUBLICATIONS COMMITTEE 1988-1989   John J. Pikulski, University of Delaware, *Chair* • Phyllis E. Brazee, University of Maine at Orono • Kent L. Brown Jr., *Highlights for Children* • Margaret K. Jensen, Madison Metropolitan School District, Madison, Wisconsin • Carole S. Johnson, Washington State University • Charles K. Kinzer, Vanderbilt University • Gloria M. McDonell, Fairfax County Schools, Fairfax, Virginia • Ronald W. Mitchell, IRA • Allan R. Neilsen, Mount St. Vincent University • Tom Nicholson, University of Waikato, New Zealand • Donna Ogle, National College of Education • Jennifer A. Stevenson, IRA • Anne C. Tarleton, Albuquerque Public Schools, Albuquerque, New Mexico

The International Reading Association attempts, through its publications, to provide a forum for a wide spectrum of opinions on reading. This policy permits divergent viewpoints without assuming the endorsement of the Association.

CHAPTER ONE

Emergent Literacy: New Perspectives

William H. Teale

Elizabeth Sulzby

In this chapter, we examine the concept of emergent literacy for the new insights it provides on young children's literacy learning. We focus on what young children do with literacy, what they know about reading and writing, and how they develop literacy knowledge and literate practices. We conclude by considering what an emergent literacy perspective implies for how young children should be taught in day care, preschool, or school classrooms.

In December, when he was five, Esteban presented to his parents the piece of paper shown below. He had, he told them, listed what he wanted for Christmas. As further insurance that nothing would go wrong in obtaining his presents, Esteban also numbered the items on the list and indicated who was responsible for getting what, first by writing "Mommy" or "Daddy" beside each item and also by drawing pictures of Mom and Dad atop the two columns of toys. This child was leaving nothing to chance.

From the time Jennifer was a year old, she was read to regularly by her mother. At three years, three months of age, Jennifer was visited by a researcher (R), who asked her to read *Are You My Mother?* (Eastman, 1967), a book that had been read to her many times. In an enthusiastic manner and with a reading intonation, she read the entire book, a portion of which follows:

Jennifer	Text
Out pop the baby birdie.	Out came the baby bird.
He says, "Where is my mother?" (aside to R) He's looking for it.	"Where is my mother?" he said. He looked for her.
Looked up; did not see her.	He looked up. He did not see her.
And he looked down; he didn't see it.	He looked down. He did not see her.
So he said he's gonna go look for her.	"I will go and look for her," he said.
- -	- -
Came to a kitten and he said, "Are you my mother?"	He came to a kitten. "Are you my mother?" he said to the kitten.
'N...and he didn't say anything. He just looked and looked.	The kitten just looked and looked. It did not say a thing.
Then he came to a hen and he said, "Are you my mother?" "No."	The kitten was not his mother, so he went on. Then he came to a hen. "Are you my mother?" he said to the hen. "No," said the hen.

From Aaron, age fourteen months, we have data of a different sort. Aaron's mother made audio tape recordings of his vocalizations in a variety of activities. The tape recordings contain babbling, not words or sentences. But even in Aaron's babbling, one hears distinctive differences in intonation patterns between occasions when he is turning the pages of a book and those when there is no book present.

During the past decade or so, an intense interest has arisen in the early literacy behaviors of typical children like Esteban, Jennifer, and Aaron. When we observe children who have grown up with reading and writing around them, we see that they know about literacy and exhibit literate behaviors. Results of many studies of children from birth to six years of age have caused teachers and researchers to change some of their ideas about young children's reading and writing development from what was commonly believed as recently as

the 1970s. A new perspective on early reading and writing has developed; it has come to be known as *emergent literacy*. In this chapter, we examine the concept of emergent literacy for the new insights it provides on young children's literacy learning. We explore what young children do with literacy, what they know about reading and writing, and how they develop literacy knowledge and literate practices. We conclude the chapter by considering what an emergent literacy perspective implies for how young children should be taught in day care, preschool, or school classrooms.

Emergent Literacy Overview

Emergent literacy is a concept that has become prominent only recently, even though there is a long history of research in young children's reading and writing. Some of the research from past decades has contributed to an emergent literacy perspective. For example, studies of early readers (Clark, 1976; Durkin, 1966), research documenting the importance of storybook reading in early childhood literacy development (Fodor, 1966; Irwin, 1960; Templin, 1957), and pioneer work by individuals like Legrün (1932) and Clay (1967) all support an emergent literacy perspective.

It is primarily studies of the past few years, however, that have shaped the current outlook. During this period, researchers have approached their work differently. For one thing, the age range of the children studied has been extended to include children fourteen months of age and younger. Researchers also have begun to study literacy development in a fuller sense. Literacy is not regarded as simply a cognitive skill to be learned, but as a complex sociopsycholinguistic activity. Thus, the social aspects of literacy have become significant, and literacy learning is investigated not just in the researcher's laboratory, but also in home and community settings.

Perhaps the most important factor is that literacy learning has been studied in fresh ways. A concerted effort has been made to examine literacy development from the child's perspective. Researchers are now attempting to understand what is going on in the child's head and in the child's world.

We have come to see that logical analyses of the task of literacy learning, such as conclusions about the literacy behaviors of young children based on adult perspectives, are not very useful in accounting for early childhood reading and writing development. Instead, studies that seek to understand literacy learning from the child's point of view have provided much more insight into the process. These studies have observed children engaged in literacy activities and interpreted what was seen from multidisciplinary perspectives grounded in cognitive psychology, anthropology, child development, and social interaction theory. As a result of employing these perspectives, we understand early childhood literacy learning in new ways. This understanding enables us to sketch a portrait of young children as literacy learners.

Portrait of Young Children as Literacy Learners

The first thing to recognize is that, for almost all children in a literate society, learning to read and write begins very early in life. Even during the first few months of life, children come in contact with written language as parents place soft alphabet blocks in their environments or read them books. These early contacts with print can be thought of as the beginning of a lifelong process of learning to read and write. By the time they are two or three, many children can identify signs, labels, and logos they see in their homes and communities (Goodman, 1986; Hiebert, 1981; Kastler, Roser, & Hoffman, 1987). Many children are fortunate enough to be read to regularly and therefore experience books and the sights and sounds of written language from an early age.

Young children also experiment with writing. Even their scribbles display characteristics of the writing system of their culture, and therefore the writings of four year olds from Saudi Arabia, Egypt, Israel, and America will look different long before the children can write conventionally (Harste & Carey, 1979). Examples like these, as well as the behaviors of Esteban, Jennifer, and Aaron (discussed earlier), clearly show that the process of learning to read and write is under way.

The more closely one looks, the more difficult it is to pinpoint a time when literacy learning begins. Certainly, it starts long before the child enters kindergarten or prekindergarten. Many would argue that even children as young as one year are processors and users of written language. The understandings and the behaviors may differ significantly from those of older children or adults. Nonetheless, young children have already begun learning to read and write.

A second characteristic of the portrait is that the functions of literacy are an integral part of the learning process that is taking place. Literacy develops from real life settings in which reading and writing are used to accomplish goals. Observational studies have shown that the vast majority of literacy experienced by young children is embedded in activities directed toward some goal beyond the literacy itself (Heath, 1983; Taylor, 1983; Taylor & Dorsey-Gaines, 1988; Teale, 1986). For example, children may see adults reading newspapers or greeting cards, writing checks, completing crossword puzzles, or using the *TV Guide*. They may find that a recipe is an integral part of helping a parent bake cookies or that written directions are used in putting a toy together. Books may be intimately involved in the religious activities of the family.

In these and other ways, young children are ushered into the world of literacy viewing reading and writing as aspects of a much larger system for accomplishing goals. The orientation to literacy as a goal directed activity is an important part of the portrait to remember because it shows that the foundation for children's growth in reading and writing rests upon viewing literacy as functional rather than as a set of abstract, isolated skills to be learned.

The third dimension of great importance in our portrait is that reading and writing develop concurrently and interrelatedly in young children. Since children do not first learn to read and then learn to write, we need to speak of literacy development, not of reading readiness or of prereading. Figure 1 attempts to depict how oral language, reading, and writing relate in young children's literacy learning.

Figure 1

Certainly, children's oral language proficiency is related to their growth in reading and to the ways in which they write. Educators have long seen that a strong oral language base facilitates literacy learning. Furthermore, it is clear that children's developing reading abilities influence their writing. However, we also must recognize that reading experiences influence oral language (e.g., reading books to children enhances vocabulary), and writing actually improves children's reading skills (e.g., allowing kindergartners to write builds decoding skills). For young children, the language arts mutually reinforce one another in development.

The fourth major characteristic of young children as literacy learners is that they learn through active engagement, constructing their understanding of how written language works. Young children's emergent readings of favorite storybooks (Sulzby, 1985), for example, are not mere memorizations of books. Notice from Jennifer's reading of *Are You My Mother?* that she reconstructs the meaning of the book even though her words often deviate from the actual text.

Young children's spellings also exhibit the attempt to construct knowledge. Five year old Kayla's use of LAEYMABCODLPK to write "I like rainbows because they have so many colors" appears to be random until we add that observations of Kayla writing revealed that she used one letter to represent each syllable of the message she was encoding. The sounds conventionally associated with each of the letters bore little resemblance to the sounds of the words being written, but, nevertheless, there was a system to Kayla's writing. In other words, her emergent literacy behaviors were conceptual. The behaviors were wrong by adult standards, showing that the process of becoming literate is developmental, but Kayla was not behaving randomly. Numerous studies of invented spellings (e.g., L or LIK for like; J or JUP for jump; HRP for chirp) also provide substantial evidence of the conceptual basis of emergent writing behaviors (Henderson & Beers, 1981; Read, 1971).

Thus, the portrait shows that in a positive literacy learning environment young children grow up experiencing reading and writing in many facets of their everyday lives, primarily as purposeful, goal directed activities. As children encounter written language, they try to figure out how it works. In so doing, they form and test hypotheses, attempting to discern the differences between drawing and writing; to understand the meanings, structures, and cadences of written language; to learn the symbols of writing; and to sort out the relationships between these symbols and the sounds of oral language. The knowledge and procedures young children develop for solving the literacy puzzle often are different from adult conventions and strategies, but they are logical and understandable, once we take the children's perspectives. Furthermore, their understandings and strategies change over time, showing that literacy learning is a developmental process.

This depiction of young children as active learners, as constructors of understandings about written language, is central to the concept of emergent literacy. But the new perspectives on early childhood reading and writing development also have shown the key role parents and other literate persons play in facilitating early literacy learning. One way adults help is by demonstrating literacy. For example, as they write a shopping list, use a bus schedule, write a letter, help a school child with homework, or read the newspaper, parents demonstrate the act of literacy. From these and other demonstrations, children can discern the purposes and some of the actions involved in reading and writing. **Even more important than the demonstra-**

tions of literacy are the times parents and children interact around print. In these interactions, children can learn a lot because parents work with them to jointly achieve the goal of the activity. Through language and actions, parents make obvious to children what is involved in the activity because they want the children to participate.

In the example of the shopping list, the construction phase comes first. Sharita, age four years, three months, and her parents are sitting at the kitchen table. Father reminds the family that tomorrow is grocery shopping day, and together they begin to construct the shopping list. Mother and Father discuss the meals for the next week and then determine the necessary ingredients. As they note the needed items, they check the refrigerator and cupboards, and items not on hand are added to the list. Both parents talk to Sharita about the construction of the list, and Father, who is actually writing the list, consciously externalizes the process by saying things like, "Okay, parsley. Let's write that here. Parsley starts with a *p*—parsley" as Sharita sits beside him and watches. After the list is constructed, Sharita accompanies her father to the store for the shopping phase. The list is an integral part of shopping, and again the adult makes using the list a joint activity.

It is not surprising that children's independent uses of print grow out of such adult-child interactions. Sharita has written her own lists while playing by herself, and seven months after the above episode, she wrote a list using scribble at the same time her parents were constructing one. A similar phenomenon is common among children who are read to regularly. Interactive storybook readings between adults and children have powerful effects on the children's literacy development (Teale, 1987) and lead to independent reenactments of books like the one by Jennifer described earlier (Sulzby & Teale, 1987). Thus, adult scaffolding (Bruner, 1983; Cazden, 1983) of the activity is an important means of promoting literacy learning in young children (Teale, 1982, 1986) and of establishing independent reading and writing habits.

In summary, young children's literacy learning grows out of a wide variety of experiences. Children construct their knowledge about print and their strategies for reading and writing from their independent explorations of written language, from interactions with parents and other literate persons, and from their observations of others engaged in literacy activities.

Literacy Instruction for Young Children

Such a perspective on young children's literacy learning carries with it significant implications for teaching reading and writing in the early childhood classroom. We begin by identifying basic principles that should guide instruction, then identify an approach to literacy learning activities suggested by classroom based investigations.

Basic Principles

An understanding of young children as literacy learners is crucial to decisions about curriculum in school settings. When we see that legitimate literacy learning occurs during the early years, we realize that the question of when to begin reading and writing instruction is absurd. We should be teaching reading and writing to all children in day care facilities, in child development centers, in Head Start programs, in preschools, in prekindergarten programs, and in kindergartens.

But as we examine the implications just presented of the portrait of young children as literacy learners, we also should realize that the ways in which we teach reading and writing in early childhood programs must be developmentally appropriate. We cannot merely shove the first grade program down a notch or two into the kindergarten or prekindergarten and expect it to work. Traditional, formal reading instruction typical of first grade is simply inappropriate for young children. So is the worksheet dominated reading curriculum (which pays major attention to letter naming and letter sound matching) that Durkin (1987) found to be typical of the kindergarten classrooms in one state and that informal observations and reports tell us is widely practiced throughout the United States.

Priorities are out of balance and out of keeping with the nature of young children as literacy learners when kindergarten and readiness books concentrate on letter sound matching, letter

Reading is an adventure for young children.

discrimination, and letter names and give only scant attention to activities that involve children with stories (Hiebert & McWhorter, 1987). The early childhood literacy program must adopt as its foundation functional, meaningful activities that involve reading and writing in a wide variety of ways. A priority for the early childhood curriculum should be ensuring that all children become capable and willing participants in the literate society of the classroom, home, and community. Even before children can read and write conventionally, the curriculum can foster these knowledges and attitudes. Overall skill in reading and writing grows from this kind of start.

The curriculum also must set high priority on getting children actively involved in literacy. Children of all ages need opportunities to experiment

daily with reading and writing. The classroom should provide rich demonstrations, interactions, and independent explorations. The link of literacy with experience and the active use of language must be stressed.

A final principle for the early childhood literacy curriculum is that learning should not be confused with teaching. The focus always should be on the child's learning. With zeal from administrators and state legislatures in the U.S. for direct instruction and teacher centered models of instruction, it is easy for the young child to be forgotten in the teaching process. It is especially important that the teacher understand each child's emergent literacy abilities and strategies. In this way, learning and teaching can come together. Rather than teaching reading and writing in an early childhood program, our focus should be on teaching children to read and write.

Teaching for Literacy Learning

An emergent literacy perspective on young children's reading and writing development carries with it many implications for classroom instruction. Space permits only a general description of the emergent literacy classroom. We discuss particular activities in this section, but do not wish to give the impression that the emergent literacy classroom is merely a bag of gimmicks or a series of separate activities. In reality, the focus should not be on a literacy curriculum per se. Instead, literacy should be an integral part of the overall curriculum. Seen in this perspective, the following types of activities can be especially productive for enhancing young children's reading and writing development.

Storybook reading. Getting children to interact with books should be the key way in which children experience print in the early childhood classroom. We recommend that teachers plan two dimensions for the storybook reading programs: reading aloud daily to the children and providing opportunities for children to independently "read" books by themselves (and to one another).

Testaments to the importance of reading aloud to young children abound in the professional literature; correlational (Wells, 1985) and experimental (Feitelson, Kita, & Goldstein, 1986) research support these testaments. In other words, reading aloud to young children *teaches* them about reading.

A discussion of storybook reading raises questions such as when, what, and how to read. We recommend reading to young children at least once a day, and more often if possible. As a valued and regular part of the curriculum, storybook reading takes on great significance to the children. Children's literature—everything from folktales and fables to contemporary pieces—should be the main reading fare.

A special effort should be made to include expository books, too. Young children can learn much about how the world works from informational books, and as research has clearly shown, background knowledge and experience with processing expository text are critical to continued success in reading (Anderson et al., 1985). Predictable books (Bridge, 1986) can be profitably used for read alouds, as several authors have described (Heald-Taylor, 1987; Rhodes, 1981; Tompkins & Webeler, 1983).

There is no one best way to read to children, but several useful strategies have been widely recommended: preview the book, establish a receptive story listening context, briefly introduce the book, and read with expression. We would add two further suggestions. First, be sure to engage the children in discussion about what is being read. Talk about the characters and their motivations and responses, make predictions and then listen to confirm or disconfirm them, draw inferences, discuss the themes of books, link information in books to real life experiences, examine the author's use of language, and draw connections among various books. It is this talk about books that gives storybook reading its powerful influence on young children's literacy development (Heath, 1982; Teale, 1987). Also, read the children's favorite books again and again, just as parents who read to their children do. Repeated readings encourage indepth exploration of books, and promote children's independent, emergent readings of those books (Sulzby & Teale, 1987).

Emergent storybook readings constitute the second dimension of classroom storybook reading. Long before they are able to read conventionally, children who have been read to will "read" books on their own (Sulzby & Teale, 1987). Called emergent storybook readings or independent reenactments of books (Sulzby, 1985), these readings seem to facilitate growth in reading because they give children opportunities to practice what they learned in interactive storybook readings, and they allow children to explore new dimensions of books and reading (Holdaway, 1979; Teale & Sulzby, 1987).

Teacher practices and even the physical set up of the classroom can promote these independent reenactments. The repeated readings by the teacher are especially important. After children have heard a book read several times, they are more likely to read it themselves. Along with systematically rereading certain books, teachers also occasionally can give children "assignments" to promote emergent storybook readings. For example, children can be asked to read a book to a partner, act out a previously read book using flannel board characters, or practice in preparation to "read" a book to the class or another group of children.

The classroom set up also can encourage children's independent reading. A key aspect is the classroom library—a collection of children's trade books that provides children with immediate access to books. There are a number of design features that encourage children's use of books in a classroom library (Morrow, 1982; Morrow & Weinstein, 1982). We encourage teachers to:

• Make the classroom library a focal area of the room, partition it, making it large enough to accommodate four or five children at a time, and provide comfortable seating.

• Use open-faced book shelves.

• Provide many types of books (stories, informational books, poetry, alphabet, counting, concept, and wordless picture books).

• Use literature oriented displays (posters, bulletin boards) and props (flannel boards, taped stories).

Teacher storybook reading practices also tie in with children's use of books in the classroom library. Books used in group storybook readings are chosen by children more often than those never read aloud by the teacher, and books read repeatedly are used even more frequently than those read only once (Martinez & Teale, 1988). In summary, group storybook reading and children's independent reading of books do reinforce one another in the classroom and promote children's literacy development.

Other opportunities to read. In addition to storybooks, environmental print, and other activities like "The Morning Message" (Crowell, Kawakami, & Wong, 1986) or "The News" offer young children valuable opportunities to read print in meaningful contexts in the classroom. Schickedanz (1986) has described how environmental print—signs, labels, charts—can be used to organize the classroom environment and also provide written language experiences. Labels and signs can indicate children's cubbies, where different classroom items belong, and directions to help the classroom run smoothly (such as how many children are allowed in a center at one time or how to operate the

Reading to young children helps them develop a love of books.

tape recorder). Charts can list various classroom jobs, the daily schedule, or attendance records. At first, the teacher will have to interpret and model the use of these printed materials, but the children will soon use them in their everyday activities.

The Morning Message and the News give children opportunities to see meaningful written language being constructed and to reread what has been written. A morning or afternoon message, written as the children watch, briefly tells significant things that will be happening in the classroom that day. For example:

Good morning. It's Tuesday, February 16. We will be going on our trash walk today. Also, we have a special book about a mystery for story time today.

Once the message is written, the children are encouraged to read along with the teacher and discuss the message or the kinds of things that people do when writing and reading messages. Crowell, Kawakami, & Wong (1986) and Kawakami-Arakaki, Oshiro, & Farran (1989) have discussed how the Morning Message is used in kindergarten classrooms. It also can work well with other age levels to provide yet another relatively informal way in which children can learn about literacy through meaningful activities.

The idea of reporting and recording news takes various forms in various classrooms. One teacher actually creates a newspaper on a large chart, writing headlines that capture the children's weekend experiences. In another classroom, the News is a time for examining what happened in the community, nation, or world (Martinez et al., in press). On Friday, the teacher invites children to predict weekend news, based either on their planned weekend activities or exciting events such as shuttle launchings, approaching hurricanes, or prominent sporting events. The predictions are written on chart paper. On Monday, a chart containing the weekend's actual news events is made and read. After six months of participation in the News, one kindergarten child even began to write her own news, using inventive spellings and collecting stories from classmates.

Through vehicles such as environmental print, the Morning Message, and the News, teachers provide a variety of opportunities for children to read significant, functional print in the classroom. In these and other ways, children can gain a wide understanding of the purposes and processes of reading.

Response to texts. A variety of response, or extension, activities can complement and enhance the effects of group storybook readings. Art and drama are two especially powerful techniques. For example, after reading *The Very Hungry Caterpillar* (Carle, 1981), children might make thumbprint caterpillars or water color paintings of the various items the caterpillar ate. Students can punch holes through the paintings (indicating that the items were eaten through), string them together, and attach a caterpillar face, ending up with a caterpillar composed of all the things he ate.

For dramatic activities, children can reenact stories with flannel board characters or puppets, or even play the roles themselves using simple props and costumes (perhaps ones that they have designed). One of the most successful response activities in one classroom was having the children dramatize *The Three Billy Goats Gruff* on the clatter bridge in the school playground. Another class made stick puppets of Mr. Gumpy, his motor car, and all the characters who accompanied him on his ride in *Mr. Gumpy's Motor Car* (Burningham, 1973). The children reenacted the book, placing the characters in the car one by one, getting everyone out to push the car out of the mud after it rains, and finally having a swim together.

Books also can be extended through activities such as cooking and even eating. There's nothing quite like making and sampling stone soup after reading Marcia Brown's (1947) version of the story. Morever, her rendition can be neatly tied into a nutrition lesson or unit because she includes all of the major food groups in the book.

Many expository books for young children like those from the Let's-Read-and-Find-Out Book™ series contain experiments illustrating concepts discussed in the books. For example, an excellent way to make *Air Is All Around You* (Branley, 1986) have an even greater impact is to invert a glass containing a napkin crumbled in the bottom and place it into a bowl of water to see what happens, just as described in the book. Another effective tactic is to have children draw and write "learning logs" about what they learned from an informational book. As part of a unit on rodeos, one kindergarten teacher read the National Geographic book *Cowboys* (Filcott, 1979). The children enthusiastically produced drawings of chaps, spurs, and other things relating to cowboys. It was apparent when they reread what they had written about their drawings (often writing in scribble or random letters) that they had learned a lot.

Writing. In this section, we focus on the composing and spelling aspects of writing development. Research cited earlier shows that these facts of writing development begin early in a child's life and that

The News

Based on years of experience in working with young children and knowing how they love to talk about themselves, I have developed a project that takes advantage of the "my" world of kindergarteners. On the first day of kindergarten, the children dictate their concepts of what will happen during the school year. This dictation is recorded on a large chart tablet and is always available for the children to view. Also, each Monday throughout the school year, the entire class dictates weekend news for the experience chart. This chart records what actually has happened in their lives: "Jonathon went to Pistol Pete's Pizza," or "Roslyn rode her bike."

Approximately one month into the school year, the class also begins to dictate news on Friday. This news may cover any relevant topic, such as a classroom project, but most often provides a prediction of what the children will be doing on the weekend.

On Monday, after the weekend news is charted, students often compare their predictions with the actual happenings. This promotes higher level thinking skills by distinguishing predictions from fact. The chart is used throughout the week, often reread in its entirety. The children also take turns identifying features of what has been written, such as the names of students in the class, the letters of the alphabet, or sight words. The children love to read the news, and throughout the year I notice them dictating news to other students. In addition, I have had children volunteer to be the news writer.

As the school year draws to a close, all the news charts are reread, beginning with the entries from the first day of school. What fun the children have as they recall events that took place during their year in kindergarten. It is interesting to note the advanced development of the news content as the children use improved communication skills.

The project has many benefits. It allows children to seek familiar words used in context. Students also take an active role in reading and writing. They learn that letters form words and that words have meaning, therefore adding to the usefulness of writing.

All this project requires is patience in listening to and charting the news. The reward is the smiles on the children's faces as they are able to recognize words and say "I can read!"

Ann Hemmeter
Kindergarten Teacher
San Antonio Independent School District
San Antonio, Texas

reading and writing develop concurrently. Furthermore, research confirms what has often been stated: Children learn to write by writing. Therefore, the early childhood curriculum should encourage children to write often and to write for a wide variety of purposes and audiences. Much has already been written about how to establish writing as part of the early childhood program (e.g., Kawakami-Arakaki, Oshiro, & Farran, 1989; Martinez & Teale, 1987; Salinger, 1988; Schickedanz, 1986; Teale & Martinez, 1989). Here are some general ways in which writing may be incorporated into the curriculum in preschool, prekindergarten, and kindergarten.

First, we recommend that a writing center be an integral part of every classroom. The writing center is a place where children can experiment with writing, collaborate with others through writing, and have an audience to whom they can read their writing and get responses. A writing center should contain a variety of writing instruments and materials: chalkboard; magnetic letters; unlined, lined, and story paper; typewriter; computer; markers; crayons; pens; and pencils. Children can visit the writing center frequently and write on topics they choose and topics assigned by the teacher that fit into the themes of the curriculum units. Of course, young children will use a variety of forms (scribbling, drawing, random letters, inventive spelling) in their writing. The writing center is the key necessary for building a community of writers in the early childhood classroom. It makes writing a visible part of the curriculum and serves as a place where children can write for a wide variety of reasons.

Martinez & Teale (1987) have described how to introduce a writing center in a kindergarten classroom, and Schickedanz (1986) provides guidelines for using writing in a preschool setting. Children will write many types of stories, ranging from personal narratives to takeoffs on familiar books or television shows to fanciful, original creations. Also, the utility of other types of writing should not be overlooked. Children may write letters, make lists, create signs, write invitations, and do many other things.

Once writing becomes established in the classroom, it will carry over into a variety of activities, such as becoming an integral part of children's dramatic play. Also children will engage in self-sponsored writing at home. After the first few weeks of school in the classroom of one kindergarten teacher who emphasized writing, the children literally lined up each morning to give the teacher (and read to her) personal notes they had written the night before.

Other ways in which the teacher can promote writing is by establishing a postal system in the classroom or organizing a pen pals program (Teale & Martinez, 1989). Also, writing can be an excellent way of responding to books (see previous section). For instance, after reading *Go and Hush the Baby* (Byars, 1973), the children could write about how they would hush the baby. A response activity to *King Bidgood's in the Bathtub* (Wood, 1985) that incorporates art, drama, and writing is to have children write what they would do if they were king and then make crowns for themselves and act out their scenarios.

Literacy and play. As a final and related topic, we highlight the importance of integrating literacy into children's play activities in the early childhood classroom. Filling children's play with reading and writing is a primary means of ensuring that literacy instruction is developmentally appropriate. We already have discussed one kind of play in talking about dramatization as a response activity. In addition to thematic fantasy play like that, sociodramatic play can be profitably incorporated into the curriculum.

Sociodramatic play involves two or more children adopting roles and acting out a situation. To promote children's knowledge of the functions and uses of literacy, real life situations can be especially useful. For example, the teacher might set up the dramatic play area of the classroom as an airport or travel agency. Included in such a setting could be a great deal of print—travel posters and brochures, a schedule board indicating destinations, times and numbers of flights, airline tickets, and magazines. Of course, writing materials would be present so that children could write phone messages, tickets, boarding passes, and itineraries, and make signs for the area.

A dramatic play area can be set up in any number of ways, depending upon the theme being stressed in the curriculum. For a nutrition unit, it could become a restaurant, bakery, or supermarket. A dinosaur museum would complement the study of dinosaurs. A fire or police station, doctor's office, or post office could be used for a unit on community helpers. Written language can be made an integral part of all these settings. The teacher provides the props and models the use of print or writing if necessary, but basically allows children to create their own scripts and scenarios. With such preparation, and with occasional praise and suggestions from the teacher, the extent to which literacy becomes a part of this sociodramatic play can be remarkable.

Conclusion

Although this chapter is designed to provide new perspectives on young children's reading and writing development, readers no doubt will recognize much familiar information. Many early childhood educators, especially those acting from a child centered, holistic perspective on learning and teaching, have proposed similar views and advocated similar practices since the late 1800s. We have learned a great deal in the past decade that supports these educators. We also have gained new understandings that help refine and extend such ideas.

There is much yet to be learned, but an emergent literacy perspective rests on a solid research foundation. It certainly challenges the current status quo in early childhood education, as revealed in studies of the way reading is typically taught in the kindergarten (Durkin, 1987; Hiebert & McWhorter, 1987). The goal now is to make this new perspective the way in which teachers and publishers think about young children's literacy development. Then we can have early childhood programs that are indeed developmentally appropriate.

I · D · E · A · S

You Can Use

Guest Story Reader

The Guest Story Reader program is one way to bring reading into the lives of those children in my kindergarten classroom who come from families in which little parent-child storybook reading is done. The guest story reader is an enjoyable supplement to our regular classroom storytime.

Early in the school year, my students and I discuss questions about reading, such as: "What is reading? Why do people read? What kinds of things do people read? What people can we think of who read?" I then tell the children that we are going to invite some different people to visit our classroom and read us stories. At first, I usually make the decisions about who we will invite, but later on the children begin suggesting guests they would like to have. Together we write the invitation and, if possible, a couple of the students deliver it themselves. We often receive an immediate written or in-person acceptance message, which is nice because it provides the students with visible evidence that their writing (the invitation) is powerful enough to elicit a response from someone else.

Although occasionally we have provided classroom library books from which to choose, our guest story readers usually bring a book of their own to share. As they tell why they chose their particular story and what makes it special to them, the guest readers are helping the children understand the affective link between people and literature. One guest selected *The Little Engine That Could* because it is her grandson's favorite story, and he asks her to read it on every visit. Another guest brought an eighteen year old copy of *The Night Before Christmas (In Texas That Is)*. She showed the children the inside cover where she had written a message to her daughter eighteen years before when the book had been a first Christmas present for the (then) baby. Loving ties between grandmother and grandson or mother and daughter are easily understood by young children, no matter how bountiful or barren their prior literacy experiences have been. This sharing about the book adds to the enjoyment and impact of the story itself.

As the story is being read, I take a photograph of the guest reader with the group of students. Afterward, I take a picture of the guest reader holding the book so that its title can be seen. These pictures are displayed in the classroom as visual reminders of a pleasurable shared literacy experience.

Before our guest story reader leaves, we usually ask if he or she has time to listen to us perform a song, poem, fingerplay, or story that we know. Our guest readers always respond so graciously and appreciatively that the children are thrilled. Through reciprocating in the sharing experience, the children are provided an opportunity to feel like "members of the (literacy) club."

In the days after the guest reader's visit, we follow up with a discussion of the experience. Children have a chance to tell their reactions to the visit. Comments have focused on story plot, characters, illustrations, text, style, and voice of the reader. Eventually, the children begin to notice and comment on similarities and differences between stories and between readers. We also try to get a copy of the book to have in our classroom library for closer inspection and repeated readings.

Of course, we also write a thank you note. The students are quick to learn a "formula" for this and are quite pleased with themselves for this accomplishment. Our thank you notes usually contain a "thank you" sentence and a sentence or two about what we especially liked about the story. Then the children invariably insist on a sentence along the lines of "We hope you'll come back and read again."

I believe there are three benefits to the guest story reader program in addition to those already mentioned.

1. It enhances self-concept. The children get the message that they are important enough for others to take time for them. One guest reader came to us straight from a meeting with a state senator.
2. It builds awareness that the social aspect of literacy experiences can be shared and enjoyed with a community beyond the home and the classroom.
3. It provides exposure to positive reading behaviors and readers—parents, older students, and other teachers. It helps children see that reading is for everyone.

Nancy Pfrang
Ridgeview Elementary School
Northeast Independent School District
San Antonio, Texas

References

Anderson, R.C., Hiebert, E.H., Scott, J.A., and Wilkinson, I.A.G. *Becoming a nation of readers*. Champaign, IL: Center for the Study of Reading, National Institute of Education, and National Academy of Education, 1985.

Branley, F.M. *Air is all around you*. New York: Thomas Y. Crowell, 1986.

Bridge, C. Predictable books for beginning readers and writers. In M. Sampson (Ed.), *The pursuit of literacy: Early reading and writing*. Dubuque, IA: Kendall/Hunt, 1986, 81-96.

Brown, M. *Stone soup*. New York: Macmillan, 1947.

Bruner, J.S. *Child's talk*. New York: Norton, 1983.

Burningham, J. *Mr. Gumpy's motor car*. New York: Thomas Y. Crowell, 1973.

Byars, B. *Go and hush the baby*. New York: Viking, 1971.

Carle, E. *The very hungry caterpillar*. New York: Philomel Books, 1981.

Cazden, C.B. Adult assistance to language development: Scaffolds, models, and direct instruction. In R.P. Parker and F.A. Davis (Eds.), *Developing literacy: Young children's use of language*. Newark, DE: International Reading Association, 1983.

Clark, M.M. *Young fluent readers*. London: Heinemann, 1976.

Clay, M.M. The reading behavior of five year old children: A research report. *New Zealand Journal of Education Studies*, 1967, *2*, 11-31.

Crowell, D.C., Kawakami, A., and Wong, J. Emerging literacy: Reading-writing experiences in a kindergarten classroom. *The Reading Teacher*, 1986, *40*, 144-151.

Durkin, D. *Children who read early*. New York: Teachers College Press, 1966.

Durkin, D. A classroom-observation study of reading instruction in kindergarten. *Early Childhood Research Quarterly*, 1987, *2*, 275-300.

Eastman, P. *Are you my mother?* New York: Random House, 1967.

Feitelson, D., Kita, B., and Goldstein, Z. Effects of listening to stories on first graders' comprehension and use of language. *Research in the Teaching of English*, 1986, *20*, 339-356.

Filcott, P. *Cowboys*. Washington, DC: National Geographic, 1979.

Fodor, M. *The effect of systematic reading of stories on the language development of culturally deprived children*. Unpublished doctoral dissertation, Cornell University, 1966.

Goodman, Y.M. Children coming to know literacy. In W.H. Teale and E. Sulzby (Eds.) *Emergent literacy: Writing and reading*. Norwood, NJ: Ablex, 1986, 1-14.

Harste, J.C., and Carey, R.F. Comprehension as setting. In J.C. Harste and R.F. Carey (Eds.), *New perspectives in comprehension*. Bloomington, IN: Indiana University School of Education, 1979.

Heald-Taylor, G. Predictable literature selections and activities for language arts instruction. *The Reading Teacher*, 1987, *41*, 6-12.

Heath, S.B. *Ways with words: Language, life, and work in communities and classrooms*. New York: Cambridge University Press, 1983.

Heath, S.B. What no bedtime story means: Narrative skills at home and school. *Language in Society*, 1982, *11*, 49-76.

Henderson, E.H., and Beers, J. (Eds.). *Developmental and cognitive aspects of learning to spell*. Newark, DE: International Reading Association, 1980.

Hiebert, E.H. Developmental patterns and interrelationships of preschool children's print awareness. *Reading Research Quarterly*, 1981, *16*, 236-260.

Hiebert, E.H., and McWhorter, L. *The content of kindergarten and readiness books in four basal reading programs*. Paper presented at the annual meeting of the American Educational Research Association, Washington, DC, 1987.

Holdaway, D. *The foundations of literacy*. Sydney, Australia: Ashton Scholastic, 1979.

Irwin, O. Infant speech: Effect of systematic reading of stories. *Journal of Speech and Hearing Research*, 1960, *3*, 187-190.

Kastler, L.A., Roser, N.L., and Hoffman, J.V. Understanding of the forms and functions of written language: Insights from children and parents. In J.E. Readance and R.S. Baldwin (Eds.), *Research in literacy: Merging perspectives*. Rochester, NY: National Reading Conference, 1987.

Kawakami-Arakaki, A., Oshiro, M.I., and Farran, D.C. Research into practice: Integrating reading and writing in a kindergarten curriculum. In J. Mason (Ed.), *Reading and writing connections*. Newton, MA: Allyn & Bacon, 1989.

Legrün, A. Wie und was "schrieben" kindergartenzoglinge? *Zeitschrift fur Padagogische*, 1932, *33*, 322-331.

Martinez, M.G., and Teale, W.H. The ins and outs of a kindergarten writing program. *The Reading Teacher*, 1987, *40*, 444-451.

Martinez, M.G., and Teale, W.H. Reading in a kindergarten classroom library. *The Reading Teacher*, 1988, *41*, 568-573.

Martinez, M.G., Cheyney, M., McBroom, C., Hemmeter, A., and Teale, W.H. No risk kindergarten literacy environments for at risk children. In J. Allen and J. Mason (Eds.), *Reducing the risks for young learners: Literacy practices and policies*. Portsmouth, NH: Heinemann, in press.

Morrow, L.M. Relationships between literature programs, library corner designs, and children's use of literature. *Journal of Educational Research*, 1982, *75*, 339-344.

Morrow, L.M., and Weinstein, C.S. Increasing children's use of literature through program and physical design changes. *Elementary School Journal*, 1982, *83*, 131-137.

Preston, E.M. *The temper tantrum book*. New York: Viking, 1969.

Read, C. Preschool children's knowledge of English phonology. *Harvard Educational Review*, 1971, *41*, 1-4.

Rhodes, L.K. I can read! Predictable books as resources for reading and writing instruction. *The Reading Teacher*, 1981, *34*, 511-518.

Salinger, T. *Language arts and literacy for young children*. Columbus, OH: Merrill, 1988.

Schickedanz, J.A. *More than the ABCs: The early stages of reading and writing*. Washington, DC: NAEYC, 1986.

Sulzby, E. Children's emergent reading of favorite storybooks: A developmental study. *Reading Research Quarterly*, 1985, *20*, 458-481.

Sulzby, E., and Teale, W.H. *Young children's storybook reading: Longitudinal study of parent-child interaction and children's independent functioning*. Final Report to the Spencer Foundation. Ann Arbor, MI: University of Michigan, 1987.

Taylor, D. *Family literacy: Young children learning to read and write*. Portsmouth, NH: Heinemann, 1983.

Taylor, D., and Dorsey-Gaines, C. *Growing up literate: Learning from innercity families*. Portsmouth, NH: Heinemann, 1988.

Teale, W.H. Emergent literacy: Reading and writing development in early childhood. In J. Readance and R.S. Baldwin (Eds.), *Research in literacy: Merging perspectives*. Rochester, NY: National Reading Conference, 1987.

Teale, W.H. Home background and young children's literacy learning. In W.H. Teale and E. Sulzby (Eds.), *Emergent literacy: Writing and reading*. Norwood, NJ: Ablex, 1986.

Teale, W.H. Toward a theory of how children learn to read and write naturally. *Language Arts*, 1982, *59*, 555-570.

Teale, W.H., and Martinez, M.G. Connecting writing: Fostering emergent literacy in kindergarten children. In J. Mason (Ed.), *Reading and writing connections*. Newton, MA: Allyn & Bacon, 1989.

Teale, W.H., and Sulzby, E. Literacy acquisition in early childhood: The roles of access and mediation in storybook reading. In D.A. Wagner (Ed.), *The future of literacy in a changing world*. New York: Pergamon Press, 1987, 111-130.

Templin, M. *Certain language skills in children*. Minneapolis: University of Minnesota Press, 1957.

Tompkins, G.E., and Webeler, M. What will happen next? Using predictable books with young children. *The Reading Teacher*, 1983, *36*, 498-502.

Wood, A. *King Bidgood's in the bathtub*. San Diego, CA: Harcourt Brace Jovanovich, 1985.

CHAPTER TWO

Oral Language and Literacy Development

Susan Mandel Glazer

This chapter has three purposes. First, I present theories about how children learn oral language and outline the stages of development of talk. I also discuss the relationship between learning to talk and thinking. Second, I focus on the relationship of oral language to the broader contexts of literacy, specifically learning to read and write. Third, I present practical ideas based on research theories, in the areas of dramatic play, literature, and artistic experiences. These ideas can be used by caregivers to guide the oral language development of young children. Descriptive passages and dialogues present examples of oral expressions.

Adults greet children's first words with enthusiasm. Each new word or phrase is a momentous occasion. Even more important, words represent the beginning of long and exciting changes and accomplishments for children and their caregivers. Words open worlds for children. Youngsters rediscover familiar objects when they learn their names. They receive pleasure from rhymes, chants, and songs. Someday they will be able to argue, learn to read, make promises, and even write poems, lesson plans, or medical prescriptions.

The adults in children's lives use language extensively to interact with children and to induct them into the social life of communities. Children themselves become absorbed with using language and exploring what they can do with words.

The amazing process of language acquisition has fascinated linguists, psychologists, and educators for years. The fact that an infant's cooing and babbling develops into a meaningful language without any type of formal instruction is awesome. It is astounding to think that within two years of life most children in all parts of the world use language to share ideas and feelings. This chapter will help describe how this happens by focusing on three questions.

- How do children learn oral language?
- How is oral language related to the broader concepts of literacy?
- How can adults guide children to use oral language effectively?

How Do Children Learn Oral Language?

Linguists and psychologists have debated for years how children acquire language, what influences its development, if language acquisition is innate, and if language growth depends on the environment. Several have attempted to explain the origin of oral language. Three theories seem important to discuss in an attempt to explain the acquisition of language: behaviorist, nativist, and interactionist.

Behaviorists believe that language is learned through environmental conditioning and imitation of adult models (Skinner, 1957). The child hears a word and imitates its sound, even without knowing its meaning. The adult praises the child in order to reward the attempt to use language. Behaviorists believe that thought is an internal, unheard part of oral language. According to this theory, the learning equation is simply "listen, imitate, receive a reward, and repeat for recall." Nowhere does this theory account for the astonishing speed with which children learn to speak or for language children invent (I throweded away my dinosaur).

Nativists believe that language is native, natural, and innate to human beings. Every child is born with a "built-in" device for acquiring language (Chomsky, 1974). This theory explains why children are able to invent language they've never heard. A three year old might say, "He scratched my feets," generalizing forms about plurals. Children build an intricate rule system which enables them to generate interesting and complex oral language, in many cases without adult modeling. Lenneberg (1967) believes this creative language usage suggests there is a biological element in all human babies that provides them with the knowledge about language that is necessary in order to create structures.

Interactionists seem to combine the ideas of behaviorists and nativists. These theorists propose that language is a product of both genetic and environmental factors (McCormick & Schiefelbusch, 1984). Infants are born with the ability to produce and learn language by using their genetic abilities and by interacting with caregivers.

Their ability to think helps them learn to speak. Language stimulates thought, and interactions with adults help them develop concepts (what "hot" means, for example).

Others have proposed theories, but Halliday (1973, 1975) in particular has had great influence concerning children's language acquisition. Halliday sees language acquisition as an active process. Children learn language in order to function in their worlds. They create language through social engagements with other language users (Newman, 1985).

Halliday proposed that children acquire language as they need it in order to make their presence known to those around them, to find out about things in their environment, to tell others their ideas, to accomplish goals, or to socialize. Halliday and others (Heath, 1983; Harste, Woodward, & Burke, 1984) support the assumption that language is learned because of what one can do with it. Halliday categorizes language functions as (1) language instrumental for meeting needs, (2) language used to regulate the behavior of others, (3) language used to establish social relationships, (4) language used to express ideas and feelings, (5) imaginative language used to express fantasies, (6) language used to investigate in order to gain information, and (7) language used for sharing. Oral language is learned as needed, and it develops in stages.

Stages of Language Development

The descriptions below represent typical stages of language development, but parents and caregivers should remember that rates of language development vary greatly among individual children.

Birth to One. Babies play with sounds, cooing and babbling. At about six months, sounds begin to take on meaning. Babies begin to select those that are important and to eliminate those that are not. "Ma Ma," for example, will be retained, for it creates a response. At about nine months, babies use single words, sounds, or several sounds together that express whole ideas. They learn words used daily. Milk, Mommy, Daddy, up, no, and bye-bye become part of their vocabularies.

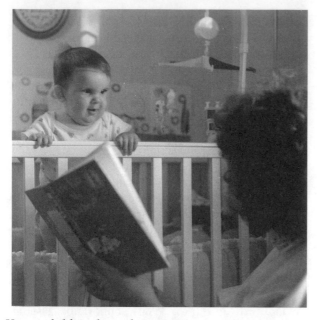
Young children learn language at an amazing rate.

One to Two. Children's language grows boundlessly during this second year. Children begin to imitate their caregivers, modeling their intonations and gestures. They begin to put two words together, and the effects are almost like reading a telegram. Children use important words to meet a need or share information like "Mommy up," or "Aaron fall down." This telegram format is referred to as "telegraphic language."

Two to Three. By the end of their third year, children can use about 1,000 words and can understand even more. Telegraphic language begins to evolve into more traditional and complex forms of oral language. Children begin to listen to language and use language more dramatically. Many words are used to describe one object or idea. One youngster two years, eleven months old described her stuffed toy bear by saying, "He cuddly, he cute, he brown, he soft." This descriptive language was followed with oral language defining the function of the bear in the child's life. She said, "He hugs, he kisses, he nice, nice teddy."

Three to Four. At this age, children use complex sentences that include pronouns, adjectives, adverbs, possessives, and plurals. They generalize knowledge about language. "I wented to the zoo on my birthday" denotes past tense. At this stage, children recall that "ed" represents past tense. Although they probably have not heard the word "wented," and it is grammatically incorrect, they have appropriately used the "ed" ending to tell about a past experience. Children at this age possess a 1,500 word speaking vocabulary.

Four to Five. By four, children have acquired most of the elements of adult language. Sentences are grammatically correct, and oral vocabulary includes approximately 3,000 words. During this year, children begin to tell about their lives—what they do and how they do it, as if words and behavior were one. It's often difficult to tell whether the language functions as a result of the behavior, or the behavior functions to result in language. Morrow (1989) describes a child of four painting and at the same time describing his actions. As he speaks, he simultaneously does what his oral language describes. "I'm making colors all over, I'm painting, pit, pat, pit, pat. I'm going back and forth and up and down." The child's words and activity became one (p. 47).

Five to Six. By age five, children's language and adult language are similar. Most grammatical rules have been mastered, and language patterns are complex and intricate. Language is creative and sometimes humorous. One kindergarten child, when talking about a locomotive, said, "It just takes a big breath of air and holds it inside and that's what makes it go so fast. It's like when you put air in a balloon and, poof, it blows itself away." Action is justified with language (Glazer, 1980).

Differences in Development

Although these developmental stages can be applied to most children, many factors affect oral language acquisition. Children's sex, age, and ethnicity, as well as the socioeconomic class, status, customs, and values of the adults with whom they communicate are some of these (Holzman, 1983). Oral language forms reflect the settings in which they are used. For example, one would not say to a professional colleague, "How's my cute, cuddly teacher's aide feeling this sunny morning?" It would be inappropriate.

Children seem to have problems in school when (1) their first language is different from that used in school, (2) they speak a form of dialect with different grammatical structures and meanings from standard English, and (3) their oral language develops more slowly than other children's. Many adults consider these differences deficiencies. This is unfortunate, for language differences often reflect the child's environment and cultural and regional backgrounds.

I recall stopping at a fast food restaurant in Nebraska and asking for a diet soda. The waitress looked at me askance and responded, "Gee, you have a funny accent. What is a soda?" As a New Yorker in Kearney, Nebraska, I was a cultural misfit. I'd never heard the word "pop" used in place of "soda." Pop was my grandfather's name! My dialect and accent were difficult for the waitress to understand. Even as an adult with knowledge about language differences, I felt embarrassed.

To look at language differences problematically means seeing the children as problems. Language differences *must* be respected. These differences ought to lead to a curriculum designed for helping others understand the uniqueness of each child's culture and traditions.

**Thought and Its Relationship
to Language Acquisition**

Piaget's (Piaget & Inhelder, 1969) and Vygotsky's (1978) theories seem to be most acceptable for explaining the relationship between the development of thought and language. According to Piaget, children acquire language in association with their activities. Babies will learn the words "socks and shoes" before "coat and hat," for they will put on socks and shoes by themselves first. Piaget believes that not only language but all activities that involve thought are learned as the result of activity and interactions. Children see, hear, touch, taste, and smell objects and events in their worlds in order to learn conceptually about them and the language they represent.

Vygotsky (1978) described communication as "zones of proximal development." Zones are ranges of social interactions between children and adults. Adults, considered to be more literate, push children from an actual stage of development toward their potential. Adult models provide names for things and events. Vygotsky was convinced that children learn language *only* with the assistance of an adult.

Many believe that oral language is the basis for becoming literate. Without oral language, it might be impossible to develop the ability to read and write.

How Is Oral Language Related to the Broader Context of Literacy?

It makes sense to say that oral language is a vehicle for the development of writing and reading. It serves as a companion to the development of both. Studies have demonstrated that early readers, for example, come from homes where diverse oral language is used (Snow & Perlmann, 1985). Teale (1987) observed that literacy is a functional component of daily living in these homes. Speaking, reading, and writing all are associated with daily activities. Parents and children talk about activities, read together, and write notes to one another using pictures, letters, or words. Parents read to children often, illustrating how oral language serves as a companion for reading and writing.

I recall a time in my office speaking with a parent. Her three year old, obviously restless after twenty minutes, came up to her mother and said,

Mommy, put your coat on,
Mommy, put your coat on,
Mommy, put your coat on,
Let's go home.

That youngster has probably heard and sung "Polly Put the Kettle On" over and over again. The language of rhyme had influenced her oral text.

Oral language accompanies children's writing in the early years in drawing and painting activities. In my clinic classroom, I observed a five year old at an easel retelling about her visit to a circus. "First, me and my mom walked up to the lion. He was a big, scary one!" As she spoke, she drew her mother, herself, and a very large figure which she called the lion. "Then the lion roared. He said, 'rrr-rrr-oooooo-aaaaaaa-rrrrrrr.' Me and my mom was scared." The child twisted and turned the paint-brush near the mouth of her lion as she made the roaring sounds. Her language and the paintbrush moved together almost like the baton and voice of an orchestra conductor, leading her thoughts from ideas to speech to written text.

The relationship of oral language to reading is evident. Children who hear stories learn story language and structure. They learn that "once upon a time," for example, is the way a story begins. They learn that a story has a main character. They learn that marks on paper represent events and ideas that occur in real life or in one's thoughts. They learn that the English language moves from left to right, because they've sat in adults' laps and watched care-givers move their heads, hands, or fingers to follow the print. They learn how to recognize signs as they ride in a car.

Young children who have had book experiences from the beginning of life develop a whole range of attitudes and concepts about print. They have learned to expect special pleasure from print and also have learned oral models for language in books (Holdaway, 1979). Oral language, which occurs in natural ways in and out of school, helps children use their knowledge about language in all of their literacy activities, particularly reading and writing. They have, through oral interactions, learned to attend to language and respond to its meanings in new situations.

Guiding Children to Use Oral Language Effectively

Associating language with interesting, exciting, and pleasant experiences encourages children to talk. They will talk and talk when the environments where they live and play promote a natural need to communicate (Morrow, this volume). Young children's oral language grows when environments encourage risk taking, someone listens, and there is a need to exchange language.

Very young children trust their caregivers. This trust must be maintained in order for children to take risks using language, particularly in new and creative ways. Children need to play with familiar language, explore meanings, and test uses of

language in different settings. Familiar materials and actions encourage risky uses of words and phrases. Using new words to describe familiar objects, inventing new ways to use well known words, and discovering additional ways for telling about events and dreams all happen in interactive settings with a devoted adult who listens and responds in positive ways to reinforce the language play so that it will continue.

Activities and Materials to Guide Oral Language Growth

Activities that guide children to increase oral language include dramatic play in response to life and literature, literature experiences, and artistic experiences.

Dramatic play. Drama is a powerful vehicle for guiding the growth of oral language. Drama provides young children with a way to discover themselves, learn how to deal with new and unusual experiences, and learn how to solve problems (Glazer & Searfoss, 1988). Most of us create drama for ourselves before entering into new situations. I recall my first date. I put on my dress, looked in the mirror, and rehearsed conversations with Harold, my date. I even practiced the good-night kiss, using a pillow while observing my behavior in front of a mirror.

Young children, like adults, "role play" the dramas of life to rehearse for real times. These roles result from observing and interacting with people, books, and other media. Drama prepares children by helping them rehearse life using language in lifelike settings. Heathcote (Wagner, 1976) believes that drama evolves and helps to reduce children's anxieties about new roles. Playing roles makes them feel real and familiar.

Young children's first dramatic play activities are usually solitary and spontaneous (Moffett & Wagner, 1983). They dramatize to help themselves understand and to find out about identities through action. Children freely act and dress up like people they know from life and literature (Isenberg & Quisenberry, 1988). Dramatic play encourages imitation, conversation, and the creative expression of ideas using oral language (Fromberg, 1987; Singer, 1986).

These activities require settings and materials. The very young need only simple objects or toys to engage in role playing. As they grow, more complex materials representing lifelike situations are needed. It is in these play corners that language flourishes on its own. Areas for dramatic play in homes might be the child's bedroom or a corner of the family room or living room. In school settings, drama corners can be sectioned off with small screens or storage shelves.

Materials appropriate to each area should be visible and easily accessible to children. Areas could contain specific types of materials to foster role playing as nurses or doctors, fire fighters, law enforcement officers, dentists and patients, fast food operators, beauticians and barbers, gas station attendants, business people, lawyers, psychologists, teachers, mothers, fathers, siblings, or supermarket employees, and more. Costumes representing roles in life and in stories also encourage role playing. If space is a constraint, materials might be changed periodically to encourage diversity of dramatic play so children can rehearse roles in different aspects of life.

Materials should be child size. Small tables and chairs and shelving that is low enough to reach but just high enough for stretching can be arranged to section off play areas. Dolls, doll furniture, dress up clothing, toy appliances or "out of use" real ones, utensils, dishes, cartons, paper bags, magazines and books, note paper or pads, pencils, a camera, a bulletin board, a broom, a vacuum cleaner, tables and chairs, and an ironing board are just some of the important items that encourage children to play the roles of life. Time must be provided for children to play freely until they have completed "acting out" their roles.

Children's play reflects their curiosity and their observations of life. They act what they know. Learning how children interpret roles by observing them in solitary and interactive dramatic play experiences helps adults understand children's perceptions of roles in life.

Storytelling and reading are natural stimulants to encourage oral language through drama. Children in their preschool years will respond to stories using language through drama. Props such as stuffed animals, hand puppets, lifesize puppets, and puppetlike figures used on a flannel board often provide points of departure for young cildren to use oral language in response to stories

Hugging a Max doll dressed in his wolf suit (the main character in Maurice Sendak's *Where the Wild Things Are*) in one arm and sailing a toy boat away into "night and day" to where the wild things "roar their terrible roars and gnash their terrible teeth," or stacking caps and more caps on one's little head and shouting, "Caps for sale, 50 cents a cap," after hearing Esphyur Slobodkina's *Caps for Sale* are responses to stories through props. Props suggest to children what to do; they evoke hosts of associations based on stories embedded in children's minds. Having a special place for keeping books and related props is one way to encourage spontaneous drama based on stories. The place might include lifesize story puppets, bits of costumes, and paper bags containing objects that represent stories.

Lifesize story puppets. Lifesize puppets also help children recall stories they've heard. They often guide children to live the parts of characters. These are easily constructed with cardboard and magic markers. Story objects and characters should be drawn lifesize and then cut out and covered with clear contact paper for durability. Sometimes, when the lifesize puppets arc people, a hole might be cut where a face would be drawn, so that children can put their faces in the spot and instantly become the character.

The following books easily stimulate children to role play using lifesize puppets.

Barrett, J. *Animals Should Definitely Not Wear Clothing*. Atheneum, 1970.
Illogical clothing on several animals provokes a host of funny ideas, which are well depicted through pictures and words.

Eastman, P. *Are You My Mother?* Random House, 1960.
A baby bird loses his mother and asks many unlikely candidates, "Are you my mother?"

Johnson, C. *Harold and the Purple Crayon*. Harper & Row, 1959.
Harold draws himself in and out of adventures, using his purple crayon.

Paper bag prop stories. Paper bag prop stories

Grocery Store

In one classroom, a teacher created a grocery store. There were shelves defining the area, and on those shelves were empty cereal boxes and food cans. A supermarket food cart was placed and designated as the store's entrance. A magazine rack displayed old copies of *TV Guide, Woman's Day, Life, Cosmopolitan*, and several newspapers. An "Entrance" sign hung at one side of the shelving and an "Exit" sign at the other. An outdated cash register was placed on top of a table, and paper bags were neatly stacked next to it. Two four year old girls entered the play area, one pushing the cart and the second holding onto the cart's handle. One was acting as the mother, the other as the child. A four year old boy was standing at the cash register. He had put on an apron which was stored on the shelf. He attentively watched the two shoppers.

Child: (speaking like a much younger child) I want to ride in the cart.
Mother: You can't, sweety, you're too big.
Child: No I'm not (shaking head in an assertive way).
Mother: But you will make it fall over.
Child: (acting out with a pouting facial expression) No. I am little like Jamie.
Mother: No, you are bigger, 'cause you are the big sister.
Child: No (stamping her foot), I want to go in, I want to be the little sister.
Mother: Well, OK 'tend you are littler, and don't move. Get in and sit still (said in a firm voice, with stern facial expression, and pointing a finger).
Child: (smiling) I'll be good.

The "mother" pushes the cart around the small area, selecting merchandise.

Mother: I think we'll have rice for dinner (taking an empty rice box). It's good for when your stomach is upset.
Child: I want that candy (in a whining voice).
Mother: I told you (pointing with frown on face) to be still!
Child: P-L-E-A-S-E! May I have one little candy? (in a pleading, soft spoken manner).
Mother: Well, 'cause you are soooo good and said "please" you can have one piece. Here, take this one (selects an empty candy box).
Child: I want that one (pointing to another).
Mother: (in an angry tone) Take this, or nothing.

The shopping continued with similar dialogue exchanges, while the cashier observed. The role playing continued for approximately ten minutes before they approached his counter.

Mother: (taking things out of the basket and putting them on the table) Help me put the food here, Melissa.
Boy: (Takes large brown bag and looks at a box, as if observing the price, then taps some keys on the cash register and places the box in the bag. He continues this process and each time he places a box in the bag, he says a number and writes it on the bag. When the packing is completed, the boy again calls each number that he has written. He draws a horizontal line at the bottom of the column.)   I am adding up all the prices of all the foods so you know what to pay. OK? You owe $14.00.
Mother: That's a lot of money, but things cost more today than when I was little.

Figure 1
Repetitive Story in Rhyme, *This Is the House That Jack Built*

also can stimulate role playing. Put a book familiar to the children in each of three to five different paper bags. Fasten the book jacket or a photocopy of one picture from the book onto the front of the bag. Put props associated with each story into the appropriate bag. Props should represent story objects, characters, settings, sequence, and other elements important for the child's role playing. Paul Galdone's *The Three Billy Goats Gruff* could be made into a paper bag prop story by placing into the bag three stuffed animals that resemble goats and a doll that resembles an old troll. More intricate dramatic play based on this story would occur if a toy bridge and scraps of blue paper to represent water under the bridge also were in the bag. Props should be simple, already assembled, and easily available for children to use during free times. The following books represent wonderful stories for paper bag prop story experiences.

Carle, E. *The Very Hungry Caterpillar*. Scholastic, 1974.

A caterpillar eats through unlikely foods on his way to becoming a butterfly.

Hyman, T.S. *Little Red Riding Hood*. Holiday, 1983.

Beautiful illustrations tell the story of a little girl's encounters with a big, bad wolf.

Zelinsky, P. *Rumpelstiltskin*. Dutton, 1986.

This classic fairy tale tells of a girl who must spin straw into gold.

Literature Experiences

Books that encourage children to respond to the story because of interesting and exciting language help stimulate language growth. Participation stories, poetry and rhymes, and song books help immerse children into language. The language is repetitive and predictable. Because children are able to anticipate the language, they join the reader and become part of the storybook activity. The language catches their ears and captures their hearts and minds. These suggestions for using participation stories with children are recommended for all preschoolers.

1. Hold the child on your lap in a cozy manner. Put your arms around the child, and together hold the book as you read the story. If the book is a song (Go tell Aunt Rhody, Go tell Aunt Rhody) with repetitive language, reading the repetitive passage once or twice should entice the child to read it with you each time it appears in the text. Very young children will make sounds that follow the tempo, intonation, and pitch used by the adult.

2. When reading to a group of children, sit as they do, on the floor, on a rug, or in a small chair. Use books with repetitive rhyming text. Read the story, and as you approach the language that repeats, look at the children. Begin the repetitive, rhyming sequence slowly, suggesting that you need them to help you say it. Have the children repeat the sequence each time it appears in the text. You might want to turn the book toward the children as they "chant" the rhyme, so that those who are ready can notice the repetitive words and phrases.

3. Tape record yourself reading a favorite book. Then place the book and the tape in a special place. Be sure the children know that the book and tape recording go together, and show the youngsters how to start the tape playing. The children will be encouraged to listen, look at, and say the story along with your voice. Here are some suggested books with repetitive language that encourage participation.

de Regniers, B. *May I Bring a Friend?* Atheneum, 1964.
This repetitive rhyme describes a small boy's invitation to tea with royalty.

Gerrard, R. *Sir Cedric.* Farrar, Straus & Giroux, 1984.
This rhyming story tells of a gentle knight searching for adventure.

Hoopes, L.L. *Mommy, Daddy, Me.* Harper & Row, 1988.
A story in rhyme of a small boy and his parents who sail to visit his grandfather on a summer day.

Martin, B Jr *Brown Bear, Brown Bear, What Do You See?* Holt, Rinehart, & Winston, 1967.
The bear asks several animals, "What do you see?"

Prelutsky, J. *The Baby Uugs Are Hatching.* Greenwillow, 1982.
Silly creatures come alive with repeated, rhyming words.

Robart, R. *The Cake That Mack Ate.* Little, Brown/Joy Street Books, 1987.
This cumulative tale with a funny ending tells how to prepare a birthday cake.

Wordless books are important for children's language development. These books tell stories with pictures, and the illustrations encourage oral language use. A series of pictures that describe a simple activity in sequence directs the reluctant speaker. Children, when nurtured by a loving adult, match words to the pictures and create the oral text. Encouraging children to tell stories using picture books increases oral language while building their self confidence about using language to create stories.

The following wordless books provide pictures that easily provoke children to tell their stories.

Krahn, F. *First Snow.* Clarion, 1982.
A boy catches a strange "thing" while fishing, and it escapes.

McCully, E. *New Baby.* Harper & Row, 1988.
A mouse family has a new baby, and the youngest is excited and also frustrated as the new baby gets everyone's attention.

Artistic Experiences

In addition to storybooks, music and songs and arts and crafts help oral language thrive. Musical instruments for the young child include rhythm instruments (drums, sticks, etc.) used for keeping the tempo of the rhythmic language of poems and chants. Songs and song books that have been prepared as storybooks lure children to use language. Many kinds of paper, felt tip pens, large crayons, or clay are among the materials that help children express themselves through arts and crafts.

Here are some specific suggestions for using music, dance, and the arts to stimulate language.

1. Songs and chants are wonderful. Select one such as:

Michael row the boat ashore, Hallelujah,
Michael row the boat ashore, Hallelujah,
Brother, lend a helping hand, Hallelujah,
Brother, lend a helping hand, Hallelujah.

Figure 2
A Wordless Story in Sequence

Chant the poem, moving your head and arms with the beat of the language. Repeat it several times. Then substitute the child's name for the one in the poem. Actions can also accompany the words.

Chants also may be used to guide children to follow directions. For example: "Mathew put the toy away, Hallelujah, Mathew put the toy away, Hallelujah." Provide time for children to create their own words to chant in the language of song.

2. Listening to recordings also encourages language growth. In addition, it provides sound and tempo for body movement. Select tapes or records that include songs with repeated language patterns, songs that rhyme, songs about families and things around the child, and songs that tell stories. Keeping tempo with rhythm instruments while singing helps children associate the sounds of language with physical activity, and they feel the language.

The favorite folk song, "Here we go looby-loo, Here we go looby-light, Here we go looby-loo, All on a Saturday night" may be used to help children dance to words. Actions can change to match new words that children create. For example: "Here we go skipping, skip."

3. Clay is wonderful for developing strength in little hands. The molding helps children feel shapes and talk about them. If you mold materials with children and talk about your actions as you proceed, children will probably do the same. Many youngsters will talk and mold simultaneously.

Talking is an important human activity. It is always part of some environment, and to a large extent it derives its importance from the setting in which it occurs. Talking is a way to conduct social events, and it is sensitive to its context and purpose. It serves to help both children and adults work out the curiosities, problems, and intricacies of life.

References

Aliki. Illustrator. *Go tell Aunt Rhody*. New York: Macmillan, 1973.

Chomsky, N. *Aspects of the theory of syntax*. Cambridge, MA: MIT Press, 1974.

Fromberg, D.P. Play. In C. Seefeldt (Ed.), *The early childhood curriculum*. New York: Teachers College Press, 1987.

Glazer, S.M. *Getting ready to read: Creating readers from birth through six*. Englewood Cliffs, NJ: Prentice Hall, 1980.

Glazer, S.M., and Searfoss, L.W. *Reading diagnosis and instruction: A C-A-L-M approach*. Englewood Cliffs, NJ: Prentice Hall, 1988.

Halliday, M.A.K. *Explorations in the function of language*. London: Edward Arnold, 1973.

Halliday, M.A.K. *Learning how to mean: Explorations in the development of language*. London: Edward Arnold, 1975.

Harste, J., Woodward, V., and Burke, C. *Language stories and literacy lessons*. Portsmouth, NH: Heinemann, 1984.

Heath, S.B. *Ways with words: Language, life, and work in communities and classrooms*. Cambridge, MA: Cambridge University, 1983.

Holdaway, D. *The foundations of literacy*. New York: Ashton Scholastic, 1979.

Holzman, M. *The language of children: Development in home and school*. Englewood Cliffs, NJ: Prentice Hall, 1983.

Isenberg, J., and Quisenberry, N.L. Play a necessity for children. *Childhood Education, 64* (3), 138-145, 1988.

Lenneberg, E.H. *Biological foundations of language*. New York: Wiley, 1967.

McCormick, L., and Schiefelbusch, R.L. *Early language intervention*. Columbus, OH: Charles E. Merrill, 1984.

Moffett, J., and Wagner, B.J. *Student centered language arts and reading, K-13: A handbook for teachers*. Boston: Houghton Mifflin, 1983.

Morrow, L.M. *Literacy development in the early years: Helping children read and write*. Englewood Cliffs, NJ: Prentice Hall, 1989.

Newman, J.M. Insights from recent reading and writing research and their implications for developing whole language curriculum. In J.M. Newman (Ed.), *Whole language: Theory in use*. Portsmouth, NH: Heinemann, 1985, 17-36.

Piaget, J., and Inhelder, B. *The psychology of the child*. New York: Basic Books, 1969.

Sendak, M. *Where the wild things are*. New York: Harper, 1963.

Singer, D.G. Make-believe play and learning. In J.S. McKee (Ed.), *Play: Working partner of growth*. Wheaton, MD: Association of Childhood Education International, 1986, 8-14.

Skinner, B.F. *Verbal behavior*. Boston: Appleton-Century-Crofts, 1957.

Slobodkina, E. *Caps for sale*. Glenview, IL: Scott, Foresman, 1947.

Snow, E., and Perlmann, R. Assessing children's knowledge about bookreading. In L. Galda and A. Pelligrini (Eds.), *Play, language, and stories*. Norwood, NJ: Ablex, 1958.

Teale, W.H. Emergent literacy: Reading and writing development in early childhood. In J.E. Readence and R.S. Baldwin (Eds.), *Research in literacy: Merging perspectives*. Rochester, NY: National Reading Conference, 1987, 45-74.

Vygotsky, L.S. *Mind in society: The development of psychological processes*. Cambridge, MA: Harvard University Press, 1978.

Wagner, B.J. *Dorothy Health Cote, drama as learning medium*. Washington, DC: National Education Association, 1976.

CHAPTER THREE

Family Storybook Reading: Implications for Children, Families, and Curriculum

Dorothy S. Strickland
Denny Taylor

This chapter describes what we have learned about the dynamic interaction between children and adults when they share books at home and what that implies for educational settings outside the home. We begin with a discussion of how family storybook reading supports children's language and literacy development and how it acts as a socializing process within families. We conclude with descriptions of classrooms that suggest how caregivers and teachers can capitalize on what is known about the nature of children's learning during storybook reading at home.

For many years, educators have known that children who come from homes in which storybook reading takes place have an educational advantage over those who do not. These children are more likely to read before they are given formal instruction, and those who are not early readers are more likely to learn to read with ease when formal instruction does begin. In recent years, educators have learned a great deal about the acquisition of reading and writing, and much of this knowledge helps us to explain why shared book experiences are important to early language and literacy development. (For an introduction or update on this emergent literacy research, see texts edited by Sampson and by Teale and Sulzby, 1986.)

As researchers interested in the literacy development of young children both at home and in school, we have had a lasting interest in what makes family storybook reading work. We have asked ourselves what actually happens when parents share books with their children. Why is it such a powerful factor in the literacy development of young children? How does the research support parents' natural instincts about what is right for them and their children?

We were aware of some of the conditions under which first language learning occurs, and we sought to determine how these conditions were supported by family storybook reading. For example, in first language learning, the following conditions are generally maintained.

First, there is an atmosphere of success. The child acquires spoken language in a warm, rewarding atmosphere. The nature of the learning environment is positive. Parents are generally delighted with whatever the child accomplishes, and they show it. Anxiety about first language acquisition is rare. The young child's miscues or mistakes not only are accepted, they are the subject of family stories for years to come.

The child acquires spoken language in an atmosphere that conveys respect for the uniqueness of each individual, with little temptation to make children fit a group standard. Individual styles and approaches to the task of first language learning generally are respected. Young children are not asked to alter their approach to learning in order to conform to a preconceived method. Instead, parents usually judge children's achievements in terms of what their children are doing today that they could not do yesterday.

Second, children acquire spoken language in an atmosphere that is largely child centered. Adults use language with the child and interact individually with the learner. The child is an active, curious participant, asking questions and wanting answers. First language learning inherently demands feedback, and it is largely guided by children's purpose or intent.

Third, children acquire spoken language in a meaningful context. First language learning and concept development are always related to meaningful activities, objects, and situations in children's environments. If the new word or concept makes no sense, it is discarded. Each new idea or element of language must find its place in children's existing schema of knowledge. It must have meaning for the children or it is discarded. Here, the adult's role is that of encoder of what children are experiencing. Throughout, adults are using language to do something besides just teach the language. And since the focus is on what is being experienced or accomplished, correcting is aimed at the content of language expression rather than its form.

Fourth, and perhaps most important, in first language learning children are presented with the whole system of what is to be learned. Language is not sequenced; it is not arranged by skills or put into an elaborate management system. All of the subsystems or components of the language are presented as they exist—as an interrelated, integrated whole.

Finally, it is important to note that none of these features inherently requires standard forms. What is required is adult-child interaction where the focus is on whole language used in a meaningful context. As we explored the family storybook reading phenomenon, we kept these factors in mind as fundamental to the dynamics of language learning.

Family Storybook Reading Aids Literacy Development

Christina was almost three when she and her mother, Karen, shared *The Story of Babar*, by Jean de Brunhoff. Sometimes reading and sometimes talking about the story, Karen conveyed the extraordinary happenings in the life of Babar and sensitively related them to the everyday world of her little girl. In the story, Babar's mother is killed by hunters and Babar runs away. He runs and runs until he comes to a town and is befriended by a rich elderly lady who gives him money to buy a fine suit of clothes.

Karen tells Christina what is happening in the story. "He goes into the store," she says, "and he goes into the elevator." Karen points to the elevator and asks Christina, "Does this look like the old broken down elevator in Mommy's office?"

"Yes," replies Christina.

"But this one's not broken," her mother says. "It goes up and down." Karen returns to the story. "And the man says, 'This is not a toy, Mr. Elephant. You must get out and do your shopping'."

In this way, the strange looking elevator, which is filled with an elephant and is supposed to go up and down on the page of the book, is likened to an elevator that is familiar to Christina.

Karen continues reading the story, and a few pages later she reads, "Well satisfied with his purchases and feeling very elegant indeed, Babar now goes to the photographer to have his picture taken."

Fathers as well as mothers should participate in family storybook reading.

Christina looks at the picture of the photographer and says, "He fur on him?"

"Well, that is the photographer's hair," her mother explains. "It looks like fur, doesn't it?"

"Um-hum," says Christina.

Karen reads the writing that appears on the page under the photograph of Babar. "And here is his photograph," she says to Christina.

Christina doesn't understand, and she questions her mom. "Photograph?" she says.

"That's his photograph, that's his picture," Karen answers.

Christina is still unsure, and she asks, "Is that him?"

"Um-hum," Karen replies. Then, changing the subject, she continues talking to Christina. "This is the man's camera," she says. "It's an old-fashioned camera. Cameras used to be big like that.

Christina is back to the photographer, and she questions her mother again about the person in the picture.

"That's the photographer," Karen explains. "Remember the photographer who came to your class and took your picture? Did he have a camera like that?"

"Yes," replies Christina.

"And did he say, 'Everyone look at the camera'?"

"Yes," says Christina, and she and her mother continue with the story.

This pleasant, though unremarkable, exchange between a mother and her child as they share a storybook is a wonderful example of what is undoubtedly one of the most powerful catalysts for young children's language and literacy development. It illustrates several of the many ways that children benefit from sharing books. What is more, the insights it reveals have been evident to some degree in the shared experiences of every family with whom we have worked.

For example, parents frequently help their children understand a new word or concept by relating it to something the child already knows. By referring to "the old broken down elevator in Mommy's office," Karen helps Christina understand Babar's elevator experience in the story. Karen does the same thing in a more elaborate way as she attempts to help Christina with the concept of Babar going to the photographer to have his picture taken. "Remember the photographer who came to your class and took your picture? Did he have a camera like that?"

Not only the text, but also the talk surrounding the text, helps expand Christina's vocabulary and concepts. She begins to assimilate the language of picture taking—photograph, photographer, picture, and camera—into her listening vocabulary, and she expands her awareness of what having one's picture taken means. In every instance, it is this mother's intimate knowledge (see Erikson, 1982) of her child's background of experience that enables her to help her child move from the known to the unknown.

Like most parents, Karen is tuned in to her daughter. She augments the text in places where she intuitively anticipates that there may be a problem. By adding "And the man says" before reading " 'This is not a toy, Mr. Elephant'," Karen establishes who is speaking at that point in the story. In this way, quite possibly without even thinking about it, she helps to avoid a potential source of confusion for Christina. Later, she responds to Christina's puzzled query, "He fur on him?" by explaining that the photographer has a lot of hair. Then she sensitively adds, "It looks like fur, doesn't it?"

In gathering families to participate in our research (Taylor & Strickland, 1986a), we purposely included parents and children of various ethnic and educational backgrounds, socioeconomic levels, geographic locations, and family configurations. Yet, with all this diversity, certain universals were maintained. We found that parents who share books with their children often expand and extend the content of the stories in natural and meaningful ways. Parents seem to sense when such expansions are necessary, or when an unembellished reading is the best way to share a particular story.

We have found that when parents and children talk about a story they are reading, there is a give-and-take, with family discussions reflecting what we may think of as genuine conversation. Parents appear to talk *with* their children, not *at* them, and they are more likely to follow their children's lead rather than some preconceived agenda of their own.

It is the child centered, personalized nature of family storybook reading that is most evident in these families and perhaps that is its greatest asset. Yet, as researchers interested in the development of literacy, we had no difficulty appreciating the cognitive benefits that were occurring. We knew that through family storybook reading, these parents were supporting their children's language development. New words and new expressions beyond their everyday talk continually appeared in even the simplest storybooks. Children's background knowledge also was given an opportunity to expand as they read about familiar things in new contexts, and pondered unfamiliar things and happenings.

These families love stories, and both the children and the parents have favorites. Becoming acquainted with many stories and "book binging" on a particular story help to strengthen the children's sense of what makes a story. An awareness of story structure is critical both for comprehending and composing stories. We have observed that as more books are shared, children begin to attend to the print on the page. They learn that print carries messages. Children talk about the meanings of some of the words they encounter in print, and ask questions about words and letters as they attempt to match speech with the text. In very natural ways, their awareness of print and the reading process begins to take shape. We have found positive attitudes and a curiosity about books and reading develop as parents openly display their enjoyment during the sharing.

While educators ponder the underlying reasons why family storybook reading is so important to the language and literacy development of young children, parents usually do not. Our observations suggest that most parents approach storybook reading as they might approach any pleasurable activity. This is precisely why the activity is so important, for storybook reading is primarily a family occasion, and when parents share stories with their children they do not deliberately set out to give language lessons. Nevertheless, all kinds of lessons about language and thinking do occur. Learning begins with the genuine interest that parents and children have in one another. It takes place as family members share the content of the story, and extends beyond the story as parents and children talk about the words written on the page.

Sharing Storybooks: A Socializing Process

In many ways, sharing storybooks with young children is a celebration of family life. As parents and children listen, talk, read, and play together, they learn about themselves, one another, and the social world in which they live. It is an intimate occasion that cannot be staged. Family storybook reading grows quietly in the home until it becomes a part of everyday life, with rituals and routines that seem to fit the needs and interests of individual family members.

Marie Ellen works three days a week, and her daughter, Rachel, is in a family day care program. Marie Ellen leaves Rachel with the day care family on her way to work and picks her up on her way home. Rachel has listened to stories since she was born, and both her mother and father read to her. When Marie Ellen talks of sharing books, she calls it "our golden time," and says, "It's something that we really like to do." For Marie Ellen, storybook reading is almost an extension of breast-feeding her little girl. Storybook reading provides Rachel's father, Larry, with the opportunity to learn more about his daughter. Larry and Rachel have learned to have fun together as they share books, and now they have their own way of reading as they joke and play.

The Garcia family also has found a special way of sharing books. Books are read in both English and Spanish. Raphael, age six, listens to the stories with his little sister, Maria, age two. When their mother, Carmen, begins reading the story of *Hester the Jester* by Ben Shecter, she starts in English. Raphael and Maria listen, and ask questions about the story. Carmen answers them, and then she gives a Spanish translation of the story. It is a family time, and the children enjoy listening to their mother as she reads and talks to them in the English and Spanish of their bilingual home.

Some parents have told us that they found it hard to talk to their tiny babies, and spoke of having to learn how to play with them. Several parents said that storybook reading helped them relax. One young mother commented that reading to her child helped ease the first lonely months of staying home with a new baby. Working parents said that storytime became a special time of closeness that would be difficult to achieve in any other way. Families managed to adjust their routines as new children came into the picture, and a range of interests and abilities began to emerge. Whatever the individual styles and preferences of parents and children, the sharing of storybooks developed over time and gradually became an important part of family life.

The communication surrounding storybook reading is one means by which families establish relationships and a sense of family. Although book sharing is only one way families transmit ideas, attitudes, and values, it is an important one. Parents rarely select a book to read because of a particular message it conveys; nevertheless, they often emphasize the message if it agrees with their own view of life. The use of books to convey attitudes and ideals is an important part of the message itself. In effect, the parent is saying, "We can read about important ideas, and we can talk about them. We can relate what the book says to our own lives. Books help our family communicate."

Storybook Reading in the Schools

Caregivers and classroom teachers can use what has been learned about the dynamics of family storybook reading to plan for and analyze shared book experiences in their classrooms. Most early childhood teachers include storybook reading in their daily plans, and most value read aloud sessions as an enjoyable activity that fosters language development.

Frequently, teachers are unaware or only vaguely aware of the many cognitive and social dimensions of storytime, and therefore they may not make the most of it. More importantly, when teachers underestimate the value of reading aloud to children, they often turn to skills related worksheets and workbooks to meet the ever increasing demands for formal literacy programs. A literature based language and literacy program from the very earliest years provides a structure that is both developmentally appropriate and effective in helping children acquire language and literacy.

In Janice Odom's urban prekindergarten, the read aloud time is followed each day by a period in which children may select books to "read" independently in groups or as individuals. It is not surprising that most of the books selected have been previously read to the group as a whole. Children find a book, a pillow, and one or two friends to share a story. Readers may be heard to ask, "And what do you think will happen next?" as they reenact the teacher's reading aloud of a familiar story. Two children may snuggle in a corner taking turns "reading" to one another.

Next door to Janice, the two and three year olds in Maxie Perry's group love to share books with adults one-to-one. Reading aloud takes place at various times during the day, often upon a child's request. Because Maxie believes one-to-one reading to be an essential daily experience, she recruits numerous volunteers to supplement the teachers and aides available.

Maxie is aware that many of the adult volunteers have limited reading abilities themselves and may be shy about reading aloud. She delicately encourages them to share books by helping children name objects and talk about the pictures. It is not uncommon to see a senior citizen seated in the rocking chair in this classroom with one child perched on his or her lap and another peering over the arm of the chair listening intently. Maxie recognizes that much of the value of these exchanges lies in the personalized social interaction and oral language opportunities they offer.

Joyce Jennings, a teacher of four and five year olds in a suburban kindergarten, starts each year by using storybook reading to develop a sense of community in her classroom. She selects books such as *Will I Have a Friend?* (Cohen, 1967) and *The Growing Story* (Krauss, 1947) to stimulate children to talk about themselves. The books provide a springboard to talk about who they are, what is special about each of them, what they want to learn, and what they can do now that they couldn't do when they were little. These discussions help her to

get to know the children and to help them get to know one another. Each child is encouraged to develop a sense of self both as an individual and as a member of a group. Joyce sees the bonding begin to take place within a few days.

Throughout the year, Joyce keeps storytime as relaxed and as cozy as possible. She purposely selects books that allow the group to share feelings as well as information. The children are anxious and sad when they share a story in which a small child loses her dog; they giggle with delight when they hear of the plant that grows right through the ceiling; they understand the feelings of the child who is afraid to spend the night away from home without his teddy bear.

The children respond to literature in a variety of ways. Most often, they simply discuss the story, both during and after the reading. Sometimes they may draw pictures of something relating to the book, or they may draw or write about a favorite part of the story. Sometimes they dictate a group chart. The chart may be a group retelling, a list of ideas relating to the reading, or a series of sentences telling what they liked about the story. Some stories lend themselves to creative dramatics, and some naturally seem to suggest various art and music activities for follow up.

Whenever possible, Joyce interviews two or three children after a read aloud session in order to personalize their responses. Telling them that she is very interested in what *they* think, she uses a pad and pencil to take notes during their brief one-to-one conversations. When the children see her writing, they know she genuinely cares. Joyce uses these interviews as informal observations of children's language and concept development. This procedure helps her to "tune in" to the children as individuals as she attempts to stimulate the personalized quality of storybook reading.

Suzanne Wiedenheft, who teaches in a small rural school, reads aloud at least once a day to her kindergarten children. Often, the books she selects complement a theme that the children are studying. Recently, Suzanne and her children read books about mice. Their interest began when they shared a version of *The Country Mouse and the City Mouse* that was a part of the readiness program used in the school system. Suzanne elaborated on the theme by

Functional Uses of Print

Children need to be given frequent opportunities to use print and to see print being used functionally. Here are two examples from classrooms where teachers are providing these opportunities.

This sign up sheet was located on the door to Deborah Davis's second grade classroom. Her students became very adept at reading aloud, telling stories, and reciting poetry for other classes.

Please sign up if you would like a
    Poet
    Storyteller
    Book read aloud to your class

Teacher's Name	Poet	Storyteller	Read Aloud
Mrs. Jason	✓		
Mr. Brownley			✓

The chart below was located on the wall of Annette Ayers's first grade classroom. Children were encouraged to enter their favorite titles whenever they wished.

Recommended Book List		
Title	Author	Reader

Deborah Davis and Annette Ayers
P. S. 220
New York, New York

introducing other versions of the story.

The children found many differences between the various versions. For instance, in one version the mice were female, and in another they were male. In one story, the country mouse lived in a tree stump, and in another, it lived on the edge of a field. After Suzanne and the children had read and talked about the stories, they talked about the makeup of the books. They discussed the different sizes and shapes of the books, the layout of the pages, and the artwork.

When Suzanne works on a theme in this way, she tries to read poetry, folk literature, and a variety of storybooks. On this occasion, one of the "mice" books that she read was *Mooch the Messy* (Sharmat, 1976). The children looked at the cover of the book, and Suzanne talked with them about the title and the author. When they came to the dedication page, they talked about how an author dedicates a book to someone special. Suzanne explained that this particular dedication meant that the author, Marjorie Weinman Sharmat (and she showed them the name on the cover), had written *Mooch the Messy* especially for Fritz. Immediately, one student asked, "So how come you've got it?" This comment stimulated further discussion, and Suzanne gained new insights into the children's thinking.

Suzanne's children are particularly lively and talkative during read aloud time. Although some might consider the talk distracting, Suzanne skillfully manages to accept all the children's questions and comments, while still keeping them on target. As we have indicated, she is particularly adept at using storybook reading to develop her children's thinking. She may begin the reading by using the book jacket and title to elicit predictions about the story. She asks children to give reasons for their guesses through questions such as, "What was it about the title or the picture that made you think of that?" In this informal way, Suzanne guides the children toward thinking about supporting evidence for their inferences. All predictions are accepted and then confirmed or disconfirmed as the story proceeds. During the reading, children also may be asked to make predictions about what will happen next.

Suzanne also uses these stories to extend first-hand experiences, but never to replace them. As she reads, she relates the information in the stories to everyday experiences. The mice in the stories lead to discussions about real mice, which are abundant in their rural location. The children draw pictures of mice, and each child makes a "mouse house." The front door of the house becomes the cover of a story that the child writes on the pages stapled inside.

Like parents who constantly draw on the experiences they have shared with their children, these teachers use classroom experiences as a basis for relating new ideas to old. Listening to and responding to books is viewed as a vital resource for building background knowledge, fostering language development, linking reading to writing, developing a sense of story, and building positive attitudes about books and print (Strickland, 1987; Taylor & Strickland, 1986b).

Admittedly, storybook reading in the classroom will never replace family storybook reading at home, nor should it. We do believe, however, that schools can benefit from studying how young children learn in other settings, especially the home, and can apply that information to improve the learning environment.

References

Cohen, M. *Will I have a friend?* New York: Macmillan, 1967.

Erikson, F. Taught cognitive learning in its immediate environments: A neglected topic in the anthropology of education. *Anthropology and Education Quarterly*, 1982, *13*, 149-180.

Krauss, R. *The growing story.* New York: Harper & Row, 1947.

Sampson, M. (Ed.). *The pursuit of literacy: Early reading and writing.* Dubuque, IA: Kendall/Hunt, 1986.

Sharmat, M.W. *Mooch the messy.* New York: Harper & Row, 1976.

Shecter, B. *Hester the jester.* New York: Harper & Row, 1977.

Strickland, D. Sharing books with young children. *Pre-K Today*, 1987, *1* (4), 16-19.

Taylor, D., and Strickland, D.S. *Family storybook reading.* Portsmouth, NH: Heinemann, 1986a.

Taylor, D., and Strickland, D.S. Family literacy: Myths and magic. In M. Sampson (Ed.), *The pursuit of literacy: Early reading and writing.* Dubuque, IA: Kendall/Hunt, 1986b.

Teale, W.H., and Sulzby, E. (Eds.). *Emergent literacy: Writing and reading.* Norwood, NJ: Ablex, 1986.

CHAPTER FOUR

Literature for Young Children

Bernice E. Cullinan

A superabundance of good books awaits children due to a virtual explosion in publishing for the very young. Brightly colored books or soft flannel pillow books can become a part of a child's life from the very beginning. Board books, participation books, and easy to read books pave children's way to independence in reading. Whether children benefit from this vast array of beautiful books depends entirely upon the adults in their lives. If you have young children of your own or work with them in day care centers or nursery schools, it is important that you find out about children's books and make them available. You will enrich children's lives and your own as well.

On my desk, I have a photograph of my friend Kathy Harwood reading to her daughter Elizabeth on the day she was born. I take great pleasure in looking at that photograph, not only because it shows people I love, but also because it represents something I firmly believe in—reading to children. Books will be an important part of Elizabeth's life. I know that Kathy continues to read to Elizabeth every day and that both mother and daughter take great joy in their shared experience.

Childhood is a time of joy and a period of great learning. What can we do during the early childhood years to assure learning in the midst of joy? I find that the answers to this and other such questions lead me to literature. This chapter explores various types of literature for young children and documents the ways in which books can make a difference in children's lives.

The purpose of this chapter is to (1) show that literature makes a difference in children's lives, (2) develop criteria for selecting books for young children, and (3) identify outstanding books by notable authors and illustrators that help us give the gift of literacy to our children. Books can play a significant role in the life of a young child, but the extent to which they do so depends entirely upon adults. Our children have a literary heritage; adults must see that they receive their legacy.

Literature Makes a Difference in Children's Lives

Children who learn to read early are ones who have been read to. Although just how early a child needs to learn to read leads to a philosophical debate, we do know how it happens. Learning to read naturally is quite different from being "taught" to read. Studies of early readers looked at children who "picked it up on their own" without direct instruction. Relationships between learning to read at an early age and being read to have been documented again and again.

An early study by Durkin (1966) showed that children who learned to read before entering first grade had been read to by siblings, parents, or another caring adult. Neither race, ethnicity, socio-economic level, nor IQ distinguished between readers and nonreaders; the differences lay in access to print, being read to, valuing education, and early writing. Durkin called the readers "paper and pencil kids" who liked to make marks on paper. Studies by Clark (1976, 1984), Hall (1987), Morrow (1983), Teale (1984), and White (1984, 1954) underscore and extend Durkin's findings.

Children's language development is enriched by exposure to literature. Chukovsky (1963), a Russian poet, said that beginning at age two, every child becomes a "linguistic genius" — one who learns language rapidly and plays with its forms. In one of Chukovsky's examples, Yurochka asks her mother, "Say, Mother, when I was born, how did you find out that I was — Yurochka?" (p. 36). In another, three year old Nata pleads, "Mommie, sing me a lullaby-ly song!" (p. 4).

The phenomenal growth in children's language causes us to wonder where and how children discover so much so fast. Although language is not learned solely by imitation, a rich language environment stimulates growth (Cazden, 1972). Chomsky (1972) found a strong positive relationship between children's linguistic development and their exposure to literature. The more advanced the stage of linguistic development, the greater the exposure to literature.

Children's later educational achievement is related to early experiences of listening to stories. Wells (1986), a British linguist, spent fifteen years conducting a longitudinal study of thirty-two children from shortly after their first birthday until the last year of their elementary schooling. In *The Meaning Makers*, Wells presents case studies of six of those children to identify the major linguistic influences on their later educational achievement.

Wells found that stories are the way children make sense of life; stories give meaning to observable events by making connections between them.

It is clear that the number of stories children heard before schooling had a lasting effect. Rosie, who listened to no stories prior to school entrance, continued to lag at the end of elementary school. Jonathan, who had listened to more than 5,000 stories in that same period, was at the top of the class in literacy related activities. Jonathan understood his world in a way that Rosie never could know. He felt the joy of making sense of the mystery of print in the sudden realization, "I can read," a major step in the process of growing up. Knowledge of literacy at age five was directly related to reading comprehension at age seven. Repeated demonstrations of literate behavior serve as models for young learners.

In a similarly convincing study, Butler (1980), a New Zealand researcher, described the part played by books in the early development of Cushla, a severely handicapped child. Books became important to Cushla at a surprisingly early age, and almost by accident. Because she was unable to hold objects, crawl, sit up, or watch what happened around her, books became her chief means of learning as well as her chief source of delight. Although doctors believed that Cushla was mentally retarded, when she was tested at three years, eight months, her intelligence was assessed as being well above average. She was a happy child, well liked by other children and able to join in many of their games. Her parents' patience, acceptance, and love had borne fruit. They had used stories to calm her through long hospital stays and sleepless nights. Studies by Clay (1979), Butler and Clay (1979), Doake (1985, 1986), Taylor (1983), Taylor and Strickland (1986), Baghban (1984), Teale (1984), Heath (1982), Ferreiro and Teberosky (1982), Goodman and Altwerger (1981), and Mason (1980, 1983, 1984) support and extend these dramatic findings.

Children build their storehouse of language from their communicative experiences and develop their concept of story from the stories they hear. Harste, Burke, and Woodward (1984) describe children feeding their "linguistic data pool" from language encounters and drawing what they need from that data pool in subsequent language encounters. King and Rentel (1981, 1982, 1983) found that children imitate and adapt from stories they hear as they create their own stories. One child borrowed freely from "The Ugly Duckling," *Frog and Toad*, "The Gingerbread Boy," and "Little Red Riding Hood" as he packed elements from each into his own original creation. Literature is reflected in the content and form of children's language and their stories. Blackburn (1985) described children's use of stories they had heard in stories they wrote as "borrowings" in a cycle where stories never end.

Criteria for Selecting Books for Young Children

Good books for young children have interesting language. Since children are "language sponges" that soak up words around them, we want the language in their books to be worthy of emulation. The words should have a rhythm of their own and fall harmoniously on the ear. There is no need to worry about the level of difficulty of books read aloud since children readily adopt words they hear as a part of their own vocabulary. The context and the illustrations make the meanings of these words clear. Moe (1978) found that many excellent picture books use only thirty to forty different words but are far richer than most of the controlled vocabulary books. Look for books with language that sounds the way natural language sounds.

Books for young children should present experiences that have a connection to their lives. This does not mean that books should deal only with familiar experiences since books are experiences in themselves, and learning from books is a time proven strategy. Children draw parallels from books, however, to the events and characters in their daily life. Dorothy White kept a diary in which she recorded the books she read to her daughter Carol from birth to age five and noted Carol's responses to these *Books before Five* (1954, 1984). In one entry made when Carol was three and one-half, White reflects

> *Animals of Farmer Jones* became that year one of Carol's best loved books and Farmer Jones himself a household myth

like Mother Goose. She developed a passionate interest in animal diets. "What do tigers eat? What do fishes eat? What do birds?" Throughout [the year] we were answering such questions, and although I have not read her this story for the last six months it is still part of her background. A good children's book is like a gifted man in an obscure place. It is not easy for an observer outside the circle to estimate just how far or how deep that influence may reach.

Because young children's coordination is not well developed, they need books with sturdy durable pages. Sturdy books for babies are made from cardboard (board books), cloth, or plastic fabrics. Such books withstand chewing, dribbles, and other mishandlings.

Finally, in choosing books for children, select those that you yourself like. Your enthusiasm in sharing books with a child will influence the child's response. Pick a book that appeals to you, match it to your child's interests and level of development, and you're sure to have a winner. In summary, you may wish to use these criteria in selecting books for young children: (1) rhythmic language, interesting vocabulary; (2) within the conceptual level of the child; (3) sturdily constructed; and (4) ones you like yourself.

Outstanding Books for Young Children

The books listed are reviewed in three major clusters: books for infants (birth to twelve months); books for toddlers (one to three years); and books for preschoolers (three to six years). These broad developmental ages provide rough guidelines for selecting books. It should be noted, however, that children cling to favorite books for many years after they have supposedly outgrown them. In the same way, children will reach up for a book that is purportedly "too old" for them.

Restricting books for a particular age group is sheer nonsense; follow your child's lead in selecting appropriate books. For convenience, poetry and folklore are listed under a specific age group, but this in no way should limit their use. Children need poetry and folklore every day and at every age.

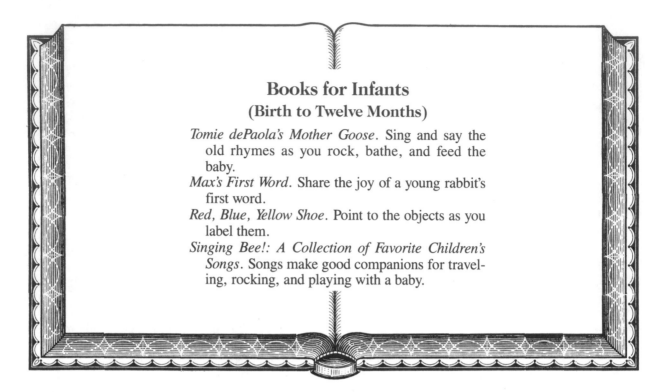

Books for Infants
(Birth to Twelve Months)

Tomie dePaola's Mother Goose. Sing and say the old rhymes as you rock, bathe, and feed the baby.

Max's First Word. Share the joy of a young rabbit's first word.

Red, Blue, Yellow Shoe. Point to the objects as you label them.

Singing Bee!: A Collection of Favorite Children's Songs. Songs make good companions for traveling, rocking, and playing with a baby.

Mother Goose and Nursery Rhymes

The earliest literature shared with children, more often sung and recited from memory than read, often consists of Mother Goose and nursery rhymes. Some modern young parents missed the nursery rhymes themselves because they were born in the television generation and learned Big Bird's songs instead of the old verses. Although contemporary rhymes are fine, our children deserve the touchstones of a literary education encompassed in the old verses. The books will help parents and children share the legacy of Mother Goose together.

Tomie dePaola. *Tomie dePaola's Mother Goose* (Putnam, 1985) contains the stamp of his distinctive art with sharp, bold, clear lines and generous use of white space. All the old familiar verses dePaola includes become favorites that children want to hear repeatedly and learn by heart quickly.

Arnold Lobel. *The Random House Book of Mother Goose* (Random House, 1986) is an illustrated collection of familiar and less familiar rhymes. Lobel breathes new life into the traditional rhymes with his comic illustrations and graphic art.

Marguerite de Angeli. *Marguerite de Angeli's Book of Nursery and Mother Goose Rhymes* (Doubleday, 1954) is a comprehensive collection of the old verses illustrated with charming muted vignettes of quaint children. This book is considered something of a classic among Mother Goose books.

Brian Wildsmith. *Brian Wildsmith's Mother Goose* (Oxford University Press, 1982) is a bold contrast to de Angeli's muted tones. Wildsmith depicts his characters and their plights with deep purples, fuchsias, and strong geometric patterns such as hexagons.

Books for Babies

New mothers often ask me when they should start giving books to their children, and I reply, "right now," no matter how young the child. I tell them about Kathy Harwood and turn to the photo-documentary of David Doake's son, Raja, who was read to on the day he was born and virtually every day following (Doake, 1986).

Both Doake's and Harwood's children learned early that books provide a special way of communicating with parents. Although babies and toddlers will not understand every word, just as they don't understand every word spoken to them, they eventually will begin to pick up meaning from the context of the situation and soon can select a favorite book from among several on a shelf. In these early days, the literature is read aloud or sung as nursery songs. As soon as a child can grasp a book, however, there should be books to grasp. These books need to be durable, washable, and child proof; many are board books or made from cloth or plastic fabrics.

Helen Oxenbury. *Playing, Dressing, Working, Friends, Family* (Baby Board Book Series, Simon & Schuster, 1981) all feature a droll plumpish baby with wispy hair doing what babies do—banging on pots, putting clothes on backwards, or "helping" with the housework. The books are perfect for the labeling and pointing stage when children repeatedly identify "baby," "Mommy," or "shoe." Other excellent series by Oxenbury include *Mother's Helper, Shopping Trip, Beach Day, Good Night, Good Morning,* and *Monkey See, Monkey Do* (Dial, 1982); *Clap Hands, All Fall Down,* and *Tickle, Tickle* (Macmillan, 1987); and *I Can, I Hear, I See,* and *I Touch* (Random House, 1986).

Rosemary Wells. *Max's First Word, Max's New Suit, Max's Ride,* and *Max's Toys: A Counting Book* (Dial, 1979) were the first high quality board books to be done by an established author. In fact, these books are acknowledged as making the genre respectable. Max, a child in the guise of a rabbit, remains mum while his sister Ruby tries to get him to say "cup," "egg," "broom," "fish," "apple," or "yum-yum" in *Max's First Word*. Max surprises Ruby and us when the first word he speaks is "delicious." Wells also follows Max in another series, *Max's Breakfast, Max's Bath, Max's Birthday,* and *Max's Bedtime* (Dial, 1985).

Tana Hoban. *Red, Blue, Yellow Shoe* and *Panda, Panda* (Board books, Greenwillow, 1986), *1, 2, 3: A First Book of Numbers* and *What Is It?: A First Book of Objects* (board books, Greenwillow, 1985) show what a talented photographer can do in presenting concepts to very young children. Hoban's crystal clear photographs sparkle with clarity as she focuses on animals and objects in a child's world. Children learning language will name the objects and animals as many times as you help them turn the durable, colorful pages.

Beatrix Potter. *Meet Peter Rabbit, Meet Hunca Munca, Meet Jemima Puddle-Duck,* and *Meet Tom Kitten* (Beatrix Potter Board Books, Warne, 1986) feature carefully selected and authorized illustrations from the original Beatrix Potter books to cast the beloved animals in board books for very young children. The illustrations are authentic Potter, but the text is not; simple sentences describe what is going on in the illustrations. These books cannot substitute for the real thing, but they are artistically sound and can be used much earlier than Beatrix Potter's magnificent books.

Nursery Songs

I have often said, "Give me a rocking chair, a baby, and a lullaby and I'm at the gates of heaven." Although this may not describe complete happiness for everyone, it does for me. There are many excellent books—some collections, some individual songs—that will keep you singing to your children. If you work with young children, you know the magic a good song can work.

Jane Hart (compiler). *Singing Bee!: A Collection of Favorite Children's Songs,* illustrated by Anita Lobel (Lothrop, Lee, & Shepard, 1982) is a book that everyone who works with young children needs. It is filled with 125 wonderful nursery songs (with piano accompaniments and guitar chords) that are magnificently illustrated by Anita Lobel. Lobel uses the concept of a little theater to bring unity to the book; the characters play out their scenes against stage frames and backdrops. Most of the songs are based on traditional rhymes, but a few modern favorites, such as "The Bus Song," are included.

Merle Peek. *Roll Over!: A Counting Song* (Clarion, 1981) and *Mary Wore Her Red Dress & Henry Wore His Green Sneakers* (Clarion, 1985) are rollicking songs that call for participation. In the counting song, a boy is in bed with nine animals. Each time they roll over, another animal falls out of bed. In the other, a traditional folk song appears in counterpoint to a story of Katy Bear's birthday party.

There are numerous individual songs illustrated by noted artists. Look for these: Aliki, *Go Tell Aunt Rhody* (Macmillan, 1974); Margot Zemach, *Hush, Little Baby* (Dutton, 1976); Harve Zemach, *Mommy, Buy Me a China Doll*, illustrated by Margot Zemach (Follett, 1966); John Langstaff, *Oh, A-Hunting We Will Go*, illustrated by Nancy Winslow Parker (Atheneum, 1974); and Peter Spier, *The Fox Went Out on a Chilly Night* (Doubleday, 1961).

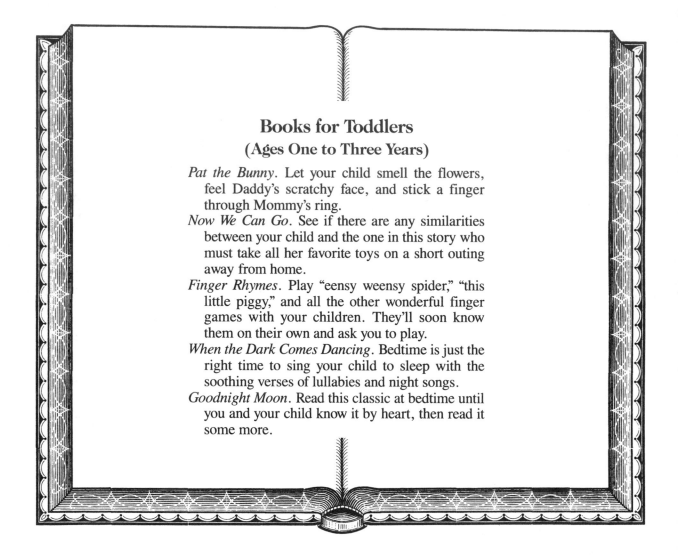

Books for Toddlers
(Ages One to Three Years)

Pat the Bunny. Let your child smell the flowers, feel Daddy's scratchy face, and stick a finger through Mommy's ring.

Now We Can Go. See if there are any similarities between your child and the one in this story who must take all her favorite toys on a short outing away from home.

Finger Rhymes. Play "eensy weensy spider," "this little piggy," and all the other wonderful finger games with your children. They'll soon know them on their own and ask you to play.

When the Dark Comes Dancing. Bedtime is just the right time to sing your child to sleep with the soothing verses of lullabies and night songs.

Goodnight Moon. Read this classic at bedtime until you and your child know it by heart, then read it some more.

Participation Books

It would be wonderful to again see the world through the eyes of a toddler: a dewdrop on a flower petal becomes a sparkle of enchantment; a crack on a sidewalk is a mystery to be explored; a surprise page turned in a book must be repeated time and again, with each repetition bringing squeals of delight. For this wondrous age, there are beautiful and exciting books waiting to be discovered.

Dorothy Kunhardt. *Pat the Bunny* (Western Publishing, 1940) has entertained three generations. It simply shows what Paul and Judy can do and invites the reader to do those things, too. Paul and Judy play peekaboo, smell flowers, wave bye-bye, and do other things children willingly try. It is a must for all toddlers.

Eric Hill. *Where's Spot?* (Putnam, 1980), *Spot's First Walk* (Putnam, 1981), *Spot Goes to the Circus* (Putnam, 1986), *Spot Goes to the Farm,* and *Spot's First Picnic* (Putnam, 1987) feature lift the flap pages that keep children searching for the lovable dog, Spot, or for the things Spot chases throughout his escapades. Children never tire of following Spot through his various adventures.

Finger Plays

Who can resist playing "this little piggy went to market" with a baby's toes? Or playing "eensy weensy spider went up the water spout" with a toddler? These old song games delight children and beg to be repeated until they are memorized. Toddlers sing them to themselves during play and as they fall asleep.

Marc Brown. *Finger Rhymes* (Dutton, 1980), *Hand Rhymes* (Dutton, 1985), and *Play Rhymes* (Dutton, 1987) are filled with bouncing lyrics that enchant youngsters. Old favorites, such as "I'm a little teapot/ short and stout/ Here is my handle/ Here is my spout," have children acting out the movements in jig time. Guides to appropriate actions appear in the illustrations.

Tom Glazer. *Eye Winker Tom Tinker Chin Chopper* (Doubleday, 1973) is indispensable because it contains so many old favorites. "Here is the church/ Here is the steeple/ Open the door/ And see all the people," "Pat-a-cake, pat-a-cake, baker's

man," and the title song illustrate the variety of the popular selections. The author gives guitar chords and piano arrangements for each rhyme. Tom Glazer adds to the variety in *Music for Ones & Twos: Songs and Games for the Very Young Child* (Doubleday, 1983), *Tom Glazer's Treasury of Songs* (Doubleday, 1988), and *Do Your Ears Hang Low?* (Doubleday, 1980).

Beginning Picture Storybooks

Beginning picture storybooks tell a story through a combination of extensive illustrations and few words. The story lines deal with everyday situations in a child's life or with animals in childlike situations. Picture storybooks are especially appropriate for the young child because the stories are simple and the illustrations are strong and clear. The books listed represent just a sampling of the wealth of picture books that await children in preschool and primary school years.

Ann Jonas. *When You Were a Baby* (Greenwillow, 1982), *Where Can It Be?* and *Now We Can Go* (Greenwillow, 1986), *The Quilt* (Greenwillow, 1984), and *The Trek* (Greenwillow, 1985) all feature just what young children need in their early picture storybooks—a clear plot, a sturdy design, and surprise! In one book, Jonas catalogs the things a child could not do *When You Were a Baby* and closes with, "But now you can!" In another, she shows a child insisting on packing all her toys before agreeing that *Now We Can Go.* In *Where Can It Be?* a child searches behind lift the flap doors and under the covers for that special blanket. In a happy ending, friend Deborah rings the doorbell and returns the blanket; it had been left at her house. An engaging child looks at *The Quilt* to recall the origin of the patchwork designs—her baby pajamas or first curtains—as she settles down for the night. In her dreams, the scenes on the quilt come to life while she searches for her stuffed dog. *The Trek* is a girl's delightful search for imaginary animals hidden in the shrubs and trees that line the path to school. Jonas is adept at pacing a plot and sure in her strong graphic images; her books celebrate universal feelings about childhood.

During the Me Museum project, Anderson and Suntken select many old favorites for story-

Me Museum

We believe that every child is a unique and special individual. Our belief reflects the philosophy of our school and is expressed through the ways we work with children in building a sense of community and through the curriculum we develop. For example, in our social studies curriculum for four and five year olds, we focus on the children's immediate world — self, home, and family.

We begin the year with the unit on self, placing a great emphasis on the uniqueness of the individual as we encourage children to develop positive self-concepts. To accomplish this, we plan a variety of activities around the question, "What's special about me?" Shared experiences help children to feel good about themselves, to know each other better, and to begin to expand their world. Through the theme of "Self," we develop several concepts: each person is a unique and special individual; people are alike in some ways but different in others; and every person has feelings and preferences. We see the study of Self as a bridge to the study of "Home" and "Family" which follow as we help children expand their views of the world.

In recognition of the uniqueness of each child, we have developed a special project to honor children in a weeklong celebration called the "Me Museum." Beginning in October, we feature two children each week in our classroom Me Museum. We send home a calendar listing dates the various children will be featured. The Me Museum, located atop two shelves in the center of the classroom, is a display of several items of special significance to the child featured. In any given week, there will be photographs of the children when they were younger, photographs of family members, carefully kept records in baby books, infant shoes, baby clothes, christening outfits, pictures or recipes of favorite foods, rattles, and favorite toys.

During the week the materials are on display, the child shares details with classmates, writes about the collection, and celebrates aspects of his or her early life. Favorite books from early childhood are frequently a part of the display. Several of these books are read to the entire class during storytime. Occasionally, a favorite recipe is prepared in the classroom and enjoyed for a snack.

When children bring in their bags full of memorabilia, one of us sits with them and asks them to talk about each item. We help organize the exhibit by labeling the items, and we encourage the child to tell the class what is special about each. We take dictation about each item and make up a descriptive card for each. When all the dictation is completed, we help children to assemble the exhibit and place things where they want them. Because parents must work with the children in compiling these treasures, the project facilitates communication between home and school and provides another opportunity for parents to become involved in what their children are learning at school.

At the end of the week, we dismantle the museum, and the featured children have a "show and tell" about each item in front of the entire class. The children always seem to derive pleasure from this and feel very special. The children have been so enthusiastic about the Me Museum that they have requested that we teachers exhibit special things from our lives.

Judith Anderson and Jane Suntken
Friends Seminary
New York, New York

time, including *Evan's Corner* (Elizabeth Hill, Holt, 1967), *Alexander & the Terrible, Horrible, No Good, Very Bad Day* (Judith Viorst, Macmillan, 1972), *Just Me* (Marie Hall Ets, Viking, 1965), *Dandelion* (Don Freeman, Viking, 1964), *Whistle for Willie* (Ezra Jack Keats, Viking, 1964), *What Mary Jo Shared* (Janice Udry, Whitman, 1966), and *Let's Be Enemies* (Janice Udry, Harper, 1961).

Nancy Tafuri. *Have You Seen My Duckling?* (Greenwillow, 1984), *Do Not Disturb* (Greenwillow, 1987), and *Early Morning in the Barn* (Greenwillow, 1983) draw the viewer's eyes to the visual subplots hidden in the pictures. In *Have You Seen My Duckling?* a baby duck scampers through the reeds and tall grass while mother duck searches high and low. The child looking at the book becomes a willing helper, pointing out, "There she is, mommy duck!" *Do Not Disturb* follows a family on a camping trip where they disturb the creatures of the forest all day long with their splashing and banging. At night, the animals retaliate by making their own nocturnal noises, causing the family to futilely hang a sign, "Do not Disturb" on their tent. *Early Morning in the Barn* pictures a proud rooster awakening the barnyard animals with a "cock-a-doodle-doo." A little chick replies, "cheep," awakening two other chicks to run through the barnyard searching for their mother. They are greeted by all the other creatures, who respond in their characteristic ways. Then, in satisfying fashion, the chicks return to their mother who has food waiting for them.

Margaret Wise Brown. *Goodnight Moon*, illustrated by Clement Hurd (Harper, 1947), has become a classic in less than fifty years. The simple bedtime story features a little rabbit who lies snug in his bed and says goodnight to everything in his room. Through the window, you can see the moon rise and cross the heavens as the light and shadow inside the room glow and glimmer on the sleepy rabbit.

Poetry

Poetry is a natural language for young children; they respond to its rhythms and bounce to its rhymes. There are several comprehensive collections especially designed for young children, but you can find many appropriate poems in collections aimed at a broader audience.

Jack Prelutsky, compiler. *Read-Aloud Rhymes for the Very Young*, illustrated by Marc Brown (Knopf, 1986), features poetry selected from the best poets across the ages. In an introduction to this collection, Jim Trelease, author of *The Read-Aloud Handbook*, says that everyone knows children are great *asking machines*, but we forget that before they become asking machines, they are great *listening machines*. They will listen to the poems in this collection, which celebrate the small joys and tragedies of children's lives: dropping a jelly sandwich in the sand, losing a sand castle to the crunch of a passing foot, and baking sand pies. Such events are made more memorable when they are cast in verse. Prelutsky has selected with the ear of a poet, and he includes six of his own poems.

Caroline Royds, compiler. *Poems For Young Children*, illustrated by Inga Moore (Doubleday, 1986), includes selections from poets Walter de la Mare, William Blake, A. A. Milne, Lewis Carroll, Edward Lear, and Robert Louis Stevenson. The collection, while not geared to the youngest child, serves as an introduction to great works.

Josette Frank, compiler. *Poems to Read to the Very Young*, illustrated by Eloise Wilkin (Random House, 1982), has many old favorites, such as "There was a little turtle./ He lived in a box./ He swam in a puddle./ He climbed on the rocks." by Vachel Lindsay. The illustrations match the quaint traditional nature of the verses.

Nancy Larrick, compiler. *When the Dark Comes Dancing: A Bedtime Poetry Book*, illustrated by John Wallner (Philomel/Putnam, 1983), is filled with forty-five wonderful poems about little creatures settling down to sleep, stars, the middle of the night, the moon, dreams, lullabies, and more. Larrick, a noted anthologist, has a sense of what it takes to help a child unwind at the end of the day and restore the inner calm that leads to restful sleep. The poems, lullabies, and lyrics she selects weave that mystical web that eases children off to sweet dreams.

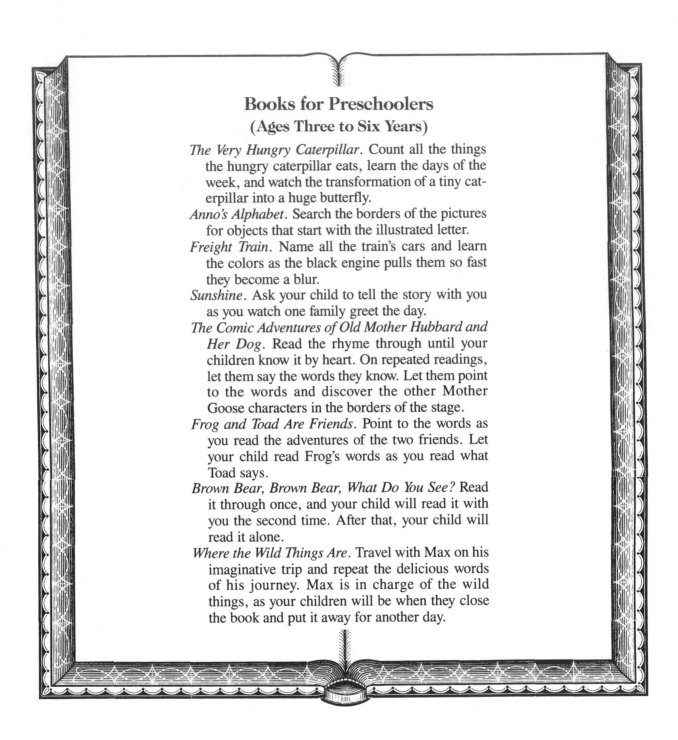

Books for Preschoolers
(Ages Three to Six Years)

The Very Hungry Caterpillar. Count all the things the hungry caterpillar eats, learn the days of the week, and watch the transformation of a tiny caterpillar into a huge butterfly.

Anno's Alphabet. Search the borders of the pictures for objects that start with the illustrated letter.

Freight Train. Name all the train's cars and learn the colors as the black engine pulls them so fast they become a blur.

Sunshine. Ask your child to tell the story with you as you watch one family greet the day.

The Comic Adventures of Old Mother Hubbard and Her Dog. Read the rhyme through until your children know it by heart. On repeated readings, let them say the words they know. Let them point to the words and discover the other Mother Goose characters in the borders of the stage.

Frog and Toad Are Friends. Point to the words as you read the adventures of the two friends. Let your child read Frog's words as you read what Toad says.

Brown Bear, Brown Bear, What Do You See? Read it through once, and your child will read it with you the second time. After that, your child will read it alone.

Where the Wild Things Are. Travel with Max on his imaginative trip and repeat the delicious words of his journey. Max is in charge of the wild things, as your children will be when they close the book and put it away for another day.

ABC and Counting Books

Some of our finest illustrators use the frame of the alphabet and numbers to sketch a plot or to show objects to label and to talk about. Children need to recognize the letters and numerals as they begin reading and writing, and there are no finer materials to instruct and delight them than the creative books described here.

Eric Carle. *The Very Hungry Caterpillar* (Philomel/Putnam, 1969; Miniature Edition, 1987) is one of children's favorite counting books. The book describes a caterpillar growing from a tiny egg into a huge butterfly by eating its way through all sorts of food. The caterpillar leaves holes in the food he eats, and all children I've shared the book with insist on sticking their finger through every hole.

Bert Kitchen. *Animal Alphabet* (Dial, 1984) and *Animal Numbers* (Dial, 1987) are a visual delight for their fine art and the cleverness of the concepts presented. In *Animal Alphabet*, the animals are entwined in the letter that begins their name. In *Animal Numbers*, the numerals are represented by the number of baby animals shown with their mothers. Large, spacious pages designed by a gallery painter make these books worth looking at time and again.

Mitsumasa Anno. *Anno's Alphabet* (Crowell, 1975), *Anno's Counting Book* (Crowell, 1977), and *Anno's Counting House* (Crowell, 1982), books by one of Japan's leading artists, can be enjoyed on many levels. Each book contains several subtle subplots that keep children returning to look again. In *Anno's Alphabet*, a woodcarver's tools foreshadow the carved letters to come, and the borders around each letter are filled with hidden objects starting with that same letter. *Anno's Counting Book* begins with zero (which is unusual), showing a frozen landscape and no objects. For the numeral 1, Anno adds one house, one tree, one bridge, one dog, one bird, one sun, one girl, one boy, and one snowman in a January setting. Each double page spread flows through the changing seasons and months of the year as Anno adds people, buildings, and objects to represent the numeral. *Anno's Counting House* is more complex, showing addition and subtraction as children move from one house to another, taking their belongings with them. Windows open as flaps to reveal the diminishing number in one house and the increasing number in the other.

Other excellent ABC and counting books include: Arnold Lobel, *On Market Street*, illustrated by Anita Lobel (Greenwillow, 1981); Mary Azarian, *A Farmer's Alphabet* (Godine, 1981); Tana Hoban, *A, B, See!* (Greenwillow, 1982), *Count and See* (Macmillan, 1972), and *26 Letters*

and 99 Cents (Greenwillow, 1987); Muriel Feelings, *Jambo Means Hello: Swahili Alphabet Book*, illustrated by Tom Feelings (Dial, 1974); and *Moja Means One: Swahili Counting Book*, illustrated by Tom Feelings (Dial, 1971); Shirley Hughes, *Lucy & Tom's 1.2.3.* (Viking, 1987); and *Lucy & Tom's A.B.C.* (Viking, 1986); Tracey Campbell Pearson, *A*Apple Pie.* (Dial, 1986); and Nancy Tafuri, *Who's Counting?* (Greenwillow, 1986).

Concept Books and Informational Boooks for Young Children

A concept book describes objects or an abstract idea, such as color, shape, size, or place. Informational books present factual information in straightforward, expository prose enriched by clear, realistic illustrations. There is not necessarily a story line, although some authors include one. Instead, the author/illustrator shows various dimensions of the concept or topic of information.

Tana Hoban. *Is It Red? Is It Yellow? Is It Blue?* (Greenwillow, 1978), *I Read Symbols* and *I Read Signs* (Greenwillow, 1983), *I Walk and Read* (Greenwillow, 1984), *Round & Round & Round* (Greenwillow, 1983), *Big Ones, Little Ones* (Greenwillow, 1976), *Shapes, Shapes, Shapes* (Greenwillow, 1986), *Dots, Spots, Speckles, & Stripes* (Greenwillow, 1987), *Is It Larger? Is It Smaller?* (Greenwillow, 1985), and *Is It Rough? Is It Smooth? Is It Shiny?* (Greenwillow, 1984) are all excellent concept books that showcase Hoban's vision and skill as a photographer. *Is It Red? Is It Yellow? Is It Blue?* shows those colors, as well as orange, green, and purple in everyday scenes in a city—stacks of fruit, umbrellas, balloons, leaves, cars, bubble gum, and heavy machinery. Hoban puts clear circles of the colors evident in the photographs at the bottom of the page so there can be no mistaking which colors are shown in the picture. The three books on reading show how much we learn from environmental print. The other books focus on shapes and textures.

Donald Crews. *Freight Train* (1978), *Truck* (1980), *School Bus* (1984), *Carousel* (1982), *Light* (1981), *Flying* (1986), *Bicycle Race* (1985), *Harbor* (1982), *Parade* (1983), *Ten Black Dots* (1986), and *We Read: A to Z* (1984)—all published by

Greenwillow—elevate design to a high art. Crews studied art and graphic design as a student, and each book features bold lines and vivid colors. *Freight Train* features a black engine, an orange tank car, a yellow hopper, a purple box car, and a red caboose that all become a blaze of glowing color as the train moves over bridges and through tunnels. *Truck* follows a big tractor trailer truck that is loaded with toys and driven cross country. Beginning readers point out all the stop signs, exit signs, and road markers as the big truck barrels along the highways. All of these books will be viewed again and again by young children.

Harlow Rockwell. *My Kitchen* (Greenwillow, 1980), *My Doctor* (Macmillan, 1973), *My Dentist* (Greenwillow, 1975), and *My Nursery School* (Greenwillow, 1976).

Anne Rockwell. *Boats* (Dutton, 1982), *Cars* (Dutton, 1984), *The Emergency Room* (Macmillan, 1985), *Fire Engines* (Dutton, 1986), *I Like The Library* (Dutton, 1977), *My Baby Sitter* (Macmillan, 1985), *Our Garage Sale* (Greenwillow, 1984), *Planes* (Dutton, 1985), *Things That Go* (Dutton, 1986), *Toolbox* (Macmillan, 1971), and *Trucks* (Dutton, 1984).

Anne and Harlow Rockwell. *My Back Yard* (Macmillan, 1984), *My Barber* (Macmillan, 1981), *The Supermarket* (Macmillan, 1979), and *Machines* (Harper, 1985), like all of the Rockwells' books, present information in clean, simple pictures on spacious white pages. Their topics have great appeal, for they deal with aspects of life that interest young children. Looking closely at the dentist, doctor, nursery school, kitchen, baby sitter, back yard, and supermarket holds tremendous appeal for children.

Gail Gibbons. *Check It Out! The Book about Libraries* (Harcourt Brace Jovanovich, 1985), *The Milk Makers* (Macmillan, 1985), *The Post Office Book: Mail and How It Moves* (Crowell, 1986), *Up Goes the Skyscraper!* (Four Winds, 1986), *Department Store* (Crowell, 1984), *Boat Book* (Holiday, 1983), *Deadline! From News to Newspaper* (Crowell, 1987), *Dinosaurs* (Holiday, 1987), *Fill It Up!* (Crowell, 1985), *Fire! Fire!* (Crowell, 1984), *Flying* and *Playgrounds* (Holiday, 1985), *Sun Up, Sun Down* (Harcourt Brace Jovanovich, 1983), *Tool Book* (Holiday, 1982), *Trains* (Holiday, 1987), *Trucks* (Crowell, 1981), *Tunnels* (Holiday, 1984), *Weather Forecasting* (Four Winds, 1987), and *Zoo* (Crowell, 1987) are all good informational books for young children. Gibbons researches her topics carefully and checks the accuracy of her information with experts. She simplifies technical information as much as possible without distorting it. Her book on dinosaurs leads to further study in some early childhood classrooms.

Aliki has produced some of the best books on dinosaurs, a subject of perennial interest to young children. Aliki's books include *My Visit to the Dinosaurs* (Crowell, 1985), *Fossils Tell of Long Ago* (Crowell, 1972), *Dinosaurs Are Different* (Crowell, 1985), *Digging Up Dinosaurs* (Crowell, 1981), and *Dinosaur Bones* (Crowell, 1988).

I·D·E·A·S
You Can Use

Dinosaur Museum

Our group of five and six year olds has shown the mysterious predilection of many young children for dinosaurs. After studying living animals earlier this year (from lap dogs to stingrays), we came around to this dramatic subject. When we asked the children to tell us and one another what they knew about dinosaurs, the responses ranged from shrugs to outpourings of (accurate) information. Not only knowledge and opinions were shared, but, even more precious to the children, their own toys and models from home. The parents were generous, lending us wonderful books and objects.

Eager to stimulate even more interest, we started making small clay models for the children to play with, along with primitive trees made from sticks found on the playground. Sticks and rocks collected by the children, along with their toys, began to fill the classroom. Spontaneous fantasy play using the collection increased, based on the information we were discussing in class. Broken models were even "fed" to the carnivorous models. At the end of our first week, Mary Lou (the director) had caught our bug and came in with a fierce looking, three feet high Tyrannosaurus Rex model, mouth wide open and looking very hungry.

Wanting to encourage the fantasy play in which intellectual and emotional interests are joined at this age, we decided to build a larger environment. We transformed our block area into an indoor sandbox (with pine bark) for the children to play in. A child brought in horsetails (a plant existing at the time of the dinosaurs) which she found in New Jersey. These provided the first vegetation; other forests and hills grew rapidly. This environment was built by the children; they figured out how to make a boundary using blocks. The landscape continues to change. Volcanoes rise; lava (represented with tissue paper) and rocks burst out of the papier-maché mountains. Playing in what the children now call our museum, they discuss and argue over intellectual and social problems, such as how the archaeologists can be *sure* they are right.

"They might have mixed up a cat and a Tyrannosaurus's bones."

"No, there were no cats then."

"Well maybe the bones got mixed up, though."

A recent heated discussion centered on how to choose a name and characteristics for a fantasy dinosaur (Jokeosaurus) drawn collaboratively for the art class.

"How do scientists pick the names?"

"The dinosaurs didn't know their names. They only got them from people."

"The names are made up from pieces. Saurus means lizard."

At the sand table, they made plaster impressions of footprints they'd "discovered" by digging them in the sand. Conversations took place while they covered up the "fossils," then carefully dug them up and brushed them off. Playing the role of archaeologists, their thinking was apparent.

"If this print is buried here and this other one is here, maybe the dinosaurs were walking together."

"And this one is broken?"

"Put it back like a puzzle."

"What made it broken?"

This unit's development provides an example of how we value collaborative, indepth work. In our class and our museum, the children have gained authority. This has promoted a democratic mood. The teachers still provide leadership (we supply the pine chips), but each child plays a part in discovering and discussing what questions to ask.

Jane Maisel and Scarlote West
Friends Seminary
New York, New York

Wordless Books

Wordless books tell a story through illustration alone. Before children learn to read print, they can read a story from the pictures of these inventive books.

Mercer Mayer. *A Boy, A Dog, and A Frog* (Dial, 1967), *Frog Where Are You?* (Dial, 1969), and *Frog Goes to Dinner* (Dial, 1974), a series about a boy and his pet frog, is hilariously funny because of the slapstick situations that arise. In *Frog Goes to Dinner*, the boy sneaks the frog into his pocket when he goes with his parents to a nice restaurant. Before the evening is over, the frog has leaped into the salad, a glass of champagne, and a saxophone. As they leave the restaurant, the parents are unhappy, but the smirks of pleasure on the frog's face and the boy's face cause readers to chuckle.

Jan Ormerod. *Sunshine* (Lothrop, Lee & Shepard, 1981) and *Moonlight* (Lothrop, Lee & Shepard, 1986) are both good books. Ormerod received critical acclaim for her first book, *Sunshine*. In it, a small girl helps her mother and father wake up, get breakfast, and get off to work in the morning. In *Moonlight*, the same family tries to get the child to go to bed. She uses all the typical ploys to stay up and ends up being the last one in the family to fall asleep. In Ormerod's books, both parents share in the housekeeping and child care tasks.

Folklore

Folkore is the body of literature handed down by word of mouth from generations past. We do not know the authors of the tales, but they continue to enchant youngsters as they are retold and illustrated by some of our outstanding artists. No child should grow up deprived of the wealth of folklore that abounds. "The Three Little Pigs," should be a part

Tomie dePaola. *The Comic Adventures of Old Mother Hubbard and Her Dog* (Harcourt Brace Jovanovich, 1981) and *Tomi dePaola's Favorite Nursery Tales* (Putnam, 1986) feature dePaola's distinctive artistic style, which enchants children with its simplicity. In *The Comic Adventures of Old Mother Hubbard and Her Dog*, he incorporates visual subplots in the borders of the pages. Setting each scene on a stage, he hides other storybook

characters in little vignettes in the folds of the curtains. Tomie dePaola's *Favorite Nursery Tales*, a beautiful collection, contains all the old favorites.

Paul Galdone. *Cat Goes Fiddle-I-Fee* (Clarion, 1985), *Cinderella* (McGraw, 1978), *The Elves and the Shoemaker* (Clarion, 1984), *The Gingerbread Boy* (Clarion, 1983), *Henny Penny* (Clarion, 1968), *Jack and the Beanstalk* (Clarion, 1982), *Little Bo Peep* (Clarion, 1986), *The Little Red Hen* (Clarion, 1973), *Rumpelstiltskin* (Clarion, 1985), *The Teeny Tiny Woman* (Clarion, 1984), *The Three Bears* (Clarion, 1985), *The Three Billy Goats Gruff* (Clarion, 1981), *The Three Little Kittens* (Clarion, 1986), *The Three Little Pigs* (Clarion, 1970), and *What's in Fox's Sack?* (Clarion, 1982) are all excellent tales in single editions. Galdone's flamboyant style seems just right for the outlandish make believe stories that children love so much.

Janet and Allan Ahlberg. *The Jolly Postman* (Little, Brown, 1986) and *Each Peach Pear Plum: An I-Spy Story* (Viking, 1979) give the old nursery rhyme characters a new life by casting them in new and ingenious books. In *The Jolly Postman*, the characters write letters to one another. There's a letter of apology from Goldilocks to the three bears, a postcard from Jack to the giant, and a lawsuit against the big bad wolf for all his huffing and puffing. In *Each Peach Pear Plum*, storybook characters play hide and seek with the reader. Children enjoy spotting them hidden among the bushes or peeking in the window.

Easy to Read Books

Easy to read books are especially designed for beginning readers. They combine the controlled vocabulary of the basal reader with creative storytelling. Although we do not need to restrict the vocabulary of books we read aloud to children, it is a different matter when children are learning to read on their own. There are many excellent books in this genre. Dr. Seuss is credited with establishing easy to read books as a genre in 1957 with *The Cat in the Hat* (Random House, 1957). The number of words is controlled, and the sentences are phrased and structured so that line breaks occur at natural places.

Else Minarik. *Little Bear* (1957), *Father Bear Comes Home* (1959), *Little Bear's Friend (1960),*

Little Bear's Visit (1961), and *A Kiss for Little Bear* (1968) are all illustrated by Maurice Sendak and published by Harper. Minarik was a first grade teacher who could find nothing exciting for her students as they were learning to read. She wrote the stories for her students and discovered that children the world over loved them. Minarik was the first to develop strong characterization, natural dialogue, and engaging plots in this restricted form. Sendak's illustrations immortalized the winsome bear family.

Arnold Lobel. *Days with Frog and Toad* (Harper, 1979), *Frog and Toad All Year* (Harper, 1976), *Frog and Toad Are Friends* (Harper, 1970), and *Frog and Toad Together* (Harper, 1972) helped Lobel's lovable Frog and Toad endear themselves to readers from the very start. Toad is something of a tease who leads his gullible, shy friend into embarrassing situations.

Predictable Books

Predictable books are ones in which children can anticipate or predict what is coming because of the books' highly patterned structures. For example, once children read or hear the first line, they almost know what is coming next. The books contain highly patterned language, repetitive phrases, and predictable plots. Bill Martin Jr is credited with establishing the genre with *Brown Bear, Brown Bear, What Do You See?* published in 1967.

Brian Wildsmith. *Cat on the Mat* (1982), *All Fall Down* (1982), *Giddy Up* (1988), *If I Were You* (1988), *The Island* (1982), *My Dream* (1988), *The Nest* (1982), *Toot, Toot* (1988), *The Trunk* (1982), *What a Tale* (1988), and *Whose Shoes?* (1988) are all published by Oxford University Press. Wildsmith's colorful and artistic style is used to tell stories with highly structured language patterns. In *Cat on the Mat*, the first sentence is "The cat sat on the mat." Only one word in the sentence changes as other animals crowd in on the mat. When the cat is totally fed up with the intruders, it hisses and spits, chasing the others away. The final sentence is an understated repeat of the first sentence.

Picture Story Books

Picture story books are ones in which the story is told through a combination of text and illustration. They make up the largest and richest body of literature for young children. Their volume makes it impossible to do justice to them; they are included here to recognize their importance. See Cullinan, *Literature and the Child*; Huck, Hepler, and Hickman, *Children's Literature in the Elementary School*; and Sutherland and Arbuthnot, *Children and Books* for a comprehensive review of picture books.

Maurice Sendak. *Where the Wild Things Are* (Harper, 1963) is an imaginative story that appeals to developing young children's sense of playfulness. When Max is scolded and sent to his room for being naughty, he invents his own world of "wild things," but he controls them with the magic trick of staring into their yellow eyes without blinking once. Sendak says that he modeled the wild things on his relatives who used to come to visit and say, "I'll eat you up, you're so sweet."

Esphyr Slobodkina. *Caps for Sale* (Scott, Foresman, 1947) is an oldie but goodie in which a salesman wanders into a village trying to sell caps he has stacked upon his head. When no one buys his wares, he falls asleep under a tree. Mischievous monkeys hiding in the tree steal his caps for their own and imitate the salesman's attempts to get the caps back. A perfect story for creative drama, repetition, and just plain fun.

Big Books

Big books are oversized copies of picture story books with patterned language and repetitive phrases. Don Holdaway (1979) proposed that we transfer the routines of the bedtime story to the classroom since we know that many children learn to read from hearing the words and following along with the print. This is called shared reading. In order to transfer shared reading to the classroom, we need enlarged texts, called big books, so that a group of children can see the print.

When teachers use big books, they follow the routines of talking about the relevant concepts in the book; call attention to the title, author, and illustrator; and ask children to predict what they think the story may be about. Then they read the story aloud, tracking the print with their hand or a pointer. During the reading, they may think aloud about their understanding of the story, ask children to fill in predictable words or phrases, and ask them what might happen next.

After reading aloud, teachers guide discussion about key ideas in the text, asking children to recall important points and to find the corresponding part in the text. They guide the group in rereading, use cloze activities to involve children in meaningful prediction of words, and focus children's attention on distinctive features and patterns in the text. Teachers ask children to look for repeated words, word beginnings, consonant clusters, punctuation marks, and distinctive features of the text (Strickland, 1988). Many teachers create their own big books, but there are several available commercially. Here are some of the best.

Wright Group Story Box. *Mrs. Wishy-Washy* (Wright Group, 1984) features tireless Mrs. Wishy-Washy who scrubs barnyard animals who like to play in mud puddles.

Mem Fox. *Hattie and the Fox* (Bradbury, 1987) tells the story of Hattie, a bright white hen who spies the eyes of a fox in the bushes. She alerts her barnyard friends, but they ignore her warnings. Hattie continues her cries of alarm as the fox's nose, ears, and body show through the bushes. When her friends pay attention, it's too late!

Bill Martin Jr. *Brown Bear, Brown Bear, What Do You See?* illustrated by Eric Carle (Holt, 1983). The answer to the title question is "I see a redbird looking at me." Of course, the next question is "Redbird, Redbird, what do you see?" and on through a series of animals, ending with a group of children and their teacher looking at one another in a lovely, bouncy, predictable refrain of questions and answers. Many of the books cited under predictable books or patterned books are good ones to re-create in big book format.

In Summary

Clearly, there is a great store of riches in books for young children. There are developmentally different stages in childhood and an array of books for each developmental level. Unfortunately, children may never benefit from this wealth of books unless adults do their part. Children need adults who share their literary heritage and lead them into literacy.

Story has great power in human lives. We know that it is a primary act of mind; it is the way we organize our minds and understand our world. We also know that story touches the heartstrings in a way that facts never can do. A great poet said, "What the heart knows today, the head will understand tomorrow." Give your children literature; it is a part of their heritage.

References

Baghban, M. *Our daughter learns to read and write: A case study from birth to three.* Newark, DE: International Reading Association, 1984.

Blackburn, E. Stories never end. In J. Hansen, T. Newkirk, and D. Graves (Eds.), *Breaking ground: Teachers relate reading and writing in the elementary school.* Portsmouth, NH: Heinemann, 1985, 3-13.

Butler, D. *Cushla and her books.* Boston, MA: Horn Book, Inc., 1980.

Butler, D., and Clay, M. *Reading begins at home.* Portsmouth, NH: Heinemann, 1979.

Cazden, C. *Child language and education.* New York: Holt, 1972.

Chomsky, C. Stages in language development and reading exposure. *Harvard Educational Review,* 1972, *42,* 1-33.

Chukovsky, K. *From two to five.* Berkeley, CA: University of California Press, 1963.

Clark, M.M. Literacy at home and at school: Insights from a study of young fluent readers. In H. Goelman, A.A. Oberg, and F. Smith (Eds.), *Awakening to literacy.* Portsmouth, NH: Heinemann, 1984.

Clark, M.M. *Young fluent readers.* Portsmouth, NH: Heinemann, 1976.

Clay, M. *Reading: The patterning of complex behavior.* Portsmouth, NH: Heinemann, 1979.

Doake, D.B. Learning to read: It starts in the home. In D.R. Tovey and J.E. Kerber (Eds.), *Roles in literacy learning: A new perspective.* Newark, DE: International Reading Association, 1986, 2-9.

Doake, D.B. Reading like behavior: Its role in learning to read. In A.M. Jaggar and M.T. Smith-Burke (Eds.), *Observing the language learner.* Newark, DE: International Reading Association, 1985, 82-98.

Durkin, D. *Children who read early.* New York: Teachers College Press, 1966.

Ferreiro, E., and Teberosky, A. *Literacy before schooling.* Portsmouth, NH: Heinemann, 1982.

Goodman, Y., and Altwerger, B. *Print awareness in preschool children: A study of the development of literacy in preschool children.* Occasional paper, Program in Language and Literacy. Tucson, AZ: University of Arizona, 1981.

Hall, N. *The emergence of literacy*. Portsmouth, NH: Heinemann, 1987.

Harste, J., Woodward, V., and Burke, C. *Language stories and literacy lessons*. Portsmouth, NH: Heinemann, 1984.

Heath, S.B. What no bedtime story means: Narrative skills at home and school. *Language in Society*, 1982, *11*, 49-76.

Holdaway, D. *The foundations of literacy*. New York: Ashton Scholastic, 1979.

King, M.L., and Rentel, V. *Transition to writing*. Columbus, OH: National Institute of Education Grant G-79-0039, 1982. (ED 240603)

King, M.L., Rentel, V., Pappas, C., Pettigrew, B., and Zutell, J. *How children learn to write: A longitudinal study*. Columbus, OH: National Institute of Education Grant G-79-0137, 1981. (ED 213050)

Mason, J.M. *Acquisition of knowledge about reading in the preschool period: An update and extension*. Paper presented at the Society of Research in Child Development Convention, Detroit, 1983.

Mason, J.M. When do children begin to read: An exploration of four year old children's letter and word reading competencies. *Reading Research Quarterly*, 1980, *15* (2), 203-221.

Mason, J.M., McCormick, C., and Bhavnagri, N. How are you going to help me learn? Lesson negotiations between a teacher and preschool children. In D.B. Yaden and S. Templeton (Eds.), *Metalinguistic awareness and begin-ning literacy*. Portsmouth, NH: Heinemann, 1986, 159-172.

Morrow, L.M. Home and school correlates of early interest in literature. *Journal of Educational Research*, 1983, *76*, 24-30.

Morrow, L.M. Young children's responses to one to one story readings in school settings. *Reading Research Quarterly*, 1988, *23* (1), 89-107.

Rentel, V., and King, M.L. *A longitudinal study of coherence in children's written narratives*. Columbus, OH: National Institute of Education Grant G-8-0063, 1983. (ED 327089)

Strickland, D. Some tips for using big books. *The Reading Teacher*, 1988, *41* (9), 966-968.

Taylor, D. *Family literacy*. Portsmouth, NH: Heinemann, 1983.

Taylor, D., and Strickland, D. Family storybook reading. Portsmouth, NH: Heinemann, 1986.

Teale, W.H. Reading to young children: Its significance for literacy development. In H. Goelman, A.A. Oberg, and F. Smith (Eds.), *Awakening to literacy*. Portsmouth, NH: Heinemann, 1984.

Wells, G. *The meaning makers: Children learning language and using language to learn*. Portsmouth, NH: Heinemann, 1986.

White, D. *Books before five*. Portsmouth, NH: Heinemann, 1954, 1984.

CHAPTER FIVE

Reading to Kindergarten Children

Jana M. Mason

Carol L. Peterman

Bonnie M. Kerr

Our chapter describes the importance of reading to kindergarten children. We provide examples of effective instructional techniques using storybooks, informational books, and picture phrase books. Actual transcripts of teacher-student interactions and guidelines for teachers to use before, during, and after reading provide valuable information.

Many parents read to their children at home. Usually, their intent is simply to provide a warm, loving setting for book reading and to share a special time with their children. This activity also has greater benefits.

When parents read stories to children at home, their children's later language and reading achievement are positively influenced (Chomsky, 1972; Greaney, 1986; Moon and Wells, 1979; Wells, 1981, 1986). Furthermore, reading aids children's story retelling (Sulzby, 1985) and extends their enjoyment of reading (White, 1954). It is a valuable way for parents to support developing literacy while also influencing their children's later reading achievement.

Teachers also help children learn about reading by reading to them. Feitelson, Kita, and Goldstein (1986) found that reading stories daily to students influenced their story understanding and retelling ability. Morrow (1988) found that one-on-one reading to day care children improved their ability to talk about stories. Dunning and Mason (1984) found that reading through a story and then reviewing the key ideas improved children's ability to recall the story.

Assuming that teachers should read to children, how might they go about it? Should they read without comment, should they discuss the text ideas during or after reading, or should they use some other approach? Suppose they are reading a classic children's picture book or a fact book about nature. Should these two books be read differently? How about a picture book that has been enlarged so that children can see the print (a big book of the type described by Holdaway, 1979) or a book in which the print is in large letters and is conspicuous because there are only two or three words on a page? How should books of this type be read? At the present time, educators do not agree about the answers to these questions, and there is little or no research to guide teachers.

We wondered if experienced kindergarten teachers could help us answer these questions by demonstrating their book reading styles as they read different types of texts to whole classroom groups. We asked six teachers to read aloud to their students so we could capture what they said, how they interacted with their students, and what types of related activities their students engaged in. We analyzed what these teachers said and did before, during, and after each of three bookreading sessions by videotaping the sessions and making transcripts from the tapes.

Three children's books were chosen for the teachers to read—a well known Caldecott Honor picture storybook, *Strega Nona* (dePaola, 1975); an informational picture book about shadows, *Shadows: Here, There, and Everywhere* (Goor & Goor, 1981); and a six page picture phrase book that describes a child's preparation for bed, *Time for Bed* (Mason & McCormick, 1984). Teachers read the books to their classes in their usual manner as we videotaped the sessions. They all read the three texts to their entire classes (about twenty-five children), with the youngsters sitting on a rug in front of them as they read, showed the pictures, and talked with the children about the content.

The teachers devised a number of effective techniques to introduce each book, to help children comprehend during the book reading, and to summarize the book afterward, We describe their techniques for each book and each section of the presentation separately (before, during, and after reading).

Beginning with the storybook, moving to the informational text, and ending with the picture phrase book, we describe the techniques the teachers used for fostering word reading and comprehension. Our examples are taken directly from the transcripts where the letter *T*, followed by a number, identifies the teacher, and *C* indicates a response by one or more children. Material in quotation marks indicates that a teacher is reading the text. After describing how the books were read, we provide a list of guidelines in tables for teachers to use when reading to children.

Storybook Reading

Before Reading the Storybook

First, the teachers led discussions about what the children were going to hear. Children learned about the book in general (including discussions about the author, title, and illustrator), the type of text, the main character or other aspects about the setting, and goals for listening to the book.

Typically, when discussing the book, the teachers provided information or asked for predictions about the name of the story, an aspect of the story, or about the author and the illustrator. For example, in the following transcript excerpt, the teacher asked her children to predict the name of the story by studying the picture on the front cover of the book. Since the main character's name was also the name of the book, and since the children had been exposed to the character in another book by the same author, they were able to identify the name.

T2: What's the name of this story?
C: Basketti.
T: Oh, it's not spaghetti.
C: Pasta pot.
C: Strega-noff
T: Strega-noff? No, that's close.
C: Strega Nona.
T: Strega Nona. Very good.

Notice how the following teacher talked about the author and elicited from the children what the silver seal means on the front cover of the book.

T4: The author of this story is a man named Tomie dePaola, and there's something special about this book. Can you tell? Who can tell me?
C: It's a prize.
T: It won a prize. Do you remember what this prize is? This is a Caldecott award for having very, very nice pictures.

Teachers also discussed the type of text to be read. One teacher noted that, for *Strega Nona,* the author also was the illustrator, and this story is an old folktale.

T6: So it looks like the same man, Tomie, drew the pictures, and he retold an old tale. What is it to retell an old tale— Alex?

C: It means—to read it all over.

T: To retell is to read it over again or tell it over again. So he's retelling. He is telling it over again. What is a tale, Matthew?

C: A tale is some old story that is not true. It won't never, never happen.

T: Oh, a tale is a story that will never, never happen.

Teachers presented information about the setting of the story, introduced the main characters, discussed the point of view of the characters within the time period of the story, and commented about where the story takes place. In this example, notice how the teacher helped children relate the text character to an experience they had shared.

T3: Well, the cover of this book shows a picture of a lady who is a grandmother. I'll bet you can see her.

C: Yeah.

T: And the word *nona* means grand—no, let's see, the word *strega* means grandmother. But, she's more than that.

C: She's a mommy.

T: She is real special because she's a witch.

C: O-o-o-o-o

T: The witch you saw this morning in *The Wizard of Oz* was a bad witch, wasn't she? Strega Nona is a good witch. She has magic powers, but she is not bad.

In one discussion about the setting, notice how one teacher fostered discussions that kept the children working on an idea until they produced a sufficiently complete answer.

T6: What is the clue that tells you that she lived long ago rather than now? (The children look at the cover picture.)

C: 'Cause she's old.

T: She looks old. Don't we have any old people now?

C: Yeah.

T: We do. When we went to the nursing home, we saw old people. So we do have old people. What do you think, Justin? Why do you think this happened long ago?

C: Her dresses go all the way down to her feet.

T: Her dress goes all the way down. Did we see the people at the nursing home with dresses all the way down to their feet?

C: No.

T: So. But a long time ago, they did wear dresses that were long, didn't they?

Finally, teachers set goals for listening to the story. This also operated as a signal that the story reading was about to begin and that children should listen attentively. It brought closure to this segment of the book reading session.

T6: I want you to think about what happens to the boy in the story and what special kind of person this lady is—what she can do that no one else can do. I want you to listen to the story.

C: What's it called?

T: The title of the story is *Strega Nona*.

During the Reading of the Story

While reading, teachers helped children comprehend the story by modifying their voices to create emphasis and effect, by stopping to elaborate when they thought children needed additional information, and by having children interpret text information. They monitored children's understanding by asking them questions about the text and pictures.

Elaboration often occurred through comments about important text events. For example, by rephrasing the text, one teacher explained that "a pot that could cook all by itself (means that) you didn't have to put anything into it." Another teacher demonstrated how a picture in the book can help extend the text, especially when it illustrates an important event in the story.

T4: "He didn't see Strega Nona blow three kisses to the pasta pot." She's going in (points to picture), and then she went back to the pasta pot and blew three kisses.

Teachers asked four types of questions during story reading. The questions helped children: (1) understand the meanings of unfamiliar words, (2) make predictions about text events, (3) interpret the thoughts and feelings of the characters, and (4) understand potentially difficult concepts through explanation. In the examples that follow, the number in parentheses indicates the type of question.

(1) T2: What's a potion?
   C: It's kind of like a thing you drink or other—something like that.
   T: Sort of a special medicine.
   C: And when—and when you drink it you might turn into a frog.
(1) T5: Pasta's like what?
   C: Spaghetti.
   T: Spaghetti, that's right.
(2) T4: How do you think she's going to feel (about the spilled pasta)?
   C: Angry.
   T: At who?
   C: Big Anthony.
   T: Why do you think she'll be angry with him?
   C: Because he touched the pot.
   T: Let's see. (Here, the purpose setting question signals a return to the reading.)
(3) T5: What do you think he was thinking?
   C: I'll steal the pot.
   C: I'll make the pot work.
   T: He'll make the pot work? Okay, let's see what happens.
(3) T5: How do you think the people feel toward Big Anthony?
   C: Afraid, 'cause they think it's—I don't know.
   T: Well, go on. That's a pretty good start. You want to help him out, Dennis?
   C: I think he's gonna fall under the pasta and he's gonna suffercate.
   C: Well, I think they're mad. Probably mad.

   C: Yeah.
   T: Why, Eli?
   C: 'Cause—'cause they thought he knew—he would be able to take control of it.
   C: He knew what he was doing (inaudible) I think.
(4) T5: Why is she going to make him eat it (the pasta)?
   C: He made the mess.
   T: He made the mess. But why do you think she wants him to eat it? Eli?
   C: For the punishment.

After Reading the Story

Teachers usually ended the session by encouraging and recognizing children's comments about the completed story. They continued to ask questions as a way of checking and extending comprehension. Some teachers reiterated their earlier discussion about the type of text, as in the following example.

   T5: Is this a real story or a pretend story?
   C: False—false.
   C: A fairy tale.
   T: Yeah, it's an old tale. It really isn't true, is it? Is there such a thing as a witch?
   C: No.
   T: You don't think so?
   C: A witch can [inaudible].
   C: There can't be—there can't be a magic pot.

Most teachers asked a series of questions in order to review the principal story elements. Review questions often probed the setting of the story, the main character's problem, attempts to resolve the problem, and the resolution. The following example shows how teachers pushed children for explanations as well.

   T4: Do you think that Big Anthony should have been punished?
   C: Yes.
   T: Do you think that was a good punishment?
   C: Yes.
   T: Why do you think it was a good punishment, Nick?

C: I think it was a good punishment 'cause if he did it he would have to clean it up and so that it was a good punishment.

In addition, teachers often asked questions that helped children relate the events occurring in the story to events they had experienced themselves. In the example that follows, the teacher drew out children's feelings so they would better understand the motivation of an important character.

T6: How do you think it feels to have someone laugh at you?

C: Bad.

T: When Big Anthony went to the town square and he told them all he could make the pot do magic, and they laughed at him—he probably felt real sad. Has anybody ever laughed at you?

C: Yeah.

T: When did they laugh at you? (She continues with questions and comments, soliciting responses from children about their feelings and relating these back to the story.)

Finally, some teachers had children engage in follow up activities.

T3: Do you think you could make a picture showing Big Anthony?

C: I want to do the lady.

T: Strega Nona.

C: Could we draw like when he was fat?

T: Yes.

C: Do you think we could look at the pictures?

T: You can look some more at the pictures, too. Right.

Summary of Storybook Reading

Teachers read stories in much the same interactive way parents read to their children at home, with comments and questions that led children to comment and answer and ask questions about the story. Teachers often led a discussion about the author, illustrator, and type of text before reading the book. They provided information about the setting of the story, and set a purpose for listening. During the reading, teachers responded to children's comments and reactions, elaborated on the storylines, and asked comprehension questions to check for understanding. After the story, they reviewed the story and arranged for follow up activities.

Because of these procedures, children readily answered questions and initiated comments throughout the story reading presentation. By elaborating on the text and by asking pertinent questions, children began to understand new words and ideas, and they attended to the important story ideas. Children described their own similar background experiences and became able to express their own understanding or interpretation of the story from their own perspective. These techniques are summarized in Table 1.

Informational Text Reading

Before Reading the Informational Text

The teachers prepared children for listening to the informational text by using some of the same techniques they used for the storybook. They provided children with information about the book in general, and about the title, author, and illustrator, and they set a purpose for listening. For the most part, though, they used the introduction time to develop close connections between the text concepts and children's background experiences, as follows.

T4: What I want to hear about is what you saw (on the playground). What I asked you to look for. Something—what did you see? Ben?

C: When I was running on the sidewalk, I saw my shadow.

T: And what was it doing?

C: It was moving with me.

T: Did you try to catch it?

C: Yes.

T: Cedric?

C: When I was—when I just come out and Nick was running, I was running, too. I said, "Nick, do you see your shadow?" And I didn't know the shadow was there, so I had to look down and then I saw my shadow.

T: Why do you think you could see your shadow so well today?

Table 1
Guidelines for Classroom Reading
of Storybooks to Children

Before Reading

- Show the cover of the book to the children. Encourage predictions of the book's content.
- Discuss the book's author and illustrator.
- Allow children to discuss their own experiences that are related to those in the book.
- Discuss the type of text the children will be hearing (folktale, fable, fantasy, realistic fiction).
- Introduce children to the main characters and setting.
- Set a purpose for the children to listen to the story.

During Reading

- Encourage children to react to and comment on the story as they listen.
- Elaborate on the text, when appropriate, in order to help children understand the written language used in the story and the critical story components.
- Ask questions occasionally to monitor children's comprehension of the story.
- Rephrase the text when it is apparent that children do not understand the ideas.
- At appropriate points in the story, ask children to predict what might happen next.
- Allow children to voice their own interpretations of the story.

After Reading

- Review the story components (setting, problem, goal, resolution).
- Help children make connections between events involving the main character and similar events in their own lives.
- Engage children in a follow up activity that involves thinking about the text.

C: The sun.

T: Because the sun is very bright. What do you need in order to have a shadow? What do you have to have? Katy?

C: Like a person.

T: You have to have an object, don't you? It could be a person or a building. And what else do you have to have? Brian?

C: Lots of sun.

T: And lots of sun. And what makes the shadow, then, when you have the sun and an object—how do you get a shadow? (The teacher tries next to elicit the idea that a surface is needed, but children don't say that, so she waits for a later opportunity to evoke that information from them.)

Teachers also introduced the topic and related concepts through demonstrations. Because these took time, the preparation for informational reading was much longer and included more interactions than did the prereading presentation for the storybook. Notice this in the following elaborated demonstration of how light and objects make shadows.

T2: You see my head on the chalkboard? My head's not on the chalkboard. (The teacher holds up a desk lamp so that it casts a shadow of her face on the board.)

C: Yes it is.

T: Where? My shadow.

C: Your shadow! Your shadow!

C: Hey! Now, it's over here.

C: Light makes shadows.

T: Why does light make shadows?

C: Because it does.

C: Because they're bright and the sunlight goes right through you.

T: There are a lot of things that are bright—gold's bright.

C: Because you're just blocking the light and it can't get through and it makes a shadow because it's all the way around.

T: Oh-oh! I've got my same light—I've got my same hand. Why is my hand not up there now? (The teacher has turned the lamp sideways.)

C: Because you're putting it down.

T: Oh, so the direction has something to do with it.

C: You have to have it on a wall or something.

T: It has to be on a wall? It couldn't be on a skirt? (She moves the lamp so a shadow forms on her lap.)

C: [Inaudible.]

T: Oh, so I don't have to have a wall? I could have a skirt? What do I have to have? I have to have some sort of surface, don't I?

During the Reading of the Informational Text

Teachers used a variety of techniques to help children comprehend the text as they read it. They asked questions that functioned as a means for explaining or defining new vocabulary and concepts and, because the informational text included questions, teachers blended text questions with demonstrations of concepts. Here is one example.

T6: (After reading about what makes a shadow, the teacher brings out a flashlight.) Now let's see if I can make a shadow.

C: I got lights like that—a flashlight.

T: So, if I have a light, an object—that's my hand, and a surface—the wall, I have a shadow.

C: The farther away it is, the bigger it gets.

C: Wow!

T: So when I move my hand, the shadow changes, doesn't it?

Teachers also elaborated on relevant concepts by commenting on text or picture information. Occasionally, they asked questions to help children identify pictures in the book.

T2: And you can tell that this is a big shadow. See? That's a boat right there. And people are really in that boat. So this must be a very tall cliff, so it makes a very big shadow. And I don't know if you know what this is—

C: I know—a jack.

T: That's right. And those are little jacks you play with—jacks you play with on the sidewalk. So that's a very little thing. But it still creates a shadow.

T4: What is it that you're seeing?

C: The shadow.

T: The shadow. The light is hitting this one differently, isn't it?

Another interesting way that some teachers elaborated on the text was to suggest relevant activities for the children to engage in later in school or at home. These suggestions were no doubt derived from the important ideas in the text. For example, one teacher read, "Change the surface and the shadow changes." She then commented, "You know, when we go outside for recess today for our playtime, we're going to take a look at that. We're going to stand in different places. We're going to see how long our shadows are."

After Reading the Informational Text

Unexpectedly, there were no reviews of text ideas following the reading of the informational text. This may have been due to the length of the book and the time taken before and during the reading. Three teachers, however, did suggest follow up activities, such as directing children to look for shadows or to play shadow tag games outdoors. Here is one example.

T3: Can you think of something you're going to look for on the way home from school?

C: Shadows.

T: And when we go on the playground tomorrow, we can look for some more—

C: Shadows.

Summary of Informational Text Reading

The teachers' reading of the *Shadows* text included comments, questions, and strategies for elaboration that were similar in some ways to their reading of the storybook. They discussed the book and asked purpose setting questions, but they prepared children mainly by demonstrating relevant concepts and discussing children's experiences with the topic. During the reading of the text, teachers elaborated, principally through demonstrations and discussions of book pictures. They asked many questions that were in the book, as well as a few of their own, which led to further elaboration. After the reading, some teachers made suggestions about possible follow up activities. Overall, vocabulary

and concept building were achieved by soliciting children's responses to pictures and through demonstrations, rather than through definitions or talking about the text. Thus, these presentations focused more on visual than verbal representations of the text. A summary of the techniques used for the informational text appears in Table 2.

Picture Phrase Book Reading

In presenting picture phrase books to kindergarten children, the teachers asked considerably fewer questions than they did for the other texts. However, they involved children in shared reading. These differences were not unexpected, considering the book's length (six pages) and text simplicity (three or four words to a page).

Before Reading the Picture Phrase Book

Children were given book information and some added goals for listening to the book. This information was quite different from that used for the other books. One teacher informed children that they were really going to like the book because it was one they could learn to read. Another teacher remarked, " I would like to read it first, and I'd like you to look at the pictures and maybe someone will know the words."

Generally, teachers directed the children's attention to the cover page and asked them to read the title. One teacher had the children put the words from the title, which she had placed on cards, into the correct order.

T6: Maybe we can try together to figure out what it says.

C: Time

T: Time—

C: To get up.

C: For

T: For—

C: Bed.

T: *Time for Bed* is the name of this story. Raise your hand if you can tell me what the picture on the cover shows. (She calls on several children who describe the picture.)

T3: How many words are there in the title?

> **Table 2**
> **Guidelines for Classroom Reading of Informational Texts to Children**
>
> *Before Reading*
> - Determine children's level of understanding of the topic presented in the text through methods such as leading a discussion about the picture on the cover or children's experiences with the topic.
> - Provide demonstrations of difficult concepts.
> - Set a purpose for listening.
> - Establish a link between children's experiences with the topic and what they will be learning from the text.
>
> *During Reading*
> - Ask questions periodically to check children's understanding of the text. Questions that actually appear in the text might provide excellent opportunities for discussion and demonstration of the topic.
> - Extend new concepts to children through demonstrations, concrete examples, or pictures while reading the text information.
> - Encourage comments about the demonstrations and pictures so that children talk about unfamiliar concepts.
> - Provide suggestions about activities children might engage in later that will encourage them to explore the topic further.
>
> *After Reading*
> - Allow children to ask questions about the text.
> - Help children see how informational text can be used to learn more about their own world.
> - Offer follow up activities that will tie text concepts to children's experiences.

C: Two.

C: Three.

T: Are there two or three?

C: Three.

T: Three words. I have three words here (chalk tray), but I don't have them in the right order. That's one of the words in the title, this is one of them, and that's one of them. I didn't put them in the right order, because that doesn't say "Time for bed."

C: For bed time.

T: Thomas, do you want to see if you can get them in the right order? If I want it to say *Time for Bed,* I need it to start over here. That says "Time." What does that say?

C: "For bed."

T: And now, who will read it for us? Benjamin?

C: *Time for Bed.*

Another teacher discussed the title in relation to the cover picture.

T1: How do you know it's *Time for Bed?*

C: He's got his pajamas on.

C: And his teddy bear.

C: And his cover.

Instead of character development, teachers had children discuss their own bedtime routines or other related experiences. One teacher began, "I'd like you to close your eyes for a minute and think about when you go to bed. What is your time for bed? When you're finished thinking about your time for bed, open your eyes and we'd like to hear a little bit about your time for bed. Justin, can you tell us what you do when it's your time for bed?" She then called on children one by one to share their bedtime routine.

During the Reading of the Picture Phrase Book

The simplicity of the storyline kept teachers from making comments or asking comprehension questions. Instead, some teachers asked children to read words by looking at the initial letter. This is illustrated in the next example.

T3: (Child has misread, saying "Read a book" for "Read a story.") How do you

know it isn't "book"? This says "read" and this says "a." How do you know that isn't "book"?

C: 'Cause it's a story.

T: 'Cause it's a story. How do you know that it's a story?

C: Because there's no "b."

C: Because it starts with "s."

After Reading the Picture Phrase Book

Although two of the teachers briefly reviewed the text with the children, most teachers extended the book topic with several postreading activities. One teacher reread the story and then had children "pretend to do the things that it says." Another teacher directed, "I'll read a line and you read a line. Let's see if we can all read it together." Others had children discuss what they would do at their own bedtime. One teacher had children discuss alternative event sequences at bedtime.

T6: If we were going to change this story, we'd have to make sure that brushing your teeth comes before climbing into bed. How about after you lie down, get tucked in, say nighty-night—can you do that before you read a story?

Finally, one teacher saw an opportunity for focusing on the print by having the children engage in a small group activity during their Center Time. The activity involved the use of rubber stamp letters.

T2: We're going to take this book back to the table, and I have a brand new, never before been used, set of letters. They're very special. We're going to make the word "bed." We're going to make some other words that are a lot like bed, words that you sang about.

Summary of Picture Phrase Book Reading

With the picture phrase book, several teachers began by discussing the children's own bedtime events, whereas others had children figure out from the cover what the title ought to be or reorder words in the title. During the reading, teachers had children look at the print, try to read the text, and answer word recognition questions. After the reading, they had children act out the events, discuss the sequence of events from the book (as well as alternative sequences), and reread individually or as a group. A summary of these techniques is found in Table 3.

Table 3
**Guidelines for Classroom Reading
of Picture Phrase Books**

Before Reading

- Let children know that these books are ones they will be able to read if they listen and look carefully at pictures and print.
- Have children attempt to read the print on the cover. Talk about words they already know.
- Let children predict what the book might be about based on the title and the cover picture.
- Have children talk about their own experiences that are related to the book topic or theme.
- If children cannot see the print, provide multiple copies or enlarge the book.

During Reading

- Allow children who are able to read along.
- Challenge children to identify words in the text.
- Ask children how they are able to recognize the words they have identified.

After Reading

- Briefly review the content of the text, drawing upon the experiences of the children to highlight specific events or sequences.
- Reread the text, having the children join in as they recognize the words.
- Let children explore the print by having them attempt to write words from the book.
- Extend the presentation by having children act out the text, draw pictures to go along with the text, or compose a similar text.
- Provide opportunities for children to read the book on their own.

The Importance of Reading to Children in Kindergarten

Our analyses of the transcripts indicate that kindergarten teachers use a number of techniques to foster kindergarteners' understanding of books. They provide opportunities for listening, interpreting, and discussing text relationships, and they flexibly adjust the responsibility for reading depending on the difficulty of the text. Although the transcripts contain more examples of interactions between teachers and students (see Mason et al., 1988; or Mason, Peterman, & Kerr, in press, for fuller reports), we hope the sample examples demonstrate that teachers can interject effective comprehension and word recognition activities as they read different types of books to their students.

Although it is obvious that our six teachers fostered word recognition by pointing out words they thought children might know, by having them use the initial letter and context clues to figure out a word, and by having children reread the text with them, it is not so obvious how they fostered comprehension. We believe they did so in three ways. They (1) helped children tie new text information to their own experiences, (2) provided opportunities for children to restate text concepts, and (3) took on more responsibility for comprehension when the text was difficult and gave children more responsibility when the text was easy. We believe that these techniques, which engage children in book talk while they listen to books, are important experiences for young children. We elaborate on these three summary points next.

First, book reading facilitates connections between text information and children's background experiences. One approach is to direct children to talk about their own experiences. This occurred here when children talked about what they did before going to bed or during supper, and when they were reminded of experiences they shared at school. A similar approach is to encourage children to make unsolicited comments about text that describes their experiences. Another approach, which was prominent in the expository text lessons, is to create an experience for children to discuss through demonstrations and by staging a shared activity before reading the book (such as playing shadow tag).

Second, book reading encourages children to talk about book information. We noticed four approaches. Teachers ask questions about text words, phrases, and ideas that need elaboration or highlighting. Questions can be about word meanings, text comprehension, or picture labels. Teachers hold discussions that help children to differentiate new from old information and to comment on new concepts. Demonstrations and good questions stimulate many such comments and responses. Teachers ask questions that require thoughtful responses, such as explanation, prediction, definition, and inference. They also solicit children's descriptions of their own text related experiences.

Third, book reading sessions are adjusted to give children an appropriate amount of responsibility. With a difficult text, teachers assume most of the responsibility. They are likely to do all of the reading and demonstrate and explain most of the text ideas. They have children do easier things, such as point to pictures, label pictures, give yes or no answers, or complete their sentences. They also verbalize general concepts and simply ask children to point to or name examples. With a moderately difficult text, teachers are likely to read the entire text aloud, but have children go beyond "what" information into explanations, predictions, and interpretations. With an easy text, teachers are likely to involve children in the reading, solicit their comments, react to their suggestions, and affirm good responses.

Varied and rich book interactions that are tailored to the type of book expose children to many written language ideas. Children learn about information in books and will be introduced to written language concepts before they are readers. We think these experiences will pay off later when children read independently, because they will be better equipped to understand the texts, to monitor their understanding of them, and to juxtapose their own experiences beside the information they read.

References

Chomsky, C. Stages in language development and reading exposure. *Harvard Educational Review*, 1972, *42*, 1-33.

dePaola, T. *Strega Nona*. Englewood Cliffs, NJ: Prentice Hall, 1975.

Dunning, D., and Mason, J. *An investigation of kindergarten children's expressions of story character intentions*. Paper presented at the Annual Meeting of the National Reading Conference, St. Petersburg, Florida, 1984.

Feitelson, D., Kita, B., and Goldstein, Z. Effects of reading series stories to first graders on their comprehension and use of language. *Research on the Teaching of English*, 1986, *20*, 339-356.

Goor, R., and Goor, N. *Shadows: Here, there, and everywhere*. New York: Crowell, 1981.

Greaney, V. Parental influences on reading. *The Reading Teacher*, 1986, *39*, 813-818.

Holdaway, D. *The foundations of literacy*. New York: Ashton Scholastic, 1979.

Mason, J.M., and McCormick, C. *Time for bed*. Champaign, IL: Pint Sized Prints, 1984.

Mason, J.M., Peterman, C.L., and Kerr, B.M. *Fostering comprehension by reading books to kindergarten children*. Technical Report. Urbana, IL: Center for the Study of Reading, in press.

Mason, J.M., Peterman, C.L., Powell, B., and Kerr, B.M. *Reading and writing attempts after reading to kindergarten children*. Technical Report No. 419. Urbana, IL: Center for the Study of Reading, 1988.

Moon, C., and Wells, G. The influence of home on learning to read. *Journal of Research in Reading*, 1979, *2*, 53-62.

Morrow, L.M. Young children's responses to one-to-one story readings in school settings. *Reading Research Quarterly, 23*(1), 89-107.

Sulzby, E. Kindergartners as writers and readers. In M. Farr (Ed.), *Advances in writing research*, volume one: *Children's early writing development*. Norwood, NJ: Ablex, 1985, 127-200.

Wells, G. *Learning through interaction: The study of language development*. New York: Cambridge University Press, 1981.

Wells, G. *The meaning makers: Children learning language and using language to learn*. Portsmouth, NH: Heinemann, 1981.

White, D.N. *Books before five*. Wellington, New Zealand: Council for Educational Research, 1954.

CHAPTER SIX

Emergent Writing in the Classroom: Home and School Connections

Elizabeth Sulzby

William H. Teale

George Kamberelis

In this chapter, we focus on ways that teachers can encourage in the classroom the kinds of reading and writing activities that children do in "literacy rich homes." Our focus is on writing, as well as the reading that takes place during writing.

A challenge for early literacy education is deciding when evidence from research on literacy acquisition in the home is relevant to what should be done in schools. Researchers and educators looking at what children do in "literacy rich homes" have noted that some children engage in reading and writing activities quite freely in homes that encourage these activities in casual and playful ways. This research seems to offer important, but not direct, insights into how schools can encourage all children to use literacy that freely.

In this chapter, we describe decisions teachers have made that are intended to build upon and encourage children's emergent literacy, and we explore ways that the resulting classrooms are similar to and different from so called literacy rich homes. The chapter has two parts—recurrent themes that have been seen in the home and activities teachers can use in schools. Our focus is on writing, but that, by its nature, includes the reading that takes place during writing.

We do not think the classroom should be just like a literacy rich home, but we do think lessons can be learned by comparing children's writing behavior in the two settings. Certainly, all homes and all schools differ. We have no evidence that a particular kind or degree of literacy interaction in the home guarantees any kind or degree of literacy interaction in the school. From our observations, however, we have concluded that children who have had frequent opportunities to write and read emergently at home are more likely to enter conventional literacy as confident, risk taking readers and writers. We are concerned about children who have not had these rich opportunities, yet are often placed in instructional programs that ignore their previous experiences.

Studying home literacy raises the issue of how one goes from evidence from a home environment, in which no curriculum guide directs the parents on how to spend literacy related time with their children, to a classroom situation in which the teacher purposefully assumes responsibility for teaching/guiding children to read and write. Currently, there seems to be a lot of controversy about the role of instruction in emergent literacy. Do we simply leave children alone to develop, do we provide instructional encouragements to individual children, do we provide direct lessons about how writing works to all children just as general information, or do we try to hurry children along the developmental paths that research is uncovering?

Research in the homes of families of all income levels (Anderson & Stokes, 1984; Bissex, 1980; Doake, 1982; Sulzby & Teale, 1987; Taylor, 1983; Taylor & Dorsey-Gaines, 1988; Teale, 1984, 1986a, 1986b) has provided rich descriptions of home literacy. An interesting question is whether these descriptions can or should lead to prescriptions for the classroom. Philosophers have long debated this kind of topic under the rubric of "going from *is* to *ought*." Many people say that there is no logical way to get to prescription from description. Classroom teachers, however, have been willing and committed to prescribing, which some have called moral, rather than purely logical.

We think that the direction and character of children's development provides a sufficiently reasonable basis for building recommendations for classroom teaching. This teaching, in order to be developmentally appropriate, should include opportunities for children to read and write freely without formal instruction. Although some teachers have interpreted this idea to mean that a literacy rich environment is all that is needed, Teale (1987) noted that the so called natural development we see in homes includes teaching/learning situations, many times including direct explanation or instruction. Thus, we have concluded that classroom

teaching should include not only a literacy rich environment, but also some guidance toward further development of literacy, including direct teaching.

We have noted from our classroom observations that many teachers influenced by emergent literacy research teach in far more direct ways than most parents teach, even though these classrooms may appear very child centered and unstructured. A danger of encouraging teachers to provide direct instruction in emergent literacy, given our limited knowledge of what good teaching strategies look like, is that we might pressure children in developmentally inappropriate ways.

We believe that in good classroom instruction, young children need to be encouraged but not pushed or pressured. We interpret the concept of pushing in much the same way many classroom teachers do. When one of us offers a suggestion for what appears to be a next step in development, and the child bursts into tears or withdraws, we assume we are pushing the child unduly, and back off with our suggestions. Tears and frustration can be positive parts of development when they come from children's own initiatives and explorations, but we avoid being the cause of them. In our current research efforts, involving observations of children over time, we are attempting to chart when teachers can be fairly certain that it is time for a nudge forward. (We use "nudge" to indicate a nonpressuring push. "Push" and "nudge" aren't technical terms here; they are used to distinguish between pressuring and nonpressuring styles of interacting with children.)

Children's Writing in Literacy Rich Homes

Considering these assumptions, let us examine what we know about literacy development in the home and how teachers have applied knowledge about children's literacy development in the home to the school setting. Over the past few years—with the help of inspirational parents, teachers, and children—we have been investigating how instruction fits with natural development.

How do children write in literacy rich homes? It is possible to construct a long list of features, which researchers have already reported in detail, but here are five particularly important themes.

- Children's writing is often transient—it comes and goes.
- Children's writing is a sign of their power and is negotiated with parents and other adults.
- Children's writing takes many forms; kindergartners move across these forms easily.
- Children get engrossed in major multimedia constructions that may take days to complete.
- Children use writing for aesthetic creation.

Explanations and examples of these themes follow. Notice that many of the examples used illustrate more than a single theme.

Transience. As Taylor (1983) has pointed out, many times you must watch fast to catch children writing at home. Their writing events are often transient—a mark here and a mark there. They may call a few lines of scribble a story one moment and call those same lines a letter to Grandma the next.

Each of the writers of this chapter is a parent as well as being a researcher of literacy in the home. We have observed the kind of transience Taylor has written about and a different kind of transience—that of children's shifting interests. Children often explore writing for days and weeks on end, and then seem to abandon it for another interest, such as block construction, endless games of hide and seek, or doll play. Then their interest in literacy may return, but be concentrated on some other aspect of literacy, such as storybook reading. Still later, they may start writing again.

As with the general interest in literacy activities, children's use of various forms of writing also demonstrates transience. Individual forms (drawing, scribble, letter strings, invented spelling) may be used, abandoned, and used again. This transience seems to be rooted in the structures and functions of the writing tasks in which children are involved. A more detailed discussion of transience of forms of writing follows.

Power. Children's writing is often seen as a sign of a developing sense of self and one's own power. If you give markers to eighteen month old toddlers, they will mark on a paper (or anything else that's handy), see that mark, be intrigued by it,

and go back and do it again. This affinity for marking seems to be related in important ways to children's growing awareness of themselves as agents—as people who can make things happen. In the case of a toddler's markings, the child is leaving a trace behind. This notion of a trace is an important aspect of writing. In our culture, writing is an important means by which we make our thoughts and words permanent enough to be seen by ourselves and others. The trace becomes a symbol for self and the power of agency.

In homes with an abundance of writing materials and where adults write in front of children for reasons that seem to be intriguing, children will continue to write throughout their preschool years. Moms, dads, other relatives, and family friends get involved in children's use of writing. Such adults often encourage young children to write, showing them how to write their own name or common words. These encouragements almost always are models of conventional orthography.

But as soon as other people enter the picture with their encouragements, they also bring their own points of view and constraints. Parents typically feel they have to exercise some control so that their children do not scribble all over everything. Children's sense of self and power is tested in interesting ways in self-other negotiations that vary from support to opposition. Snow and Ninio (1986) discuss how children learn to handle storybooks through their negotiations with parents. Negotiations concerning writing also are part of family life. Just as parents and children negotiate about what storybooks are and how storybooks should be handled, Mom and Dad work hard to ensure that their little ones do not destroy family property by their eager scribbling.

This sense of negotiated power continues across the years, being reworked at many points of development. Not all negotiations are constraints such as stopping a child from scribbling on a tablecloth. When children try to write, parents often try to help, but children sometimes resist that help.

We have begun to appreciate the importance of the young child being able to work through times of frustration in literacy development. For instance, while reading a favorite book at home, a six year old girl realized that she could sound out words and recognized that there was an order to the letters of a word that corresponded to its spoken sounds. When she was trying this new feat on her own in reading, she seemed excited and motivated. When her mother tried to help her use this knowledge to write phonetically, however, the girl became frustrated, burst into tears, and ripped up her paper. Mom recognized that her help was being received as pushing. She stopped giving suggestions, and the two went on to something else. A few days later, the child became frustrated when trying to write without her mother's help. Her mother watched to see what would happen, and soon the child pushed through the frustration and wrote the words she wanted to write. Then she came to her mother, displaying her writing proudly, confident in what she had written.

We interpret this as part of the child's use of personal power. A day later, her mother was able to suggest types of words that she felt the child would find easy to write given the kind of knowledge she had demonstrated earlier. At this point, the child was willing to grant power to the adult that she had denied earlier; the help was perceived as a developmental nudge rather than a push.

This same scenario is played in many different guises in homes in which children are encouraged, but not pushed, to write. The child explores writing and encounters successes and frustrations. It appears that both successes and frustrations are common and accompany advances toward higher levels of literacy. Bissex (1980) recounted how her son Paul used signs and messages to signal his frustration with social situations (RUDF? and DO NAT KM.IN ANE.MOR.JST.LETL.KES—Are you deaf? and Do not come in any more—just little kids). These examples suggest that we need to attend both to the kinds of help we give and how the child reacts to the help.

Writing with many forms. Outside of school, young children use many different writing forms. The five most common are scribble, drawing, nonphonetic letter strings, phonetic (or invented) spelling, and conventional orthography. Often children use a number of these forms in the same piece of writing. They may, however, use forms beyond these five. Recently, in a school setting (Sulzby, 1988), one five year old kept mentioning "Siamese"

as a way of writing. Later he wrote a story. When he read it, he had used letter strings that had been crossed out, drawing, and lines of scribble. He also had used three series of dots joined by lines. These, he explained, were Siamese. When an adult asked him to "tell me about Siamese," he described Braille.

Let us examine the ages at which the five major forms of writing typically appear in home writing. Two year olds use scribble and gradually differentiate their scribble into scribble for writing and scribble for drawing. As their drawing begins to appear recognizable, their scribble also begins to look more distinctively like writing. Many three year olds use letter like features in their scribble and also begin to form conventional looking letters. Then they may compose stories or personal messages with letter strings and go back and forth among scribble, drawing, and letter strings. Children also may begin to produce conventional looking words such as their own name, Mom, or Dad.

Well after they are able to produce conventional looking letters, some children invent pseudoletters for "fast writing." As early as age four, a few children use some phonetic representation, usually when attempting to write isolated words. A few more children begin to use phonetic or invented spelling at age five, and as the fifth and sixth years progress, more and more children begin to use this form of writing.

When thinking about these forms of writing and what they say about children's development, however, we must consider what children are doing with them. In the home, children often have communicative functions to perform, even if they are in fantasy play. Occasionally, however, children seem to be writing just to be writing. Researchers have pointed out that, in order to understand a given form of writing, we need to observe how it seems to function for the child. Sulzby (1985c, Sulzby, Barnhart, & Hieshima, in press) has paid particular attention to whether children seem to be composing while producing the written form and to how children's rereading seems to relate to the form of writing used.

From our earlier description of the forms of writing, it would appear that there is a developmental progression from scribble and drawing to nonphonetic letter strings to invented spelling and finally to conventional orthography. This is not entirely true. Instead, children often move back and forth across the forms of writing well into first grade. The composition and rereading behaviors children use are critical for assessing the level of writing. Often, when children compose a complicated piece such as a many paged story, they revert to lower appearing forms such as scribble or drawing. In a somewhat similar vein, children who follow scribble with their finger while rereading, who are able to make the speech sound like reading, and who end their story when they reach the end of the scribble are showing a very advanced type of literacy behavior, despite the use of a so called lower form of writing.

Even more intriguing developments take place. Some children who write conventional pieces of writing may give quite unusual interpretations to how these pieces function as writing. Ferreiro (1986; Ferreiro & Teberosky, 1982) has described a period during which children seem to conceive of certain letters as belonging to or representing certain people or objects. These letters are almost always the first letters of the person's or object's name. This kind of one letter per unit writing might appear and be confused with the one letter per syllable writing children use later. Later in development, after children use full invented spelling mixed with conventional orthography, some children use one letter plus a period to stand for abbreviations.

Engrossing constructions. While writing at home often takes place as a fleeting mark on a newspaper or on the corner of Mom's or Dad's grocery list, young children also may get intrigued for long periods of times in multimedia constructions. These ventures may include constructing houses made of paper, popsicle sticks, or cardboard boxes; drawing decorations; and adding other kinds of marks such as scribble or strings of letters and drawings that are treated as pieces of writing.

Ruth and Katie constructed an eight page story when they were four and five, respectively. First, each drew a page of two separate stories. They taped the pages together, and Katie began to build a story across the pages. Soon afterward, Ruth physically and verbally pushed Katie aside and created her own story across the pages. Then they began working together, adding other pages and planning the structure as they went along. The plans were pliable, with the characters constantly changing, until Katie cut out a bowl of cat food. That led to cutting out a cat and a dog. Soon flowers and doors appeared. They applied a rolled up piece of tape to each cutout so they would be movable, and soon they were marching the characters and props up and down the multipage story.

One time, Katie led the cat to eat from the cat food bowl. When the cat was finished, Katie taped the food to the cat's stomach to show that the food was eaten. Thereafter, the food accompanied the cat in its marches across the story.

The girls played with this story for days, embellishing it at times but often calling one another back to the original conception. When Ruth was not present and Katie alone reenacted the story for others, she sometimes framed the story with an elaborate setting. She turned down the lights in the kitchen, focused a flashlight on the text, and introduced the relevant objects and characters before proceeding with her narrative.

No letters or scribble were ever added to the story, yet the girls' speech as they narrated the story often sounded like oral reading intonation. In addition, the story's structure was clearly literary in nature.

Dyson (1984, 1985, 1988) has repeatedly noted how children move across media in constructions in school settings. She also has argued that this type of activity creates tensions within the child's thinking about literacy that eventually enhance development. Katie and Ruth provided a home-created analogue to the school situation Dyson has reported.

Aesthetic creation. In general, aesthetic creation in language results from playing with language, making pleasurable things with it, and exploring its possibilities for expression. Examples abound of poetic language in the everyday speech of young children. Chukovsky (1963) has provided many examples of children's aesthetic language such as, "Can't you see? I'm barefoot all over," "Please don't cut down the pine tree. It makes the wind," "There's only a small piece of cake, but it's middle aged."

While much less evidence of aesthetic language in children's emergent written language has been published, more is currently being noticed. Often this evidence reflects the close, rich, and complex relationship between oral and written language development. Typically, adults have to maintain sharp eyes and ears to find the aesthetic aspects of written texts, and they have to attune themselves to the emergent forms of writing used by children. On the other hand, less sharp eyes are needed to witness the pleasure that children take in their inventions.

Even when children are focusing on graphic form rather than content, they may transform the forms. Gardner, Wolfe, and Smith (1975) provide a wonderful example of young Molly's digression as she practiced writing her first name.

> [Molly] begins by carefully forming a large M, the first letter of her name, which she is diligently learning to write. Her relative unsophistication in the graphic medium leaves her open to suggestion and she glimpses another possibility in the large letter form. Closing the giant M at the bottom, she creates a "rabbit".… "Flopsy, the talking rabbit." Folding the paper up so that the rabbit is like an actor, she remarks, in a tiny voice, "Hello, I am Flopsy the talking Rabbit, I live with my brothers in a tiny house in the woods…" (p. 20).

The authors interpreted this event in terms of Molly's "sense of pleasure and power at being able to put herself on paper," as shown both in this instance and in other stories and dramatizations in which she had used a rabbit or herself as a rabbit.

When children write connected discourse using forms that range all the way from scribble and drawing to invented or conventional spelling, they often compose graphic texts with aesthetic qualities. Similarly, they reread their texts with many formal qualities—rhythm, rhyme, intensification of form through repetition, surprise through subtle variation, onomatopoeia, and emotional impact caused by stirring up the senses. The story by Ruth and Katie is an example of a text consisting of drawing; the text and children's reactions to it were clearly aesthetic in nature.

In their aesthetic written texts, children sometimes focus on meaning or content as much as or more than they focus on graphics and sound. Some children combine writing forms to create aesthetic texts replete with evidence of some fairly sophisticated understanding of figurative language based in relationships of meanings. The contents of the texts are often related to the children's total language experience.

Recently, five year old Jake saw a dump truck on the road with a picture of the earth as its logo. He asked why the truck had the world on it. His father launched into an explanation of words with two or more meanings that he thought his son might understand. He explained that our planet has two names—world and earth, and that earth has two meanings—the world and dirt. Furthermore, he explained that the people who owned the truck probably thought that since they hauled earth (meaning two) that it would be neat to use the earth (meaning one) to show what their business was.

The look on Jake's face made the father fear that he had completely failed in his explanation. He asked his son if he understood. The response was quick and indignant: "Of course, Dad, you said that the world has two meanings, the earth and dirt." Later that day, while occupying himself in his own room, Jake produced a drawing of a truck. It had a picture of the earth on its body, and it was labeled: "wrld truk." Aesthetic understanding learned in an oral language situation was imported into Jake's writing, replete with roots of double meanings, imagery, metaphor, and surprise.

Thus, many features characterize children as verbal artists. Child artists also have some knowledge of the tools available in the language for the production of certain effects. They have some sense that there are costs and benefits to using some tools at the expense of others. Finally, children give evidence of deriving pleasure from their creations and of expecting others to take pleasure in them as well.

In summary, these five characteristics—transience, power, writing with many forms, engrossing constructions, and aesthetic creation—seem to capture important parts of children's literacy development in some, but not all, literacy rich homes.

As parents watch children develop as writers and as readers of their writing, they notice that the children do not seem to go through a straightforward, stage like development from an immature form to what looks like a mature form. Instead, children may seem to go back and forth across different forms of writing and reading. Often children show great interest in literacy and in writing, coming proudly to display their writing to parents and other members of the family. At other times, though, they seem to have absolutely no interest in literacy.

Another key feature of home literacy is the fact that children shift from the fleeting events of literacy of the toddler age into long periods of engrossed writing and reading. At times, young children read many different versions of a story or a description relating to one piece of writing they have constructed. At other times, they repeat the same composition over again to the same piece of writing. And always, they are working out the issues of who they are, of making a powerful impact, and of resolving conflicts — even the conflict of how many legs to put on an *E*.

The key issue here is that in homes children often are given sufficient time to deal with activities so they can experience them at many levels across time. And, often, the literacy events are aesthetically pleasing or entertaining, and not just functional on an information exchanging or task performing level.

Children's Writing in Schools

As we described what children do in literacy encouraging homes, we carefully indicated that children are interacting with a few interested adults and maybe a few siblings. For many children, this may be one or two parents and no siblings. Now let's think about schools. When we encourage children to write in a typical kindergarten classroom, we set up an entirely different social situation. Imagine twenty-four children, all about five years old. They see many other children their own age writing. And usually there is only one teacher. What does writing in these classrooms look like? What kinds of support and conversation go on about reading, writing, and children's other interests?

Classrooms vary, of course. In some classrooms, writing is not encouraged, except for some copying and letter formation exercises. The teacher is in charge, giving direct instruction. Most of this instruction is about "basic" skills. Such classrooms appear to be antithetical to encouraging the themes that take place in literacy rich homes. Children are often taught how to form their letters, how to hear sounds in words and how to write their names as if they know nothing. Many times, the instruction not only is misdirected relative to children's development, but also seems to interfere with the children's creativity in composition and control of written language. Most destructive, we think, is the assumption that children cannot write (that is, cannot compose) until they have mastered the mechanics and that the only way they should write is through conventional orthography.

In other classrooms, we see abundant writing, with children's emergent writing forms and functions being accepted and encouraged. In some of these classrooms, writing shows up in discrete assignments or situations. In others, writing and reading occur throughout the entire day, being woven into activities in a seamless fashion. Both kinds of teachers are integrating writing into the curriculum but in distinctly different ways (Buhle, 1987).

In a sense, all teachers who integrate writing into the classroom are trying to capitalize on what goes on in literacy encouraging homes. Yet, they must realize that school is a different setting with its own unique qualities, and they must organize literacy activities accordingly. What ties these teachers together is that they encourage and legitimize writing in the classroom.

Although it is impossible to prescribe fully what teachers should do, we do recognize methods that seem to support children's emergent literacy. In this section, we describe some of the techniques teachers are using in an attempt to create literacy rich classrooms, and we relate them to the themes observed in the homes. These teachers use numerous activities to invite children to write in emergent ways. The activities, described here in isolation, do not show how some teachers integrate them across the day and curriculum.

Activities to Invite Writing

One simple guideline is best: In situations where a teacher would ordinarily invite an older student to write, the teacher should invite a kindergartner or first grader to write as well, being sure to invite them to "do it your own way." If a teacher is uncomfortable with this broad guideline and wants a technique to formally introduce writing to begin the year in kindergarten, Sulzby (1988) suggests eliciting and modeling five major forms in the context of an invitation to "Write me a story about anything you want to."

Getting Started

How can we get children started writing in the kindergarten as easily as they do in literacy rich homes? Many people are still shocked at the ease with which children of kindergarten age (or even younger) write if they are invited and if the forms of writing which they prefer are accepted. Kindergarten is the first year of most public schooling, and it is a period during which young children are still using emergent forms of writing and reading. Therefore, we have done most of our research in kindergarten classrooms, and we have developed ways to invite children to write and read emergently in those classrooms.

From working with and observing in hundreds of classrooms, we can say confidently that all kindergartners reared in a literate culture can and will write. Sulzby (1988) offers some simple tips. First, and most important, a teacher must accept the forms of writing and reading children use. Second, and almost as important, make your request simple and straightforward. If you want children to write, say, "Write a story," or "Write a letter to your mother." Then ask the children to read what they have written: "Read us what you have written." A third guideline is to use the reassurance, "It doesn't have to be like grown up writing. Just do it your own way."

Storywriting

Inviting children to write their own stories is a key activity used in emergent literacy classrooms. Stories are a form of connected discourse, and children will use a fuller range of emergent writing/

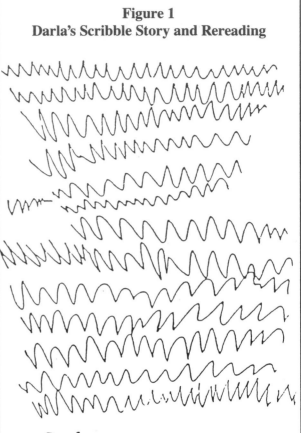

Figure 1
Darla's Scribble Story and Rereading

Darla
2/24/86

I...ride my bike to my friend's house and then when I'm ready, it's time to go home on my bike. And then I go home on my bike. And then I go home to see if anybody came for something, and if nobody came for something I I think what, what I wanted to do. And, and I think of something to do and then when I get to my friend's house _____ the little boy always scares my little bears when I am there.

Darla

Sulzby, Teale, and Kamberelis

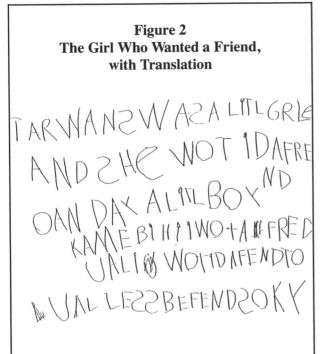

**Figure 2
The Girl Who Wanted a Friend,
with Translation**

There once was a little girl
and she wanted a friend.
One day a little boy
came by. Hi, I want a friend.
Well, I wanted a friend too.
Well, let's be friends, okay?

rereading forms in connected discourse than they will in writing isolated words or short phrases. Figures 1 and 2 show two examples of kindergartners' stories, one in scribble and the second in readable, invented spelling. Also shown are transcripts of the two stories.

Some teachers encourage storywriting as a once a week activity with little followup except displaying the children's writing. Others use story-

writing in a modified process writing format, moving from having children first share their stories individually with a receptive teacher to having them share in groups with the other children.

Children like to see their work displayed but they also like to take it home. When children first begin writing in the classroom, they need to share with the teacher fairly often. The teacher understands the importance of their emergent writing and rereading forms and sets the atmosphere for children to honor one another's writing attempts. It is a good idea to display the writing of all children. As the year progresses, teachers can vary what children do with their work, but always should honor it in some way. Some teachers encourage children to keep writing folders, others "publish" some pieces, and others display writing on bulletin boards or clothes lines.

It is amazing to see children's reactions to how teachers treat their writing. For example, Otto and Sulzby (in preparation) found that a group of preschoolers identified as academically able wrote only skimpy stories when the teacher was keeping all the stories for research purposes but not displaying them in the classroom. These same children began writing and creating long, multimedia compositions as soon as the teacher began sending stories home for the children to share with their parents.

Storywriting has been discussed at length already, but we have not discussed stories as stories. Stories, whether realistic, autobiographical, or fantasy, are wonderful avenues of creation for children (McNamee, 1987; Paley, 1981). They often involve multimedia productions that children become engrossed in. Promote this interest by encouraging children to write stories and to see themselves as authors. Treat them as authors. Provide unlined paper, pencils, crayons, markers, staplers, tape, and backing sheets—all invitations for authors to turn their stories into written productions and perhaps even into bound books. Encourage the children to read their books to the class, as well as to take them home to share.

Teachers who approach stories in this manner soon expand storybook time to include child authored as well as adult authored books. You soon see children beginning to stretch their powers to in-

I·D·E·A·S
You Can Use

Multimedia Construction

Set up your writing center for multimedia construction. Put painting and writing areas side by side. Include paper of many sizes and colors, lined and unlined. Make available lots of pencils, pens, markers, stamps, and other writing implements, along with scissors, a stapler, tape, cardboard, and glue. Encourage children to design their own "publishing" and "exhibition" areas. Children can even bind their own books. Maybe you can have a camera and tape recorder handy.

---

vent exciting and aesthetically pleasing works. You also will see them expanding their understandings of how drawings work as illustrations, not just as forms of writing. By inviting children to read their own stories, we are inviting them to remember their compositions and to treat written compositions as stable—fixed in time and space by the act of writing.

As research in emergent literacy is shared, we find that sometimes kindergarten teachers begin to build misconceptions about the levels of development to expect in their classrooms. In particular, they occasionally seem to think that all the children should be using invented spelling; we (Sulzby, Barnhart, & Hieshima, in press) have found that this is not accurate.

During kindergarten, the most typical forms of writing used in connected discourse (such as stories or letters) continue to be scribbling, drawing, and nonphonetic letter strings, with fewer children using phonetic (or invented) spelling, and conventional orthography (dictionary spelling). Children also may copy environmental print or use pseudo-letters (forms they make up after they can and do form letters conventionally). Forms such as rebus (pictures that stand for words or parts of words) usually do not show up until children are well into an understanding of the phonetic principle. Finally, Kamberelis and Sulzby (1988) have shown that even when children produce readable invented

spelling they do not always read conventionally from it at first.

Children go back and forth across the forms of writing, but teachers can begin to understand how the forms function developmentally for given children by listening while they compose and by asking them to read from their writing (Sulzby, Barnhart, & Hieshima, in press). When children write their own stories, they reread them in a variety of ways (Sulzby, 1985b; Sulzby, Barnhart, & Hieshima, in press). Children may simply label items in their writing, engage the adult in dialogue, recite an oral type story, or a story that sounds like a written monologue. (A written monologue sounds as if the child were reading independently from conventional writing.) Children may follow along with the print, accurately or inaccurately, whether the print can be read from conventionally. Finally, they may begin to read conventionally from their readable stories.

Name Writing

The previous discussion has been about story writing. We know, however, that children often use different writing forms for different tasks. If you ask children to write isolated words or lists, they tend to use (or ask for) conventional spelling or invented spelling. If you observe how they understand these forms, you may discover that they do not understand them from an adult standpoint.

Invitation to Story Writing

Invite your preschoolers and kindergartners to write a story about something exciting that happened to them. Let them talk about their ideas while sitting in a circle, then send them to their seats to write. Let them work for a while, even if some just sit and think. Be encouraging and tell them, "It doesn't have to be like grown up writing. Just write your own way."

Then, have children read their stories to a buddy and invite a few to read to the whole group. Set aside a time later in the week for more buddy and group sharing so that children get lots of chances to "read their own way" from their stories.

Conventional orthography is particularly misleading. Ferreiro (Ferreiro, 1986; Ferreiro & Teberosky, 1982; see also Barnhart, 1986) has demonstrated that children may produce correct spellings or stable strings of letters while holding quite immature concepts about written language. When asked to write stories or other forms of connected discourse, children tend to use the forms they have been using most commonly in their homes.

In traditional kindergartens, teachers often write children's names on their papers and provide models of their names on three lined strips on their desks, on cubbies, on cards, or on the blackboard. They often provide children with practice in name writing using fading techniques (often on dittoes), such as first writing the name in dark ink, next writing it with faint greyish ink, then with dots for the letters, and finally allowing children to write without aid. Such a practice assumes that children know nothing or that what they know is erroneous and that an adult model is accurate, can be learned directly, and is worth practicing.

In emergent literacy classrooms, teachers expect the children to write their own names on their belongings and, especially, on their writings and artwork. In preschools, this often means accepting scribble signatures from youngsters. One preschool teacher in Illinois proudly showed her ability to read all but two of her four year olds' scribbles. By the following week, she had learned those two as well. By year's end, all of the children were producing conventional looking signatures. In kindergarten, most children will be able to produce all or part of their first name in conventional orthography, but usually will not hold conventional understandings of writing.

Writing your own name is an important way of showing ownership of things; learning to write your name emergently seems to be an important way of being empowered in the literacy process. Ferreiro (1986) has illustrated that children negotiate with adults about what information they take in and what they reject about this seemingly simple act of learning to write one's name. In addition, she has discussed more broadly the critical importance of the concept of "name" in literacy development.

Teachers will notice that soon children not only write their own names, they also read and write the names of other children. In many curriculum materials for young children, complex words are omitted and replaced with one or two syllable, phonetically regular words. This model is misleading with respect to English orthography. It may be that having children involved in the production of the more complex patterns that appear in such names as Lukeisha, Tiffany, George, Ulana, Ian, Elizabeth, Nathaniel, Christien, or Jorge provides them with important information in a highly significant and memorable context—such as addressing Valentine's Day cards or letters to pen pals or passing out artwork to take home.

Classroom and School Libraries

Teachers in emergent literacy classrooms engage children in activities involving both reading and writing. In writing tasks, children are always reading. Reading can be done without writing, but in most reading activities children are expected to do at least some writing. The library is an important setting in which we find name writing used in a key functional way—to identify who checked out and is responsible for a book. In some traditional schools, children are not allowed to check out books until they can write their names conventionally on the card. In others, teachers or library helpers "help" children by writing their names for them. In emergent literacy classrooms, children write their own names, in their own way, on the books.

In many emergent literacy classrooms, children not only go to the library for books but also have classroom libraries for easy and ongoing access to books (Morrow, 1982). In such classroom libraries, the children write their own names. However, library activities are extended into broad ranging ways of sharing books that usually involve writing as well as other media. Children may respond to books they have read by writing and illustrating a poster, by building a shoebox mural, or by creating a dramatic re-creation of the book.

In one classroom where a teacher was hesitantly trying out emergent literacy ideas, she had been sending home nightly children's books from the classroom library but she wanted a record of all the books children were reading. The teacher and her aide were falling behind in writing the book names on the large manila envelopes children used to carry the books home when it suddenly dawned on them that children who could write stories could surely copy their own book titles. Soon they found the children reading these inventories of all the books they had read during the year. They were amazed to see that the same kinds of emergent reading behaviors they had seen with storybooks

and storywriting were used by the children in responding to complex titles such as *Marvin K. Mooney Will You Please Go Now*, *There's a Nightmare in My Closet*, or *Harry and the Terrible Whatzit*.

In addition to reading widely from the books of many authors or rereading specific books, some teachers have explored with their children the works of specific authors and illustrators. Then, in their writing, children often reflect their love for these authors' styles by imitating them. Having a classroom library and school library with ready access for children to read and reread books many times is essential in creating this kind of literary effect upon literacy development.

Letter Writing and Pen Pals

Almost all kindergarten teachers organize a field trip to the post office, create a mock post office in the classroom, or have some other event relating to correspondence just before Valentine's Day. In traditional classrooms, teachers often place model texts for students to copy. As teachers become more venturesome and child centered, they may ask the children to dictate individual messages and then to decorate them.

In emergent literacy classrooms, the children are the ones who write—their own way. Since letters and cards are connected discourse, some of the children may use scribble, drawing, or letter strings. Many children, however, have developed a set of stock phrases in conventional orthography that they use in valentines and letters. "Dear Mary" and, especially, "I love you" are important formula like phrases children use, sometimes with the rest of the letter being scribble or drawing.

One kindergarten teacher in Illinois always began her Valentine's Day celebration at the end of a social studies unit on community helpers. She took the children to a real post office just as the children became aware that Valentine's Day was approaching and led them into the idea of having a classroom post office. Even though she had begun using emergent writing sessions, when she began post office, she set up sentence models for the children to copy. Soon, however, she and the children abandoned the models and began writing their own way.

Classroom post offices can exist throughout a

school year and keep children's attention. Teale and his colleagues (Martinez & Teale, 1987; Teale & Martinez, in press) found that kindergarten children used a classroom post office as effectively as older students. Letter writing is one of the oldest functions of literacy worldwide, and it still works to tie families and friends together. No wonder youngsters are so drawn to it. Note and greeting card writing serve similar social functions. Take a count sometime of how many such missives are sent in your classroom in a year even if you do not set up a post office.

For example, in several kindergarten classrooms in the San Antonio area, teachers have children write their own invitations for special events. A Thanksgiving feast, a day for honoring guest storytellers and storybook readers, a Mother's Day tea—for all of these occasions and more, children have composed invitations and sent them to parents, school personnel, and even adults outside the school who have been involved in the classroom (students and faculty from the university and community helpers who have visited the class to share information).

In such settings, teachers introduce the task with discussions and demonstrations that focus on the purpose and format of an invitation. They also may give each child a copy of the name of the person to whom the child is writing. Then the children write their invitations using the systems we have discussed—some draw, some scribble, some use invented spellings, and some use a combination of strategies. The children reread their invitations to an adult and, if necessary, the adult produces a conventional representation of the child's rereading. Then the invitation is sent to the individual. In this manner, the children have been actively engaged in the whole writing process, and not merely practicing handwriting by copying someone else's message.

Dictation and Language Experience Techniques

Teachers who are implementing emergent literacy techniques vary in how they use traditional language experience techniques such as dictation. Sometimes dictation is an unintentional outgrowth of emergent writing. Some teachers are comfortable in accepting children's rereading only if the children are using invented spelling. When children use scribble, drawing, or letter strings, these teachers will write down what the children say when they read their pieces. This isn't intentional dictation, but it operates as dictation.

One teacher wrestled with the inconsistency she felt as a result of both honoring the child's writing and writing down the children's rereading. At first, she wrote the dictation on the front of the child's paper. She did this because she felt she needed a record of how the child reread, but then decided she was giving a mixed message to the child. Then, she decided to write what the child said in rereading on the back of the child's paper, but she was twisting the writing out of the child's view. Later, she decided to write on post-it notes in her hand and surreptitiously stick them on the back of the child's writing as she collected it. Finally, she decided she did not need that record in most cases. Still other teachers have used a checklist they devised or borrowed from researchers.

In the events described, note that the children were not invited to dictate, but the teachers nevertheless were taking dictation. Most traditional dictation activities are designed for the teacher to take dictation *instead* of asking children to write. Since we now know that children can write themselves, some teachers have concluded that there is no longer any need for dictation.

We find that the use of dictation is decreasing in many emergent literacy classrooms but that it is still a vigorous part of instruction in others. However, its purpose has usually shifted in these classrooms. The teachers try to make it clear to students that they are not using dictation because children cannot write; they are using dictation as another form of writing. Often it is used as the record of a group activity, particularly at the end of a science or social studies experience—very much in the spirit of traditional language experience but divorced from the negative assumptions about children's reading and writing abilities. Some teachers use it as a response to literacy activity. The practice of asking children to draw a picture and having the teacher circulate it and write a sentence beneath it has disappeared almost entirely.

Some teachers still treat dictation as a reading experience but not a writing experience. They use dictation as a way to get children "reading their own words." These teachers are beginning to apply understandings of emergent storybook reading (Sulzby, 1985a) to children's dictation reading, noting whether children look at the dictation while reading, whether their speech carries a storytelling or reading intonation, whether they read the story stably over time, and when and how they begin to attend to print in dictation. For these teachers, the expectations for reading from dictation have broadened. In Palatine, Illinois, we (Sulzby, 1985b) worked with teachers to understand the patterns that can be heard in children's speech while dictating, particularly noting when and where they pause during dictation and how this predicts how they will read from dictation.

Expository Writing

Expository writing should not be neglected. We know that even very young children begin to write informational pieces, just as they begin to write narratives. Many teachers move easily from using language experience charts to inviting children to write their own informational pieces. Graves (1983) suggests that every child has a topic on which he or she is an expert—or can become an expert. Inviting young children to study and write about a topic is a powerful way of involving them in literacy.

One kindergarten teacher in San Antonio did a two week unit on rodeos. Children used Learning Logs (Teale & Sulzby, this volume), and each day they drew a picture and wrote about what they learned that day. Another kindergarten teacher in Michigan worked with the school science teacher to create a bulletin board titled "Emergent Writing and Frogs" that displayed children's writing about a tadpole unit. The teachers in the school were studying children's emergent writing while the children were studying the emergence of frogs from tadpoles.

Artwork

Art provides a wonderful opportunity for children to engage in multimedia and aesthetically pleasing creations that take place over time. In many emergent literacy classrooms, art is creeping out of the easel corner into the entire room. Creations often involve writing as well as artwork. Many children create their own illustrated books as well as their own paintings, drawings, or prints.

A focus on art is important but may confuse children about the relationships between drawing and writing. Kindergartners know the difference between drawing and writing, but they still *use* drawing as a form of writing and speak in ambiguous ways about whether drawing can be writing (Sulzby, 1985c). With this in mind, when teachers invite children to write and the children draw instead, the teachers ask them to read and treat their drawing as writing until the children tell them that it is not. When they invite children to paint or draw, they treat the child's production as art unless the child tells them otherwise. One experienced emergent literacy teacher in Illinois uses neutral wording: "Jason, this is interesting. Tell me about this part," pointing to a section about which she is uncertain.

What about the common practice of asking children to draw a picture and then write something beneath it? Emergent literacy teachers we have worked with are beginning to think this practice should be treated very carefully for two reasons. First, as discussed previously, it is clear that many children use drawing as a form of writing. Not all drawing is writing but some is. Implying that drawing is different from writing and then asking children to write may create quite a conflict for those who have not yet sorted out the difference between the two ways of symbolizing. Second, Graves and his colleagues (Calkins, 1983; Graves, 1983) have found that the relationship between illustration and printed text is an important aspect to attend to when young children write. They have found that younger children draw and then write, whereas older ones write and then draw. We think this pattern is probably a later development to the forms we report. We believe that children need to sort out the drawing as writing/drawing as illustration puzzle through the practice of writing, rather than through having adults tell them "the right way." Dyson (1988) has studied how children create "picture worlds" and "text worlds" in the context of the teacher's requests to children to draw a picture and then write. Dyson also has studied how children negotiate between these worlds, both as affected by the teacher's predefined tasks and the children's enactment of the tasks.

Handwriting and Phonics

Handwriting, of course, has its own developmental patterns. Counter to the expectations of some teachers and researchers, children who are encouraged to write emergently seem to develop firm strokes, to write in left to right progression across straight lines, and to form regular size letters. Teachers using emergent literacy techniques usually allow children to write on unlined paper and only introduce lined paper *after* children are writing in straight, regular lines.

Another counterintuitive finding also has come from our studies. Traditional teachers not only give children lined paper, perhaps with ice cream cones or traffic lights to show spacing, but they also create dotted versions of letters for children to trace. (This is prevalent with the type of slanted handwriting that has been erroneously suggested for use in kindergarten to get children ready for cursive writing in third grade.) We have found that some children who have a great deal of trouble tracing such forms without frustration have nevertheless created their own dotted forms to trace. And they have accomplished this task with ease. Some emergent literacy teachers have dropped formal instruction in handwriting altogether. Others simply introduce it as a special unit—again after children are proficient in writing on their own—to help with any problems and to encourage elegant letter formation.

Most emergent literacy teachers gradually come to depend more and more upon children's writing as a means of indicating what they know about letter-sound relationships. For some teachers, instruction in phonics seems to be very important, but even they are decreasing the amount of time they spend in such drill. In addition, teachers are considering phonics instruction as an organization of what children already know rather than as new instruction in what they do not know.

Buhle (1987) reported an impressively responsive teacher who was attempting to use emergent literacy techniques. She began her traditional phonics lesson by eliciting words for sounds from her children, planning to write the words on the board. When she asked for the first word, however, holding the chalk in her hand, up popped a little boy ready to take the chalk away from her. From that moment on, the *children* wrote the words on the board their own way, and the teacher began to ask *them* to read the lists.

Conclusion

We have described some ways teachers have incorporated writing into the kindergarten curriculum. Presented more abstractly, here is what we find these teachers doing.

1. They encourage writing for ownership.
2. They encourage children to use writing in their play.
3. They encourage children to use writing in response to literature they hear or read.
4. They encourage children to share their writing and to respond to other children's writing.
5. They encourage children to use writing to communicate with other people.

We have been describing *what* teachers do and *how* they do it when they invite children to read and write in their classrooms. But let's reconsider whether the classroom can provide the same kind of social situation as the home. Clearly, the answer is no. It cannot and probably should not. Much of the research in home literacy has described writing of younger children or those in the presence of older writers. In a classroom, children see twenty to thirty other children all their age, writing in the many forms we described. They interact socially with these children, including seeing, discussing, and listening to their writing/reading attempts. Thus, there is much modeling. In emergent literacy classrooms, teachers understand and encourage the patterns of children's writing. They also have ideas about how to move children forward in developmentally appropriate ways.

Also, the teacher has a different role from the parent. Negotiations about frustrating times and power relationships will be different, although related. We have observed many teachers in emergent literacy classrooms taking a very nurturing role, but also nudging children forward. Children often accept tips and lessons from teachers in ways that they resist from parents. We do not know enough about the roles of teachers in the social-emotional development of young children, but teachers often help children make friends, share, deal with anger, and brag and joke appropriately. Similarly, they encourage children's writing and positive attitudes toward their own and other children's writing.

We know that children write with many forms and continue to use lower level forms to perform higher level functions. What about the child, though, who shows clear signs of knowing how to write in readable forms but still uses scribble, drawing, or nonphonetic letter strings? Again, we have found that the gentle touch is best. Some teachers say something like, "What a wonderful story! I really like that. Do you think you could write it so I can read it, too?" If the child balks, they encourage and accept the child's decision (nudging but not pushing): "Well, maybe next time. It's a great story. Would you like to put it on the bulletin board?"

We have left the themes of transcience, multi-media constructions, and aesthetic creations for last. We have found that these themes depend greatly upon how willing the teacher is for the children's endeavors to control the time and space use in the classroom. With brief two and one-half hour days, many kindergarten teachers feel increasing pressure to cover content. In many emergent literacy classrooms, however, the day is structured so that children have the freedom to begin projects, leave them, and return to them later. With others, this is not the case.

The transience of interest is an area that causes us even more concern. We spoke about the different social situations in the home and the school. When children are writing in a group situation, there is much positive motivation through the modeling and attention of other children. Yet, sometimes this can create pressure for the child who currently is not interested in writing but would rather be building with the big blocks. It is important to be attuned to children's interests and talents and to make available opportunitites to accommodate them.

Jennifer Heebink from California reports that

encouraging the daughter of migrant farm workers to recite oral tales seemed to be the avenue for that child to become conventionally literate. As this teacher told of her experience, it became clear how she had changed her classroom and expectations to accommodate what this child knew and could do, even though it did not fit the school curriculum's descriptions of reading readiness.

As teachers learn more about emergent writing and reading, classrooms are being filled with books and writing materials. In some emergent literacy classrooms, there seems to be a tendency to neglect other media and aesthetic interests. In others, we see teachers becoming more appreciative of children's *compositional* abilities—as artists, musicians, dramatists, and builders, as well as writers.

As we reflect upon the relationship between the home and school as places that encourage children's emergent writing, we realize that we still have much to learn—teachers, researchers, and children together. And yet we rapidly have come a long way from the day when kindergarten was a time and place to get children "ready" for reading and writing.

References

Anderson, A.B., and Stokes, S.J. Social and institutional influences on the development and practice of literacy. In H. Goelman, A. Oberg, and F. Smith (Eds.), *Awakening to literacy.* Portsmouth, NH: Heinemann, 1984, 24-37.

Barnhart, J.E. *Written language concepts and cognitive development in kindergarten children.* Unpublished doctoral dissertation, Northwestern University, 1986.

Bissex, G. GNYS AT WRK: *A child learns to write and read.* Cambridge, MA: Harvard University Press, 1980.

Buhle, R. *A study of implementation of emergent literacy by kindergarten teachers.* Unpublished master's thesis, Northwestern University, 1987.

Calkins, L. *Lessons from a child.* Portsmouth, NH: Heinemann, 1983.

Chukovsky, K. *From two to five.* M. Morton, translator. Berkeley, CA: University of California Press, 1963.

Doake, D. *Book experience and emergent reading behavior.* Unpublished doctoral dissertation, University of Alberta, Canada, 1982.

Dyson, A.H. Emerging literacy in school contexts: Toward defining the gap between school curriculum and child mind. *Written communication*, 1984, *1*, 5-53.

Dyson, A.H. Individual differences in emergent writing. In M. Farr (Ed.), *Advances in writing research: Children's early writing development*, volume 1. Norwood, NJ: Ablex, 1985, 59-126.

Dyson, A.H. Negotiating among multiple worlds: The space/time dimensions of young children's composing. *Research in the Teaching of English,* 1988, *22*(4), 355-390.

Ferreiro, E. The interplay between information and assimilation in beginning literacy. In W.H. Teale and E. Sulzby (Eds.), *Emergent literacy: Writing and reading.* Norwood, NJ: Ablex, 1986, 15-49.

Ferreiro, E., and Teberosky, A. *Literacy before schooling.* Portsmouth, NH: Heinemann, 1982.

Gardner, H., Wolfe, D., and Smith, A. Artistic symbols in early childhood. NYU *Education Quarterly*, 1975, *6*, 13-21.

Graves, D. *Writing: Teachers and children at work.* Portsmouth, NH: Heinemann, 1983.

Kamberelis, G., and Sulzby, E. Transitional knowledge in emergent literacy. In J.E. Readence and R.S. Baldwin, (Eds.), *Dialogues in literacy research,* Thirty-Seventh Yearbook of the National Reading Conference. Rochester, NY: National Reading Conference, 1988, 95-106.

Martinez, M., and Teale, W.H. The ins and outs of a kindergarten writing program. *The Reading Teacher*, 1987, *40*(4), 444-451.

McNamee, G. The social origins of narrative skills. In M. Hickmann (Ed.), *Social and functional approaches to language and thought.* Orlando, FL: Academic Press, 1987.

Morrow, L. Relationships between literature programs, library corner designs, and children's use of literature. *Journal of Educational Research*, 1982, *75*, 339-344.

Otto, B., and Sulzby, E. *Academically able preschoolers and emergent literacy.* Unpublished data, 1988.

Paley, V. *Bad guys don't have birthdays: Fantasy play at four.* Chicago, IL: University of Chicago Press, 1988.

Paley, V. *Boys and girls: Superheroes in the doll corner.* Chicago, IL: University of Chicago Press, 1986.

Paley, V. *Wally's stories: Conversations in the kindergarten.* Cambridge, MA: Harvard University Press, 1981.

Snow, C., and Ninio, A. The contracts of literacy: What children learn from learning to read books. In W.H. Teale and E. Sulzby (Eds.), *Emergent literacy: Writing and reading.* Norwood, NJ: Ablex, 1986, 116-138.

Sulzby, E. Children's development of prosodic distinctions in telling and dictating modes. In A. Matsuhashi (Ed.), *Writing in real time: Modelling production processes.* Norwood, NJ: Ablex, 1987, 133-160.

Sulzby, E. Children's emergent reading of favorite storybooks: A developmental study. *Reading Research Quarterly*, 1985a, *20*, 458-481.

Sulzby, E. *Emergent literacy: Kindergartners write and read, including Sulzby coding system.* Ann Arbor, MI: University of Michigan and North Central Regional Educational Laboratory, 1988.

Sulzby, E. *Forms of writing and rereading: Example list.* Unpublished examiner's manual, Northwestern University, 1985b.

Sulzby, E. Kindergartners as writers and readers. In M. Farr (Ed.), *Advances in writing research: Children's early writing development*, volume 1. Norwood, NJ: Ablex, 1985c, 127-200.

Sulzby, E., Barnhart, J., and Hieshima, J. Forms of writing and rereading from writing: A preliminary report. In J. Mason (Ed.), *Reading and writing connections.* Newton, MA: Allyn & Bacon, in press.

Sulzby, E., and Teale, W.H. Writing development in early childhood. *Educational Horizons*, 1985, *64*, 8-12.

Sulzby, E. and Teale, W.H. *Young children's storybook reading: Longitudinal study of parent-child interaction and children's independent functioning.* Final report to the Spencer Foundation. Ann Arbor, MI: University of Michigan, 1987.

Taylor, D. *Family literacy: The social context of learning to read and write.* Portsmouth, NH: Heinemann, 1983.

Taylor, D., and Dorsey-Gaines, C. *Growing up literate: Learning from innercity families.* Portsmouth, NJ: Heinemann, 1988.

Teale, W.H. Emergent literacy: Reading and writing development in early childhood. In J.E. Readence and R.S. Baldwin (Eds.), *Research in literacy: Merging perspectives,* Thirty-Sixth yearbook of the National Reading Conference. Rochester, NY: 1987, 45-74.

Teale, W.H. Home background and young children's literacy development. In W.H. Teale and E. Sulzby (Eds.), *Emergent literacy: Writing and reading.* Norwood, NJ: Ablex, 1986.

Teale, W.H. Reading to young children: Its significance for literacy development. In H. Goelman, A. Oberg, and F. Smith (Eds.), *Awakening to literacy.* Portsmouth, NH: Heinemann, 1984, 110-121.

Teale, W.H., and Martinez, M. Connecting writing: Fostering emergent literacy in kindergarten children. In J. Mason (Ed.), *Reading and writing connections.* Boston, MA: Allyn & Bacon, in press.

CHAPTER SEVEN

Is It Reasonable...? A Photo Essay

Nancy Roser

James Flood

Diane Lapp

In this chapter we offer a look into the classrooms of two teachers of young children, describing through the teachers' words and through photography the literacy learning that occurs. We present the teachers' notions about children's literacy growth, the influences on their teaching, and some of their instructional procedures. Across two different instructional settings, these teachers share values: showing interest in children's ideas, becoming learners in their own classrooms, sharing joy in books and reading, providing opportunities for talk and sharing, viewing learning as social and active, maximizing home and school cooperation, blurring traditional subject matter lines, and making literacy a necessity.

Is it reasonable to expect that one teacher can build a language rich, print filled, garden growing, pet tending, book reading, message writing, child nurturing, mind expanding, body building, humanities emphasizing environment and live to tell about it?

The Challenge: The Seemingly Impossible Demands on Teachers of Young Children

The professional literature is currently abuzz with advice for teachers of young children. Teachers are being reminded and encouraged to help children take an active part in their own learning (Teale & Sulzby, 1986); to plan more interesting, involving classroom experiences (Schickedanz, 1986; Strickland, 1987); to provide "as complete and complex" a learning environment as possible so that students can engage in activities they view as meaningful (Newman, 1985); to build on children's understandings and efforts (Dyson 1984; Morrow, 1988; Vygotsky, 1978); to provide for collaborative and socially constructed contexts for learning to read, to write, and to share (Cochran-Smith, 1984; Harste, Woodward, & Burke, 1984); to actively participate with children as colearners (Roser & Martinez, 1985; Tovey & Kerber, 1986); to emphasize content while not losing sight of processes (Altwerger, Edelsky, & Flores, 1987); and to become more observant of and reflective on children's behaviors (Goodman, 1986).

The Puzzle: How Can Teachers Meet These Demands?

Where do teachers find time, energy, space, and support to provide a meaningful curriculum for young children that is consistent with their own beliefs? How do teachers balance their professional values against the real world of learner differences; language differences; prescriptive materials; administrative, societal, and parental pressures; and the vicissitudes of curriculum and assessment swings (Shulman, 1986)? There is no easy answer. When we search for answers, too often we find guidelines, position statements, implementation criteria, maxims, and dictates that lack adequate description for implementation. Our intent here is to provide some descriptions by looking into the classrooms of two successful teachers we know, watching and learning, ferreting out potential applications, positions, and procedures that may inform others.

Some Successes: A Look at Classrooms in Which Practices Seem to Match the Maxims

Meet Barbara Schaefer of San Diego, California

Barbara Schaefer teaches a preschool class for four year olds as part of the California State Department Preschool Program. Children's eligibility for this program is dependent upon an annual family income of less than $10,000 and parents' agreement to participate. The twofold purpose of this state funded program is to provide a year's comprehensive preparation for kindergarten, while closely involving parents in the education of their children.

As you enter Barbara's classroom, you notice print, books, art displays, color, language charts, clutter, centers, project areas, a hubbub of activity, and opportunities for exploration. You are struck immediately with the intergenerational community of instruction—teachers, parents, babies, and grandparents all are there. Her classroom speaks her thoughts: "There are no small or insignificant literacy events in my children's lives. Each is mon-

Barbara Schaefer teaches four year olds at Valencia Park Elementary School, San Diego, California.

umental, no matter how brief."

When you ask Barbara to talk about her program, she says she believes in traditional preschool program values that encourage children's social, emotional, and academic growth. "But," she quickly adds, "I am trying to make this a special year in which my children will come to love books and have fun with the spoken and written word. I

Barbara gives a hug as she discusses the menu with Elizabeth.

want my children to feel successful, to know that they are free to try."

When she is pressed to be specific about her program, she tells you about her daily schedule. As she speaks, you find your attention drifting to the inviting library, the writing corner, the records, the posters, the children's art work, the science project area—to paints, to pets, to plants, to children and parents everywhere. You pull back, attending fully again because you hear her say, "I have so little time with the children I like to make every minute count. For example, I find lunchtime to be the very best time of the day to talk informally with my kids, to get to know them well. I enjoy them—their ideas, their perspectives, and their humor. Sometimes I think I teach them better because I know them better."

She explains that the typical day in her room follows a routine similar to that of most preschool programs. "I think routines are very important for children. They need to understand expectations as well as limits, but my real thrust is expectations. I want them to know I expect them to love books, to learn many things, and to have fun. As time goes on, I also expect them to assume responsibility for the routines. I tell them that a book a day is as important to them as water, food, and sleep. I read to them *every* day."

As we talked more, it became apparent that Barbara has certain tenets about young children's literacy development: "My program is based on a set of simple beliefs—things I learned in school, things I heard from speakers at conferences, things I've read about, and things I believe children can

Children discuss the best way to "roll a B."

Ms. Barnes, instructional aide, finds the numeral 2 with the children.

and should do. I've been influenced greatly by Sylvia Ashton-Warner, Donald Graves, Montessori, and John Dewey." Her four tenets can be framed as action oriented statements that serve as the foundation of her program: (1) Give children ample opportunities to engage in and practice all of the language arts (with direct or indirect adult involvement), (2) surround children with literature, (3) make literacy a family affair, and (4) integrate and unify a meaning filled curriculum for the children.

Give the Children Ample Opportunities to Engage in All of the Language Arts

"I think it's important for children to have time and motivation to speak, listen, read, and write. Not all of my children need the same kind of attention. Some are very shy and need special encouragement to share their ideas and opinions. I try to set up situations in which talking and listening will be as natural as possible. Sometimes I find it works if adults are only indirectly involved. For example, when we set up the tables with open ended projects, we find the children are eager to talk with and listen to one another. I want to provide situations that 'naturally' engage children's attention with compelling, purposeful things to listen to—things they need to hear in order to accomplish their objectives.

"I try to make reading a natural and frequent part of every activity, too. I label everything in the classroom so that children will learn that words can be written and read. Not every child wants to read the labels, but I have all of the labels ready for them just in case. Some children love to 'read' books, and I encourage them to sit quietly with the book of their choice. Usually before I walk away, they are happily involved with the book. It seems especially easy for them to get involved with books that I have read aloud to them. Some of my children enjoy reading and writing their own names and the names of other children in the class. Some just enjoy playing with—or should I say 'exploring'—the letters of the alphabet."

Barbara's class does a lot of writing and drawing because she agrees with people like Don Graves who have said that children "love to make their mark, declaring to the world, 'I am.'" Barbara says, "We use slates, magnetic letters, paper, pencils, and every type of drawing instrument."

Hiriece "writes" her name as Shari watches.

David explores the name card board.

Arlene finds her container.

Joshua and Leana "compare" on plate boards.

Ms. Barnes and Joshua "paint" as Arlene watches and listens.

A Photo Essay

"Sometimes my aide and I (or any adult who happens to be present at the time) directly involve ourselves with the children as they write. For example, we find that the children like it when we discuss their 'compositions' with them. Sometimes we suggest a plan. Sometimes we transcribe their thoughts to add words to their pictures. Sometimes we hold the paper still, and sometimes we just listen."

Surround the Children with Literature

"I like to have a lot of books around me. My bedroom could qualify for a small business loan to start operating as an eccentric, eclectic, very used bookstore. Now I'm reading Kozol. I decided my children should also know the joys of many types of books, so I bring in children's books of all sizes, colors, shapes, and subjects.

"Because so many of my kids were fascinated with the pandas from China at the San Diego Zoo, we decided in Circle Time to learn about bears. I don't know yet how this will work, but I'm mixing fact and fantasy books—all the way from my favorite version of "The Three Bears" to the National Geographic edition, *Baby Bears*. I'm hoping to help them learn about bears and laugh about bears all in the same unit of study. Do you think that will confuse them?

"I agree with everyone who has said that children learn from retellings. And my kids are such hams; they love a chance to tell part of the story. We start slowly with them—memorable phrases, building to details, and then major events. They love it."

Make Literacy a Family Affair

"One big reason I took this position was because of the links it mandated among the adults in the children's lives. To have a program like this, the state must want it, the district must aggressively support it, and the school must initiate it. We have to guarantee to support the program with financial, human, and physical resources. Besides that, our parents must participate fully in the classroom and/ or at home and attend monthly meetings—and the children and teachers love every minute of it.

"The parents are the cornerstone of this program; they know what the curriculum is about, and

A cornucopia of bear books—Barbara shares different genres with the children.

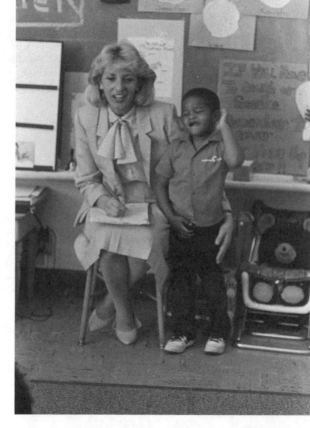

Parents and baby sister listen attentively to a retelling of "The Three Bears."

David retells "The Three Bears."

they encourage literacy at home. I work with them as partners in their child's literacy development. It's not rare when the whole family comes to school. In fact, younger brothers and sisters are here every day.

"Every day, resource teachers (speech teachers, helping teachers, counselors) freely flow in and out of here. Children come to expect that everyone is here to help them. My school principal, Carolyn Dubuque, visits often. She says, 'I want the children to view literacy and books as a vital part of everyone's life. I want them to know that everyone should take time for a good book.'

"Our late afternoon monthly parent meetings are among my favorite parts of this program. I try hard to make the parents comfortable and to draw them out. I offer suggestions, but more often I listen and plan with the parents. I need their counsel."

Integrate and Unify the Curriculum

"I think I came to an integrated view of curriculum through the back door. Before I ever had lofty thoughts about how integrated teaching helps children focus and make connections, I was in the position of struggling for enough 'minutes' to cover the state mandated curriculum. It was by clumsy 'lumping' that I first came to a view of integration, and now I couldn't teach any other way. For example, remember the panda bear study? We have a panda corner over there with books about pandas, books about China, bamboo shoots, photographs, and a globe. We planned a list of questions we'd ask a zookeeper at the San Diego Zoo. One question really sparked a lively discussion. Dominic asked about the size of panda bears when they are newborn. We scrambled through those books for answers. When we found out, I rolled a brown sock up in a ball to show the size of a newborn panda cub, and they couldn't believe it.

"Then Christine wanted to know how much the baby would weigh. Back to the books! We weighed

Barbara and the children do their growl and stretch dance.

the sock and compared the weight with what our books said a cub weighed at birth. The next task was finding enough light items in the classroom to add to a postage scale until we could measure four or five ounces—the weight of a panda bear cub. We listed all the things we weighed on a chart. Many children asked at home what they weighed at birth, so we made still another chart.

"We've read *Brown Bear, Brown Bear,* we've painted bear tracks, we've been on a bear hunt, and we're planning a *Corduroy* bear day. I must confess I've learned myself. Did you know, for example, that mother pandas weigh 800 times the weight of their babies? If you ever need a good information book, I recommend *Project Panda Watch* by Miriam Schlein.

"After rest time one day, I noticed Jessica stretching, so that's why we created this growl and stretch dance, as though we were bears waking up from our naps.

"To make a bear study a special celebration, we made bear cookies. I planned so that recipe reading, mixing, stirring, rolling, and cutting out dough would be structured enough to involve everyone in some way. These are the days I'm especially grateful for the extra hands that parents provide!"

In Retrospect

Barbara's classroom builds on a community of teachers, parents, aides, and school resource personnel working together to ensure that children learn. She believes that learning is a social process and that talk is central. Barbara is a reader, and she communicates the fact that books are important for pleasure and for getting answers to real questions. Her classroom fosters questioning, exploration, and "being free to try." She finds that children are good at informing her of their interests and their needs, so she listens carefully. She believes in responsive teaching and in students' inquiry. She acts on children's curiosity and fosters further thinking. She delights in the written word and wants to share literacy. Barbara is reflective, experimental, and herself a learner.

Meet Robin Mueller of Georgetown, Texas

Robin Mueller's classroom for four year olds is in the Learning Tree School in Georgetown, a community thirty miles north of Austin, Texas. The school is housed in a church, but operated by an independent board of directors. Robin's classroom is also a Sunday School room, so wall space, displays, and work areas are disassembled and reassembled before and after the weekend. She explains that we have come on a typical day, so before the children arrive she still has much to do. Today is "soup making" day, a special part of a healthy foods study.

Robin and her coteacher, Charlotte Rosenbaum, move about readying the classroom. They cut fresh vegetables to make vegetable prints in math time. They set the big book (Maurice Sendak's *Chicken Soup with Rice*) onto the easel, and rearrange the related picture books in the library area, among them *Stone Soup, Cloudy with a Chance of Meatballs, Growing Vegetable Soup, Watch Out for Chicken Feet in Your Soup, Strega Nona,* and of course, *Chicken Soup with Rice.* They open another big book, *Aikendrum,* which was read last week and only partially illustrated, placing it on a table top ready for other illustrators.

A cardboard box of cornmeal, as well as pens, pencils, and papers are arranged in a writing area. Paint is given a last minute stir. Robin counts to be certain that enough butcher paper soup bowls are ready for painted ingredients. She unloads a crock pot, a selection of fresh and canned vegetables, rice, knives, cutting boards, pepper, spoons, and disposable bowls from a grocery bag. The kindergarten children are making Stone Soup today, Robin explains, but the four year olds are sticking with vegetable rice. Mental lists are being ticked off. Just in time. The children arrive.

After greeting the children, saying good-bye to parents, and listening intently to many wide eyed catch up stories, Robin invites the children into a circle. Let's sing our ice cream song," she says. The children sing with gusto, while Robin points to the words:

I Want a Bowl of Ice Cream *

I want a bowl of ice cream.
I want a bowl with strawberries on it.
I want a bowl of ice cream.
Mmmm, and a little bit more.
Mmmm, and a little bit,
Mmmm, and a little bit,
Mmmm, and a little bit more.

— Raffi

*From *Raffi Singable Songbook.* Copyright © 1980 by Homeland Publishing, a Division of Troubadour Records, Ltd. Reprinted by permission of Crown Publishers, a Division of Random House, Inc.

After singing about bowls of ice cream, the children suggest variations and sing about other things they would like a bowl of. Then, they are led to notice and talk about the print.

"There's a lot of I's in that song."

"There's a lot of mmm's, too."

"How many?" "Show us." and "What else?"

Robin Mueller teaches four year olds at the Learning Tree School in Georgetown, Texas.

The children list many things they eat from bowls.

says Robin, to keep children's comments coming. Children come to the chart to point out, frame, and question.

"Remember when you told me all the things we eat from bowls?" asks Robin. She holds up a huge paper bowl, labeled with the children's ideas. They respond immediately.

"Cheerios!"
"Applesauce!"
"Popcorn!"
"Ice cream!"
"Gumbo!"
"Pasghetti!"

"Yes, and we eat soup in bowls, too." Robin reads the soup words from the bowl. "You said veg-

etable soup, tomato soup, and chicken noodle soup."

"I've brought a book to read to you about a special kind of soup." Robin turns to the homemade big book, *Chicken Soup with Rice,* by Maurice Sendak. "You can help me read this book," she tells them, and children edge closer, ready to join in. Robin announces the title and author, then reads the book to the children, taking her time, but preserving the rhythm of Sendak's lines. The book describes how nice it is to sip hot chicken soup with rice in January.

"You guys sure do know the months well!" Robin compliments the children after the second time through.

"I know what the words says," announces Grace.

"I don't think that's true," says Ben.

Robin asks, "What things go into soup?" "What ingredients?" As children make suggestions, Robin writes their ideas on a four foot high soup can cut from brown butcher paper: "rice, meat, carrots, potatoes, can." Robin writes quickly, then re-reads the children's suggestions to them.

"In work time today, some of you may help to make soup. Here's a book with a recipe we can use." Robin showed *Growing Vegetable Soup* by Lois Ehlert.

Later, in Center Time, children who gathered for soup making had many responsibilities, and the talk was task oriented:

"Who will wash a carrot for us?"

"This is an old-fashioned can opener."

"Matthew Hansen is cutting mushrooms."

"Can I stir it?"

I · D · E · A · S
You Can Use

Books Good Enough to Eat

Robin used *Chicken Soup with Rice* by Maurice Sendak and *Growing Vegetable Soup* by Lois Ehlert in her classroom for good cooking.

Other good books for classroom cooking or munching are these favorites.
Strega Nona (Tomie dePaola)
Giant Jam Sandwich (John Vernon Lord)
Cloudy with a Chance of Meatballs (Ron and Judi Barrett)
The Gingerbread Boy (Paul Galdone)
The Popcorn Book (Tomie dePaola)
Stone Soup (Marcia Brown)
Pancakes for Breakfast (Tomie dePaola)
Max's Breakfast (Rosemary Wells)
The Great Big Enormous Turnip (A. Tolstoy)
The Very Hungry Caterpillar (Eric Carle)
Benny Bakes a Cake (Eve Rice)
Bread and Jam for Frances (L. Hoban)

Cookbooks for Kids

The Little House Cookbook (Barbara Walker)
The Pooh Cook Book (J. Ellison)

Language to Literacy Project
Brownsville Independent School District
Brownsville, Texas

A Photo Essay

91

Robin and the children make soup.

A moment for my own reading.

Andrew's story.

An artist's eye: Painting the ingredients of the soup.

Roser, Flood, and Lapp

Jason and Robin read his story together.

Jason used book language: "Here goes one, here goes two, here goes chicken soup with mushrooms."

When all the ingredients were in, Robin asked, "What does the book say we do now?"

"Cook it!"

While the soup cooked, there were vegetable prints to make, celery soaking up red dye to inspect with a hand lens, "recipe books" made of bound-together paper to write in, books for reading in the library corner, and a restaurant in which to cook pretend "hamburger soup." There was a stack of bowl shaped paper near the easel for painting the ingredients of the real soup, now beginning to simmer in the crock pot. Children were deliberate in their choices, but both teachers (Robin and Charlotte) monitored movement among the work areas. Later, on the school playground, Grace and Carl dug a hole in the sand. "Now," directed Grace, "what ingredients will you put in?"

After rest time, children who had written about soup or who had vegetable prints to share signed up for a sharing time. Robin was especially

Mmmm good.

excited about Jason's work. On this January day, Jason had written his first conventional letter forms. "Do you want to read it while I hold it?" asked Robin.

"You can read it," Jason answered shyly.

"I will," said Robin. "What shall I say?"

"We made soup. We dumped in."

When it was Nick's turn, he said: "This is my snow monster. I made it at Writing Time. I wrote, 'snow monster.'"

All that was left to do was serve and eat the soup and compliment the chefs.

In Retrospect

Robin's classroom nourishes children's language and literacy growth. Thinking, expression, time, and creations are valued. As a result, the children read, write, and respond in authentic situations. "I hope you like what you've seen," Robin said. "Did it seem chaotic?" Quite the contrary. In this classroom, children read what they sang, drew what they read, wrote what they talked about, and shared what they wrote—marking a clear trail toward conventional literacy in its most meaningful sense.

We saw children interested in reading and writing their own ideas en route to becoming excellent readers and writers who see purpose and utility in what they do. We heard children use the language of books and of the teacher. We saw them involved in their learning. Robin says her professional growth is stimulated by the work of Donald Holdaway, by exchanging ideas and materials with other teachers such as Dotty Hooker, who shares her view of young children, and by Sharon Johnson, a professor at Southwestern University, whose students visit Robin's class.

I·D·E·A·S
You Can Use

Storing the Stories

When classroom chart stories accumulate, it becomes difficult to turn the pages and keep the chart story open to the selected page. Here are some tips.

1. Try removing the stories from the chart pad. Run them through the rolling laminator.
2. Hang the stories/rhymes/songs with rings onto plastic hangers.
3. Use a coat rack to collect the stories and retrieve them easily.
4. Let children "shop" for their favorites.

Chart stories hang on the coat rack for easy access.

Kathryn Otto
Learning Tree School
Georgetown, Texas

The Question Again

Yes, it is reasonable to expect that teachers can build a language rich, print filled, garden growing, pet tending, book reading, message writing, child nurturing, mind expanding, body building, humanities emphasizing environment and live to tell about it. Barbara and Robin are examples of preschool teachers who maximize the physical space in the classroom, show interest in children's ideas, become learners in their own classrooms, share joy in books and reading, provide opportunity for talk and sharing, view learning as social and active, maximize home/school cooperation, blur the traditional subject matter lines, and make literacy a necessity. Both teachers offer lively and engaging instruction that evokes joyous response to language learning. In addition, they offer valid constructs for the practices of teachers across the grades.

References

Altwerger, B., Edelsky, C., and Flores, B. Whole language: What's new. *The Reading Teacher,* 1987, *41,* 144-154.

Cochran-Smith, M. *The making of a reader.* Norwood, NJ: Ablex, 1984.

Dyson, A.H. 'N' spell my grandmama: Fostering early thinking about print. *The Reading Teacher,* 1984, *38,* 262-271.

Goodman, Y. Children coming to know literacy. In W.H. Teale and E. Sulzby (Eds.), *Emergent literacy: Writing and reading.* Norwood, NJ: Ablex, 1986, 1-14.

Harste, J., Woodward, V. and Burke, C. *Language stories and literacy lessons.* Portsmouth, NH: Heinemann, 1984.

Morrow, L.M. Young children's responses to one-to-one story readings in school settings. *Reading Research Quarterly,* 1988, *23,* 89-107.

Newman, J. *Whole language: Theory in use.* Portsmouth, NH: Heinemann, 1985.

Roser, N., and Martinez, M. Roles adults play in preschoolers' responses to literature. *Language Arts,* 1985, *62,* 485-490.

Schickedanz, J.A. *More than the ABCs: The early stages of reading and writing.* Washington, DC: National Association for the Education of Young Children, 1986.

Shulman, L.S. Those who understand: Knowledge growth in teaching. *Educational Researcher,* 1986, *15,* 4-14.

Strickland, D.S. Literature: Key element in the language and reading program. In B. Cullinan (Ed.), *Children's literature in the reading program.* Newark, DE: International Reading Association, 1987, 68-76.

Teale, W.H., and Sulzby, E. (Eds.). *Emergent literacy: Writing and reading.* Norwood, NJ: Ablex, 1986.

Tovey, D., and Kerber, J. *Roles in literacy learning: A new perspective.* Newark, DE: International Reading Association, 1986.

Vygotsky, L. *Mind in society.* Cambridge, MA: Harvard University Press, 1978.

CHAPTER EIGHT

The Place of Specific Skills in Preschool and Kindergarten

Judith A. Schickedanz

Most educators like the idea of providing young children with concrete experiences. They know that this makes learning meaningful and helps children develop a broad conceptual base. But many educators worry about this kind of education, which provides little, if any, direct training in skills. My purpose in this chapter is to illustrate how skills can be taught as children and teachers interact with materials and experiences. The chapter makes explicit some important categories of literacy skills that children can begin to master during the emergent literacy stage and explains how specific classroom incidents provide for their acquisition.

Another Day Begins

Katherine and Elise enter their preschool classroom one morning, laughing and talking. "I bet I'm a snack helper today," Katherine boasts to Elise.

"Bet I am, too," Elise boasts back.

Once inside the classroom, both girls check the Snack Helpers' chart, hanging on the wall just inside the door. "I am! I am!" yells Elise with delight.

"I'm not," says a disappointed Katherine, who continues to survey the chart, as if hoping against hope that she will find her name. Then her eyes light up as she yells, "And you're not either! It's Ellen—E-L-L-E-N, not you."

Elise moves in close to check to see if the news she has heard is true. She watches Katherine's finger trace the name from left to right and point out the evidence. "I didn't look far enough," she said. "And I thought—I thought—I was one. But I'm *not*." The teacher joins the conversation. "I think Katherine is right. I don't see any letters in that name that could say sssssss. It can't be yours, can it?"

Across the room at a small table, Andrew has been sorting through index cards from the book checkout box.

At the top of each card is a book title, written in bold, red marker. Underneath are the names of borrowers. Andrew is checking in two books. "M, M, M, M," he says to himself, as he looks for the card for *Mother, Mother, I Want Another*. He inspects the first letter of the first word written at the

Figure 1
Book Checkout Card

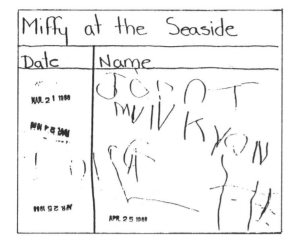

top left of each card as he goes through them, one by one. Most are put down after a quick glance, as Andrew notices that the titles do not start with the letter *M*. Then his glance lingers on one, before it, too, is rejected. It belongs to the book *Madeline*. Apparently, the *M* caught Andrew's attention. But he looked "far enough," as Elise would have said, to know that this *M* did not belong to the word he needed.

Behind Andrew, over at the fish tank, Alexis sprinkles some flakes of fish food onto the water. Alexis knew that it was her job to feed the fish today because she found a small tag attached to her pocket on the attendance chart. When finished sprinkling, Alexis returns the fish food to the shelf and dashes off toward the puzzle table. An alert teacher calls to her, "Alexis. Did you turn the sign over so everyone will know that you have fed the fish?"

"Oh. I forgot," Alexis calls back, as she dashes back to finish up. "Fish *Have* Been Fed," she says slowly to herself, as she checks each word on one side of the sign, to make sure it is not the side that says "Fish Have *Not* Been Fed."

Children and parents continue to enter during this fifteen minute Arrival Time. One parent hands a note to a teacher. Andrew's father jots a message on the clipboard hanging on the wall by the door. Michael tells the teacher he's going to Sean's house to play.

"Is that what your note says?" the teacher asks. She inspects it and begins to read it aloud. She points to the first word and pauses, as she glances at Michael with an expression that says "You start." Michael reads "Michael," but then stops and looks up at the teacher. Instead of beginning at the beginning, the teacher starts where Michael has left off, and even catches the intonation that would have been his had he continued to read the note. This is the teacher's clue that Michael is to continue to read with her, that she's not simply going to read the note to him. She stretches the words out, saying them slowly, and emphasizing the first sound or two, as she gives Michael time to read each word. When he doesn't figure out a word by the time she has sounded the last letter, she begins again or hangs onto the last sound long enough to give Michael time to piece together the information. It is Michael who ends up saying the word quickly, transforming the sounds heard into meaningful words. The note says "Michael will be going home with Sean today."

When everyone has arrived, the teacher walks through the room to tell clusters of children who are working puzzles, rereading the big print books available on a stand, inspecting and manipulating the objects included in the display on "Suction," listening to a story at the listening post, playing a game of "Chutes and Ladders" or alphabet bingo, or making designs with parquetry blocks that they must finish up now and gather in the group area for meeting time. A few parents who have lingered help the children put materials away. Parents, always welcome in this classroom, have visited so frequently that they know the routines and expectations: "Where do the blocks go?" one parent asks the child who has loaded them into their storage basket.

"Here," the child says, placing the basket on the shelf.

"Oh, of course," says the parent. "I see the sign right here. Terrific. Now, you are ready to go to Meeting."

The teacher joins the children who have gathered. "Let's say the poem we learned yesterday, while we wait for the others to join us." She turns to look at a chart, on which the poem has been written. Then she begins:

I'd Like to Be a Lighthouse *

I'd like to be a lighthouse
All scrubbed and painted white.
I'd like to be a lighthouse
And stay awake all night.
To keep my eye on everything
That sails my patch of sea;
I'd like to be a lighthouse
With the ships all watching me.

Rachel Field

*From *Taxis and Toadstools* by Rachel Field. Copyright 1926 by Doubleday and Company. Reprinted by permission of Doubleday, a Division of Bantam, Doubleday, Dell Publishing Group, Inc.

The Teacher Keeps a List

The children sit facing the teacher for Meeting Time. She sits in front of a wall where the attendance chart hangs in full view. The teacher refers to the chart and says, "Someone is sick. Who isn't here?" One name tag remains on the floor in front of the chart; one pocket on the chart is empty. Some children look at the name tag. Others scan the group of children. Still others do both, apparently trying to piece together the graphic and the contextual information. Then someone says, "Sarah!"

The teacher picks up the name tag and holds it for everyone to see. "That's right. S—ar—uh (teacher runs her finger under the name and says it slowly) is not here. Her mother called to say that she has an ear infection. We'll put Sarah's name tag in her pocket, turned over like this, to tell us that she's not coming."

Then the teacher reaches for her red tub and her list of activities. "Today," she begins, "we have many things to do. At the water table, you will find some pumps. Pumps are machines we use to move water from one level to another. I have one right here in my tub." (She searches for it and pulls it out.) "When you pull the handle this way (demonstrates), all of the air is forced out of the tube by this little part that moves down. When there's noth-

ing at all inside the tube, we say that we've created a vacuum—a place where there's nothing at all, not even air. Then if you put the end of the pump in the water and push the handle down this way to make the little part move back up, water will go up into the pump and come out the spout. You might like to try the pumps today. I'll cross out *pumps* on my list, because I've told you about them.

"Next we have a tissue paper collage project. At the blue table by the sink, we have red construction paper, glue, brushes, and baskets filled with pieces of tissue paper. To do this project, you take the brush, dip it into the glue, paint some glue on your paper, and then put tissue paper on it (demonstrates). You can even put one piece of tissue paper on top of another piece, like this. Now, I'll cross *tissue paper project* off my list, because I told you about it.

"Who knows what is next on my list?" the teacher asks, as she begins again. She holds the list up and moves it slowly in front of the children.

"Blocks!" several children say together.

"Yes, b-l-o-c-k-s," the teacher says slowly, as she runs her finger underneath the word. "Blocks are on our list every day, aren't they? They're open today, as usual, and the horseshoe magnet hanging from the pulley attached to the ceiling is there also. Jason used the magnet yesterday to pick up a big load of lids to put in his pickup truck. Someone else might like to try that today. Oh, by the way, do you know why the magnet we are using here is called a *horseshoe* magnet? It isn't a *bar* magnet, like the ones we have on the table with the tray of objects. I'll tell you what. Everybody think about the magnets, and we'll talk about them at storytime, because I have a special book that will give you some clues.

"Okay, I will cross *blocks* off my list, because we've talked about them.

"The next project is making popcorn. Four children may do that project. We'll eat the popcorn for a snack.

"Okay, now let me cross *popcorn* off.

"Now, what's the last thing on my list?" the teacher asks, as she again holds the list out for the children to see. "House Corner," several children say. "Yes. It says 'H-o-u-s-e C-o-r-n-e-r,' doesn't it? Our House Corner is open every day. You might like to play there. And, of course, the Writing Center is always open, too, if you need to make a shopping list or want to write a letter.

"Okay, now I'll ask you to choose where you'd like to start. Who would like to go to the water table to experiment with the pumps?"

The teacher calls each of the activities, in turn, and the children make their choices. If more children want to try an activity than there is space to accommodate them, the teacher makes a "turns" list and tells the children who must wait. "I'll put your name on the turns list. When there's space, you may have your turn. Start someplace else."

We Need Some Salt

The children head for their chosen projects and interest areas as Activity Time begins. The group in charge of making the popcorn gathers at the table close to the sink, where a large recipe chart hangs on a chart rack. The teacher in charge of the project points to a sign at the top of the chart and asks, "What do you do before we start to cook?"

"Wash our hands," respond the children.

The children line up to take turns washing their hands. When everyone is seated at the table, the teacher refers to the top part of the recipe chart where the heading, THINGS WE WILL NEED, appears in big, bold letters. "Let's make sure that we have everything on the tray that we are going to need," she explains. "Popcorn," she reads. "Do we have popcorn?"

"In the bag," says David, as he points to it.

"Yes. That's our popcorn. David, I'm going to ask you to hold the bag of popcorn until we need it.

"Okay. What else do we need?" the teacher asks, as she points to a second word on the list. The children look, but no one responds.

"Oi—l," the teacher says slowly, as she runs her finger under the word. "Do you see any oil on the tray?"

Children point to the bottle, and the teacher picks it up to look at its label. "Yes, it is oil," she says. "It is *corn* oil." She runs her finger under the two words written on the label. As she hands the bottle to Sheila to hold, she explains that there are other kinds of oil—peanut, safflower, soybean— and she reminds the children that they have made

peanut butter and have seen oil inside of peanuts.

The teacher continues the identification process with the other words on the list until the popcorn popper, oven mitts, measuring spoons, and bowl all have been identified. Still remaining on the tray is the cassette tape recorder. "Tape recorder is not on our list, is it?" the teacher says to the children. "We don't need a tape recorder to make popcorn," she adds, laughing, and the children laugh with her. "But we *can* use it to record how popcorn sounds when it is popping. And that's what we're going to do. In fact, I'm going to turn it on now. Let's see, where is the record button?"

The teacher turns the tape recorder so that the labels for the buttons are facing the children. They look as she points to the label above the button on the far left. "Rewind," she says, as she traces her finger under the word. "Play," she says next. "Rec..," she begins to say as her finger points to the word above the third button. Before she can finish, David shouts out, "Record! That's it!"

"That's right. Record is the word with the letter *C* in it. I don't think any of the other words have a *C*, do they? Let's take a look. P-L-A-Y. No, the word *play* doesn't have a *C*. R-E-W-I-N-D. The word *rewind* doesn't, either. FF stands for fast forward. There's an *S* in the word *fast*, but not a *C*. I think record is the only word with a *C*." With that, she moves the recorder closer to Lisa and asks her to press down on the record button.

"Okay, now we need to find out what we do to make the popcorn," the teacher explains. She again refers to the recipe chart as she points to the words WHAT TO DO. She reads each step, starting with the first: "Put 3 T. of popcorn in the popper." As each step is read, a child is asked to carry out the instruction.

The fifth step says, "Watch and listen as the corn pops." The children look closely at the large transparent lid over the popper. They wait for the soft sizzle of the oil to change into a faster, louder sizzle, and for the first pop! There are squeals when it finally comes. The squeals continue as the popping speeds up and then subside as the popping slows almost to a stop. The teacher puts on the oven mitts, takes hold of the sides of the popper, and explains that she's going to shake the popper a couple of times to send any remaining corn kernels to the bottom, where it is very hot. There are a few more pops, followed by a long silence. "It's all done popping," says David.

The teacher agrees and reaches to unplug the popper. Then she flips the popper over and lets the popped corn fall into the lid. Then the corn is emptied into a large bowl. The teacher explains that it will cool faster there than it would were it left packed tightly in the smaller bowl. "The air can circulate — move around all of the pieces of corn — better if the corn is in this larger bowl."

"Okay, our corn is ready for Snack Time," she tells the children." We need to wash and dry the dishes, and then I have a book for us to read. It explains why popcorn pops. After I read it to you, we can set up an experiment to see for ourselves if the book's explanation is right."

"But we didn't put in any salt," says Lisa. "We need some salt."

"Is salt on our recipe?" asks the teacher. She points to and reads through the THINGS WE WILL NEED list once again, going slowly so that the children can join in. " 'Popcorn, oil, popcorn popper, oven mitts, measuring spoons, large bowl,' " they all read together. "Does it say salt?" the teacher asks. "No," the children respond.

"Sometimes people do put salt on popcorn," the teacher explains. "Sometimes they don't. Today, I guess we're going to eat ours without it, because our recipe doesn't say to add salt. We'll add salt to the recipe when we make popcorn the next time. Lisa, you can put salt on the shopping list, so we will be sure to have some on hand. You can do that while the rest of us start washing the dishes."

Lisa makes her way to the piece of tagboard taped to the back of a door. OUR SHOPPING LIST, it says at the top. Lisa takes the pencil, which is stuck through two holes of an envelope, also taped to the door. Lisa writes an s. "What comes next?" she asks, calling to the teacher who is helping out at the sink.

"A," the teacher answers.

Lisa writes that and then asks, "What's next?"

The teacher vocalizes the next sound this time, instead of simply telling Lisa what letter to write.

"L," Lisa says. Then she says the word *salt* to herself, hanging onto the last sound, as she thinks for just a minute. Then she adds a T.

The children finish washing and drying the dishes, and then the teacher reads the book, as promised. It explains that the moisture — water — inside popcorn kernels turns into steam as the popper heats up the kernels. The steam explodes the outer shell of the kernel, making the corn pop. The book explains that if the kernels are dried out from being exposed to air where the moisture can evaporate, they won't pop. The teacher and children pour some corn into a jar lid. This corn will be left out in the air on the windowsill for several days. The rest of the corn is left in the tightly covered bottle. "The next time we make popcorn," the teacher explains, "we'll make two batches, one from corn in the jar, and one from corn left out in this lid. Which corn do you think will pop better?"

The children make their predictions and also check the progress of an earlier experiment, which has been left on the windowsill. Two margarine tubs, one covered and one uncovered, sit side by side. "This one has almost no water left in it," one child observes. "What about the other one, the one with the lid on it?" the teacher asks. "Does it still have a lot of water?"

Soon Activity Time ends. All of the children help to put materials away and straighten up the room. Then they gather for Group Time, where they sing songs and talk about some of the things they did during the morning.

Lisa explains that the popcorn she and the others prepared for Snack Time does not have salt. "But we're going to make it with salt the next time," she says, "so I writed it on our list."

"Oh, I'm glad you wrote it down. You know, tomorrow at Group Time we are going to go over our list to see what kinds of stores we will need to visit. I think we need to go to a supermarket to get some things, but I think we'll also need to go to a hardware store, and maybe even a stationery store, to get other things. And remember, sometimes we don't get things on our list from a store. Sometimes children take notes home to ask their parents if they can bring some things from home. We'll probably have some shopping trips to plan tomorrow when we review our list, and also some notes to take home."

The singing and the discussing continue, as long as it takes for everyone to visit the bathroom to use the toilet and wash their hands. Then everyone is off to Snack Time and then to the outdoor playground. The morning winds down with a Story Time, which is held outside under a shade tree in warm weather and inside during the winter. Next, the class goes back inside for puzzles, rereadings of books, a last look at the fish, searches through the Take Home Box to find paintings and drawings to take home, a check of personal mailbox slots to see if someone has tucked in a note or a letter, and, for some, the selection of a classroom library book to take home.

Sara checks the mailboxes, not to get her mail, but to see if the teacher has found the book she had put there as a present. The book is still there. Sara removes it and delivers it in person. The teacher

---

I · D · E · A · S
You Can Use

Dismissal Activities

Every teacher must manage the inevitable daily transitions. If teachers do not want all of the children dashing between activities at the same time, they need to devise methods to dismiss children in small groups. The following ideas help children to learn literacy skills, as well as help teachers prevent classroom chaos.

- Write children's names clearly on a set of index cards. When dismissing children from a group, hold up one card at a time. The situation becomes more interesting to children if more than one child in each group has a name that starts with a certain letter. Children often look no farther than the first letter of a name before declaring, "It's mine." Teachers can say, "Are you sure? Did you look at all of the letters?"

- Instead of using the children's names, pronounce a sound, such as *Ssssss*. All of the children whose names begin with that sound may leave the group setting. Continue to pronounce sounds until all of the children have been dismissed. This experience can lead to an interesting discussion if several children, whose names begin with the sound, actually have names that code the sound differently. For example, the names Sara, Celia, Cyndi, Sam, and Sally would present a good situation for such a discussion.

- Provide a sound and tell children that anyone with this sound in his or her name may be dismissed. In this case, the sound need not be at the beginning of the name. Children need to think through all of the sounds they hear when they say their names to see if the focal sound is contained within it.

- The teacher can say a word that rhymes with a child's name. The children whose names rhyme with the word provided by the teacher may be dismissed.

Adapted from an idea provided by Kathy Morrow
Boston Public Schools
The Early Learning Center
Brighton, Massachusetts

---

thanks her and tucks it in her pocket for later; she is too busy now to take a look.

When the children leave, the teacher and her assistant straighten things and chat. The teacher remembers Sara's book and pulls it out (see Figure 2). "Look at this," she says to her colleague. "Sara is starting to string letters together to make words; she's not coding syllabically anymore. I guess the words looked too short that way."

"I know," the assisting teacher replies. "Last week, she was playing at the Writing Center and filled an entire book with words. She kept asking, 'What word is this?' I sounded them out and, of course, most were not words."

"She'll do this for awhile, and then she'll probably start to ask for spellings or to copy them from labels and signs. I've seen this over and over for years. It's what they all go through (Genishi & Dyson, 1984; Gunderson & Shapiro, 1988; Schickedanz, in press). But Lisa is beginning to give up this strategy. She wrote salt on the shopping list today, and she asked only for letters to represent

**Figure 2
Page from Sara's Book**

**Figure 3
Word Creation Strategies Record Sheet***

Strategy Used	Description of Incident	Date
Physical Relationship		
Visual Design		
Syllabic Hypothesis		
Letter Strings (visual rules)		
Authority Based (asking for or copying spellings)		
Early Phonemic (invented spellings)		
Transitional Phonemic		

*Boston University Early Childhood Learning Laboratory

Key to Word Creation Strategies Record Sheet

Physical Relationship. Child tries to relate the number or the appearance of marks to some physical aspect of the object or person represented. The child might use three marks, for example, to write her name if she is three years old.

Visual Design. Child accepts the arbitrary nature of words—that they do not resemble their referents physically. The child tries to recreate some designs. The first design attempted is often the child's name. Placeholders—other letters, circles, solid dots, or vertical lines—often are used in the place of those letters that the child cannot form.

Syllabic Hypothesis. Child realizes there is a relationship between the oral and written versions of words and also that spoken words can be segmented into "beats" or syllables. The child codes words syllabically, using one mark for each of a word's syllables.

Letter Strings (visual rules). Children create words by stringing letters together so that they look like words. They use several rules. (1) Don't use too many letters. (2) Don't use too few letters. (3) Use a variety of letters, with not more than two of the same letter in succession. (4) Rearrange the same letters to make different words. Children also ask, "What word is this?"

Authority Based. This strategy often follows on the heels of the letter string strategy, apparently because children decide that it is more efficient to ask for spellings, since so many of their letter strings yield nonwords. Children ask for spellings of whole words, or they copy known words from environmental print or books.

Early Phonemic. Children begin to generate their own words by coding sounds they hear—an idea they might get as adults provide spellings and make letter-sound associations explicit when giving spellings during the time that children are using an Authority Based strategy. Independent spelling may be delayed in children who receive complex answers to their spelling questions during the early part of this stage. No known disadvantage is associated with a delay of this kind.

Transitional Phonemic. Children begin to realize that their sound based spellings do not look quite like words they see in the environment and that specific spellings they generate are not always identical to ones they see elsewhere. Children often become dissatisfied with their own spellings and begin again to ask for whole word spellings, or they generate a spelling on their own and ask, "Is that right?" This strategy is not common among preschoolers, although children who read early often use it, presumably because they have more visual information about words than do typical preschoolers.

Note. The order of use for the strategies typically follows the order of this list, although different environments provide different information to children, which can result in variations in children's word creation strategy development.

some of the sounds. She did the others on her own. I need to record some of this information on our word creation strategies record sheet" (see Figure 3).

What Are the Children Learning about Reading and Writing?

Children in this preschool classroom do not engage in instructional tasks that isolate learning by focusing on specific skills taught out of context. There are no assigned worksheets, no alphabet letter to be focused on each week, no counting out loud to 100 every day, and no specific practice in writing one's name. In this classroom, reading and writing skills are incorporated into every aspect of the children's daily experiences. Literacy is so vital, so much a part of the culture in this classroom, that children literally grow up with reading and writing.

But the skills are there, just the same. The teachers know what these skills are, and they know how to make them explicit in the natural course of things, so that children can latch on, instead of getting lost. What are these skills? And where can they be found in this classroom?

Children must learn that written language is an arbitrary (dictated by social convention) system for representing oral language, that written words are not, as children first think (Ferreiro & Teberosky, 1979; Schickedanz, in press), **physical representations of people and things.**

- By seeing their own and other children's names on the attendance chart, children begin to see that there is no systematic relationship between the length of names and the size of the child.
- By routinely seeing the word *fish* at the fish tank, children see that very small things can have a name as long as something that is much bigger—Adam and Sara, for example.

Children must learn that speech can be segmented into small units of sound called phonemes (Liberman et al., 1974; Mann, 1986). **This insight, "phonemic awareness," is facilitated by involvement in situations where print and speech are brought together** (Cossu et al., 1988;

Ehri & Wilce, 1980; Mann, 1986) **and where children find that they have to account for the letters they see in a word they know** (Ferreiro & Teberosky, 1979).

- The teacher read Michael's father's note by making the sounds within the words explicit and by involving Michael in looking at the words as they both read them.
- The teacher made explicit the relationship between letters and sounds in some of the words on her activity list for the day.
- The teacher provided for the rereading of familiar storybooks and big print books. The opportunity to reread familiar books helps children "get into the print" (Morrow, 1988) and try to map speech and print, which leads to their discovery of the alphabetic principle—letters code sounds.
- The teacher planned to make several shopping lists on the next day, organizing items children had written on the tagboard into store based categories. The shopping lists would be written as experience charts while the children watched. When converting a child's invented spelling into a standard form for the shopping list, the teacher would comment, "There's another way to write that word, and I'm going to write it that way here, because that might be the way you'll see it in the store." As the words were generated, the teacher would make the sounds explicit and pause to give children a chance to name the needed letter.

Children must learn to coordinate context and graphic clues when reading. Context helps children to predict what words are printed and to transform graphic phonemic information into meaningful words (Goodman & Goodman, 1977).

- The teacher allowed for the rereading of familiar books, which provides "historical context" (Snow, 1983)—knowledge of the story from previous experience with it—for the children to integrate with the graphic clues they see. Many preschoolers use picture governed rather than print governed strategies to reread storybooks (Sulzby, 1983), but the rereadings themselves help children to get into the print. Once into it, information from previous rereadings can be integrated with the children's budding graphic phonemic knowledge.

- When checking in books, children know what the titles of their books say. They often use this knowledge by pointing to the words as they say the title printed on the card.
- The many instances of familiar environmental print on the Snack Helpers' Chart, the Attendance Chart, the sign for the fish tank, the label on the shopping list, and the labels on the shelves provide children with opportunities to integrate context and graphic clues to decipher words.

Children need to learn letter names and the sounds that various letters can represent.

- The teacher pointed out to Elise that Ellen's name did not contain the letter *S*, nor was the sound typically represented by this letter heard in Ellen's name.
- The teacher pointed out the *C* in the word *record* and then named letters in the other words on the tape recorder to show that none of the others contained this letter.
- The teacher helped Lisa spell the word *salt* by providing the letter that represents a phoneme that is difficult for preschoolers to spell.
- Teachers sound out children's letter string words when the children ask, "What word is this?"
- Children are surrounded by print, including children's names. This provides opportunities for children to ask questions about letter names and to share their knowledge, such as, "My name starts with *K*."
- Alphabet materials such as letter bingo are available for use in children's play.

Children must develop a rich vocabulary and develop a deep understanding of many concepts if they are to be successful in reading words and in comprehending what they have read (Chall & Snow, 1988).

- The teacher introduced words such as vacuum, suction, machine, sizzle, measuring

spoons, oven mitts, circulate, moisture, predictions, safflower, soybean, blue, red, tomorrow, tissue paper, construction paper, spout, and pump.

- The teacher provided real experiences as the basis for concept development. Children were learning about pumps and vacuums at the water table, about why popcorn pops by making popcorn and setting up experiments, and about different kinds of stores by making shopping lists and doing the shopping.
- The teacher scheduled a Story Time every day, which provides children with the opportunity to hear and discuss new words and to find out about interesting places and things.

Children must learn about print conventions, such as the facts that English print is organized from left to right and from top to bottom on a page and that space is left between words.

- The teacher demonstrated the left to right and top to bottom organization of English print when she pointed to the text in big print books, when she underlined words on her Meeting Time list with her finger, when she wrote the shopping list experience chart with the children, and when she read the popcorn recipe chart.
- The library book check in cards have a green dot beside the first word in the title to help children know that the first word in the title is the one farthest to the left.
- The teacher put space between her own words when writing the shopping list experience chart.

Summary

This glimpse of a content and experience based classroom illustrates how some of the literacy skills known to be important for young children can be learned in a broader and richer instructional context than that provided in the typical, skills oriented classroom. In the classroom that has been described, literacy skills are embedded in every activity and interaction.

When I suggest that programs need to "move beyond skills," I do not mean that skills are unimportant. I mean, instead, that they are not enough. They are not enough to turn children into good readers, nor to give meaning to a young child's classroom life. For children who enter preschool at age three, skills oriented classrooms can span three, four, or more years, because it is not until second or third grade—after children have the basics—that schools take content seriously. That's a lot of a young child's life to squander.

In many communities, especially those that are more affluent, parents have the time and financial resources to add richness to their children's academic lives. They visit museums, go camping, assemble train sets, purchase chemistry sets, read interesting books, visit the library, and talk about things the child has seen and wondered about. Curiously, it is these children who often are offered the most richness at school, being perceived as more advanced in skills development upon school entry and being viewed as the next generation's leaders.

Other children, due to financial and family circumstances, are perceived as needing and being able to utilize much less. They are given a basic, skills oriented curriculum and little else, often with the best intentions and the children's welfare uppermost in the educators' minds. Yet these children, too, would benefit from a rich school curriculum.

Children can survive predominantly skills oriented classrooms, of course, and can learn a lot about writing and reading. It would be better, however, if they could learn to read and to write while they learn *about* reading and writing. And it would be better still if, in the process, they could learn something, instead of learning next to nothing. Teachers, as we have seen, can deal effectively with both content and skills. Children can, too.

References

Chall, J.S., and Snow, C.E. School influences on the reading development of low income children. *Harvard Educational Letter,* 1988, *4* (1), 1-4.

Clay, M. *What did I write?* Portsmouth, NH: Heinemann Educational Books, 1975.

Cossu, G., Shankweiler, D., Liberman, I., Katz, L., and Tola, G. Awareness of phonological segments and reading ability in Italian children. *Applied Psycholinguistics,* 1988, *9,* 1-16.

Ehri, L.C., and Wilce, L.S. The influence of orthography on readers' P1980, *1,* 371-385.

conceptualization of the phonemic structure of words. *Applied Ferreiro, E., and Teberosky, A. Literacy before schooling.* Portsmouth, NH: Heinemann Educational Books, 1979.

Genishi, C., and Dyson, A.H. *Language assessment in the early years.* Norwood, NJ: Ablex, 1984.

Goodman, K., and Goodman, Y. Learning about psycholinguistic processes by analyzing oral reading. *Harvard Educational Review,* 1977, *47,* 317-333.

Gunderson, L., and Shapiro, J. Whole language instruction: Writing in first grade. *The Reading Teacher,* 1988, *41* (4), 396-401.

Liberman, I.Y., Shankweiler, D., Fischer, F.W., and Carter, B. Explicit syllable and phoneme segmentation in the young child. *Journal of Experimental Child Psychology,* 1974, *18,* 201-212.

Mann, V. Phonological awareness: The role of reading experience. *Cognition,* 1986, *24,* 65-92.

Morrow, L.M. Young children's responses to one-to-one story readings in school settings. *Reading Research Quarterly,* 1988, *23* (1), 89-107.

Polushkin, M. *Mother, Mother, I want another.* New York: Crown, 1978, 1986.

Schickedanz, J. *Adam's righting revolutions.* Portsmouth, NH: Heinemann Educational Books, in press.

Snow, C. Literacy and language: Relationships during the preschool years. *Harvard Educational Review,* 1983, *53* (2), 165-189.

Sulzby, E. Children's emergent reading of favorite books: A developmental study. *Reading Research Quarterly,* 1985, *20,* 458-481.

CHAPTER NINE

Assessment of Young Children's Reading: Documentation as an Alternative to Testing

Edward Chittenden

Rosalea Courtney

In this chapter we describe aspects of a current project to develop programs of documentation as an alternative approach to the assessment of early reading. We provide steps that schools can use in establishing a program of documentation.

The need for assessment programs that are appropriate to early education has become more acute with the introduction of all day kindergarten and with increased pressures on primary teachers to account for children's "academic" learning. While teachers of young children are expected to view learning to read within the broader context of children's language and development, the standardized tests adopted by many school systems are incompatible with these expectations. The discrepancy between testing and teaching is especially pronounced for schools that develop reading programs around literature and children's own writing, rather than adopt a single basal series.

In this chapter, we describe aspects of a current project to develop programs of documentation as an alternative approach to the assessment of early reading. In cooperation with experienced teachers in several school systems, the project has explored the use of performance samples and observational methods for recording children's initial development as readers. The overall goal has been to create systematic assessment strategies as alternatives to testing that will yield descriptive records of children's learning while enhancing teachers' powers of observation and understanding of early reading.

Work described in this chapter was supported by a grant from the Jessie Smith Noyes Foundation.

Criticism of Current Testing Practices

Standardized testing in the early grades has become a prominent feature of evaluation activities in many school systems. In some districts, paper and pencil tests of reading and reading readiness are routinely administered as early as kindergarten and first grade. Despite the clear limitations of these instruments, scores from the tests—especially reading tests—come to be regarded as the definitive evidence of children's learning.

Ironically, the trend toward testing in early education occurs at a time when criticism of the tests has become more substantial. Educators of young children have restated their longstanding concerns about labeling children and about test driven curricula (NAEYC 1988). Policy analysts find little empirical support for the use of tests as screening devices to retain children who are not "ready" (Shepard & Smith, 1986). In recent years, to such criticism can be added the growing evidence from research on reading and children's literacy, which challenges assumptions about learning that underlie test construction (Valencia & Pearson, 1987).

Contemporary research (reflected in many chapters in this book) demonstrates that children's initial efforts to read and write reflect a range of experiences with books and print. Children's sense of story, their understanding of the conventions of print, and their intuitions about letters and sounds (invented spelling) are acquired gradually throughout the early school years; these and other resources support their first reading attempts. Research also demonstrates that children acquire the skill of reading in different ways, exhibiting different tempos of learning and different styles and strategies for dealing with text (Bussis et al., 1985).

Tests, by contrast, imply a narrower definition of early reading, accentuating knowledge of letters and words to the exclusion of other indicators of literacy. Moreover, norm referenced instruments allow little room for the natural variation among children in the rate at which they become relatively proficient as readers. An additional major limitation is that tests tend to be one shot attempts at assessment; by definition, they ignore evidence of learning that children exhibit in other, nontesting contexts. Children's interest in books, and their ability to listen to stories or to make sense of meaningful words (such as classmates' names or signs around the room) are not measured by tests.

Documentation

The remainder of this article describes features of an alternative approach to the assessment of early reading. We term the approach "documentation" since the methods are designed to yield a more descriptive record than test scores. The term also underscores the point that educational assessment is defined as a process (Anderson et al., 1975) that is supported by methods or instruments, but should not be defined by them.

A documentation plan can be as elaborate or as modest as time and resources permit. At its core, documentation requires participation by teachers and support staff across grade levels in an assessment program that brings them together around a common plan of observation and collection of evidence of children's learning. Unlike a testing program, which is geared to evaluating children against prescribed expectations, the first purpose of documentation is one of inquiry, of looking more closely at the thought, language, and skill children bring to their initial attempts to read. Furthermore, unlike testing, documentation builds on data collected at intervals over the years and across literacy contexts.

With respect to standardization of procedures, the methods of documentation are neither as rigid as the procedural requirements of tests nor as informal as teachers' own record keeping practices. Uniform methods and guidelines are adopted, but are stated in a way that permits the flexibility necessary when working with young children. The records of documentation are meant to be "public" in the sense that they should be open to interpretation by other teachers, administrators, and parents. The adoption of common plans and procedures makes such communication more possible; people understand what the information represents, although they don't necessarily agree upon its meaning.

Procedures for Documenting Children's Literacy Development

During the past few years, with assistance from experienced teachers, we have evaluated a variety of procedures that appeared promising as methods of documentation. Some procedures have capitalized upon teachers' everyday observations of children's behaviors in ongoing classroom settings. Other procedures are more test like and take the form of performance samples, or staged observations. The latter have included tasks related to invented spelling, word awareness, word identification strategies, sense of story, and oral reading performance. Essentially, we asked teachers to "pilot test" selected procedures and to provide critical comments regarding the methods' heuristic value. What was learned from using the procedures? What were some practical problems?

The question of institutional support for documentation also has been examined. What sorts of teacher meetings are required? How often? In what ways can the data of documentation serve the needs of evaluating pupil progress? Of reporting to parents? To what extent can records of documentation replace test data as accepted forms of information?

Teachers' Observations

In the course of an ordinary school day, teachers observe children's behaviors across a variety of instructional settings, ranging from the informal situations of play and free choice activities to the more formal contexts of reading or writing instruction. The teacher's observational database is potentially a broad one.

As a first step in developing observational procedures, we conducted a series of interviews with experienced teachers (from kindergarten, first grade, and second grade) in which two issues were raised: What cues (behavioral signals) do teachers look for when assessing children's literacy development? What records do teachers maintain that capture some of their observations?

Two findings from these discussions with teachers can be noted for their relevance to documentation. First, although all the teachers believe that observation is central to their evaluation of a child's learning, they also acknowledge that much of this information ordinarily remains unrecorded. The realities and practical pressures of classroom teaching work against maintaining systematic observational records.

A second finding has to do with the classroom contexts that provide the occasions—the settings—when teachers make some of their observations about children's literacy development. Looking across the records of the teachers' comments, it is clear that certain instructional contexts offer substantial opportunities for observation related to children's interests and skills. These settings, such as story time or free reading time, constitute almost daily features of the school day. In a sense, the teacher is a participant/observer for whom these settings are familiar situations for noting children's reactions and interests.

For purposes of illustration, consider two settings—story time and choice time. Both situations provide teachers with valid indicators of children's early development as readers. For example, when teachers read a good story to the class, they note many things about the children's facial, gestural, and vocal reactions. Children's questions and comments about the story also are revealing. Does a child's elaboration of the story line reveal an understanding of the narrative? Do the children connect this story with some personal experience? With other stories? The story time setting is a particularly good one for assessing young children's familiarity and understanding of styles of writing. It provides valid indications of children's interests and comprehension of literature.

Choice time provides a quite different perspective. What sort of books does the child choose (picture books, animal books, literature the teacher has read)? Does the child appear to be "studying" the text or looking at pictures? Is there attention to words? In the case of quite young children, is the book properly oriented? Are pages turned sequentially?

An analysis of recurring settings led to the development of an Observation Recording Form, organized around seven classroom situations. Figure 1 shows two versions of that form. In the "Ratings" version, teachers provide overall ratings of the

Figure 1
Observation Forms

Description of child's work and behavior for each context
(cite specific indications of skills or knowledge)

Settings and Activities	Examples of Child's Activities
Story Time: Teacher reads to class (responses to story line; child's comments, questions, elaborations)	
Independent Reading: Book Time (nature of books child chooses or brings in; process of selecting; quiet or social reading)	
Writing (journal stories, alphabet, dictation)	
Reading Group/Individual (oral reading strategies: discussion of text, responses to instruction)	
Reading Related Activities Tasks (responses to assignments or discussion focusing on word letter properties, word games/ experience charts)	
Informal Settings (use of language in play, jokes, story-telling, conversation)	
Books and Print as Resource (use of books for projects; attention to signs, labels, names; locating information)	
Other	

Chittenden and Courtney

Figure 1 (continued)
Observation Forms

Child _____ Grade _____ Teacher _____ Date _____

Ratings of child's interest/investment in different classroom contexts
(based on observations over a period of several weeks)

Settings and Activities	Degree of Interest/Investment				
	Very Interested, Intense		Moderately Interested		Uninterested, Attention Is Elsewhere
Story Time: Teacher reads to class (responses to story line; child's comments, questions, elaborations)	_____	_____	_____	_____	_____
Independent Reading: Book Time (nature of books child chooses or brings in, process of selecting, quiet or social reading)	_____	_____	_____	_____	_____
Writing (journal, stories, alphabet, dictation)	_____	_____	_____	_____	_____
Reading Group/Individual (oral reading strategies: discussion of text, responses to instruction)	_____	_____	_____	_____	_____
Reading Related Activities Tasks (responses to assignments or discussions focusing on word letter properties, word games/ experience charts)	_____	_____	_____	_____	_____
Informal Settings (use of language in play, jokes, story-telling, conversation)	_____	_____	_____	_____	_____
Books and Print as Resource (use of books for projects; attention to signs, labels, names; locating information)	_____		_____		_____
Other	_____		_____		_____

child's interest or "investment" in a given setting. For example, during story time is the child generally interested in the story? Does the child seem invoved with the narrative, as indicated by posture, by comments?

On the second form, teachers provide specific examples of the child's work and behavior for a given context. What kinds of reactions does the child exhibit during story time? What books are frequently chosen for independent reading? What sorts of writing activities have been undertaken? Here the focus is on the quality and level of the child's work, as distinct from degree of interest.

An observation form that uses classroom settings, or contexts, as a framework has several advantages, we believe, over observational instruments built around theoretical constructs (e.g., rating children's comprehension or listening skills). First, teachers generally agree about the broad definitions of setting, whereas it is more difficult to establish common understanding of abstractions such as ability to decode. Although no two teachers will conduct a particular setting, such as story time, in the same manner (nor should they), there is enough overlap in classroom practice so that ratings or other forms of reported observations can be meaningfully shared. In selecting the settings, an attempt was made to find some common ground across the kindergarten and primary programs.

Second, an instrument that highlights the settings of early literacy instruction appropriately reflects the several dimensions of the curriculum at this level. Literacy instruction is not confined to one sort of interaction, such as the reading group. By drawing attention to multiple settings, the instrument reminds teachers, administrators, and parents that literacy development has multiple facets. It is important that assessment instruments reflect this comprehensive view of early reading instruction.

Third, the use of multiple settings for observation allows for the inevitable unevenness in children's development. Thus, some children display keen and sensitive feeling for narrative when they listen to a story read by the teacher during story time. These children are quick to anticipate what will happen next; there is clear evidence of their ability to comprehend literature. But some of these

same children may display quite different reactions within the reading group, where their skills seem wobbly and their understanding seems tentative. A teacher who observes children in both settings is in a stronger position to evaluate their initial difficulties in decoding text.

Children will display different patterns of strengths and interests. For example, some children appear most productive and most interested in those settings that permit a fair amount of behavioral leeway, such as free reading, independent projects, and journal writing. By contrast, these same children may have trouble in the more formal settings, such as story time, reading groups, and assignments. Others, revealing a reverse pattern, thrive on teacher structure but become uncertain and less productive when called upon to read or write in more open ended situations.

Children's patterns of involvement will change over time. It is not uncommon for children to go through periods of intense interest in practice reading, selecting familiar books again and again before branching out. One teacher described how she reviews the different settings as a way of taking stock when she plans instruction or prepares for a parent conference.

> I think about how the child responds to different situations…beginning with the informal book time that happens in my classroom as the children come into the room in the morning. I have more concern about a child who is not really involved in any of the settings than I do about a child showing real energy in one area [e.g. writing] but is not strong in another.

Performance Samples

In a documentation program, performance samples of children's work provide the more tangible evidence of learning; such samples complement the observations described. Although performance sample tasks are fairly open ended and resemble instructional activities, they are nevertheless more formal and geared to assessment, to the extent that teachers adhere to agreed upon guidelines.

In projects to date, we have paid particular attention to children's early attempts to pretend read and really read. Ways of obtaining reading records are described. Other types of performance samples, such as spelling, are useful, also. For example, children's invented spellings provide a fairly reliable indication of their intuitions concerning the alphabet and how it works. In turn, this affords some insights into their progress as readers (Henderson, 1981).

On the surface, assessment of children's development as readers through listening to them read is a relatively straightforward task. Given an appropriate book and a comfortable setting, the teacher can learn much about children's skill by listening, observing, and offering help on occasion. At a rudimentary level, do the children have a stable sense of word, as indicated by finger pointing or voice pointing? Do the children's errors make sense? Do they indicate a search for meaning as well as responsiveness to letter cues?

The validity of oral reading behaviors as indicators of learning is well established in research, and certainly the practice of listening to children read has a long history in the classroom (e.g., Allington, 1984). Moreover, reading aloud is a relatively natural mode to young readers. Many children, in fact, spontaneously vocalize as an aid to keeping track.

However, although early reading is observable through oral reading, it is not necessarily easy to document. Reading aloud is noise. Unlike children's first efforts to write or spell, reading ordinarily does not leave behind any artifact or document that could become part of a child's folder, for review by the teacher or for sharing with a parent. Although teachers can make summaries of their observations of oral reading, a more concerted effort is required to obtain a full running record as a document depicting actual reading behavior.

This transparent quality of reading is one of the reasons, we believe, why teachers sometimes feel vulnerable when their evaluation of children's competence is challenged by test data or other sources. Unlike the case of writing samples, what hard copy data of reading exist that constitute tangible information about children's successes and difficulties?

In cooperation with teachers, some of the practical as well as theoretical problems associated with using running records were addressed. To facilitate the process of making records, the teachers were supplied with scripts of the books' texts and with forms for noting essential information. The teachers also adopted a notational system that could capture some of the richness of an early reading effort—long pauses, misreadings, invented text, repetitions, sounding out attempts, self corrections, and requests for help. Although teachers' notational styles differed to some extent, the system was standardized to the point where the records could be read reliably. Figure 2 depicts excerpts from a teacher's records.

The use of books as materials for assessment (instead of paragraphs or test items) makes the process a more natural one and allows children to draw upon their full repertoire of strategies. Among other criteria, it is important to choose the sort of book that enables children to learn while reading and to display their capacities for profiting from self corrections and assistance from the teacher. As Clay (1972) has noted, evidence that reading is a self improving system is an important signal of progress. Figure 3 shows how children with quite different skills can put their knowledge to work in figuring out a book's text. For young readers, picture clues (not shown in the figure) obviously are influencing their choice of words.

In the examples in Figure 3, Hillary has little trouble with text. She needs help with "into" and makes reasonable substitutions for three nouns that appear at the end of sentences. For Felicia, the text is more challenging; in the beginning sentences she hesitates in a number of places, receiving teacher assistance. She substitutes the phrase "Let's go fly over" for "Look out for" twice, but the last time says "Let's not fly again." Both the frequent hesitation and seeking help and the invention of whole phrases (that somehow fit) are characteristic of the wobbly reader. The third child, Joanne, is mostly reading the pictures, with little correspondence to the words in the text.

With practice, the process of actually making notational records is not difficult. In fact, some teachers make similar records on their own. The more significant challenge for an assessment

Figure 2
Example of a First Grade Reading Record

. . . (H)
/Once upon a time, there was a little

. . . (H)   © farm
red hen/who lived in a|farmyard.

One day the little red hen

© f.f.   . . . (H)
|found some/grains of wheat.

orange
She took them to the ~~other~~

animals in the farmyard.

"Who will help me to plant

those gardens
~~these~~ ~~grains~~ of wheat?" asked

the little red hen.

"Not I," said the cat.

"Not I," said the rat.

"Not I," said the pig.

child	text
farm	farmyard
orange	other
those	these
gardens	grains

Figure 2 (continued)
Example of a First Grade Reading Record

Oral Reading Sample

Child *Leslie*   Book/Story *The Little Red Hen*

Teacher *C. F.*   Date *2/7/88*

Choice: Comments on selecting book.
            Was it child's choice? Teacher's? Reasons?

   Child's choice

Background: How familiar was the child with this book/story?
_____ Read it previously   _____ (when?)
___✓___ Generally familiar with book but had not read it
_____ Little/no familiarity

Comments: Child's *interest* in the book and/or in reading aloud. (Was the child relaxed or anxious? Interested? To what extent is this sample representative of the child's skill and attitude regarding reading?)
   She said she knew the story and liked it.

Comments: Child's *understanding* of the material (e.g., intonation, spontaneous remarks, use of picture clues, self-correcting for meaning, responses to questions).
   She continued to have trouble with "grains"—perhaps doesn't know what it means.

Comments: Child's *strategies* for reading (e.g., willing to guess, maintains momentum, seeks support from teacher, monitors for accuracy).
   Fairly deliberate reader... does not skip words.

Figure 3

Three First Grade Children from the Same Class Read "Fly with Me" in January

Hillary	Felicia	Joanne
	w... H	up in the sky
Fly with me.	Fly/with me.	Fly ~~with me~~.
	... ... Ⓗ	up
Fly with me up and up.	Fly with me/up/and up.	Fly ~~with me up and up~~.
	...	down
Fly with me down and down.	Fly with me down/and down.	Fly ~~with me down and down~~.
...Ⓗ sky		straight, fly around
Fly with me/into the ~~clouds~~	Fly with me into the/clouds	Fly ~~with me into the clouds~~
	...Ⓗ... Ⓗ ...Ⓗ	
and around and around.	/and/around and/around.	~~and around and around~~.
	...Let's go fly over	fly over the bush
Look out for the hills.	/~~Look out for~~ the hills.	~~Look out for the hills~~.
bush	Let's go fly over	fly over
Look out for the ~~bridge~~.	~~Look out for~~ the bridge.	~~Look out for~~ the bridge.
garden	Let's not fly again.	fly down on
Look out for the ~~ground~~.	~~Look out for~~ (the) ~~ground~~.	~~Look out for~~ the ground.

program is to establish the time and setting when teachers may pay undivided attention to individual children. This is a matter of institutional support as well as teacher effort. It has been solved in various ways, depending upon teachers' styles of instruction and the use of support staff. In one school, in an interesting reversal of roles, the reading specialist assumed responsibility for the whole class for twenty minutes, giving the teacher the chance to meet individually with four or five children.

Another challenge in obtaining performance records is maintaining a balance between giving children assistance when needed, while refraining from providing too much help or instruction. A reading sample should produce evidence of the child's own strategies and resources. This means allowing children time and space to tackle the material in their own way. On the other hand, a reading sample should not become a test situation in which all support is denied. Young readers depend upon outside help as part of their repertoire; denying assistance when it is clearly needed or sought by chil-

dren would produce a distorted picture of their competence. Any help the teacher may offer should be recorded as part of the notational system. In reviewing the records, the question can be asked, "Did the children profit from such help?"

Questions also arise concerning the frequency of collecting performance samples. How many children? How often during the year? Another question concerns familiarity with the material. Is it all right to use a book the child has read, heard, or looked at before? The answer is definitely "yes." It may well be that a child's second or third reading of particular materials will tell more about the skill than will a child's first efforts to struggle with new text (see Figure 4).

Answers to such questions depend upon the overall purpose and design of a documentation program. Reading records constitute only one part of a plan for data collection and need to be evaluated accordingly. Moreover, they may play a prominent part in the documentation of initial reading, but a minor part as children become proficient and move past the point when reading aloud is a useful indicator.

Space does not permit full discussion of data interpretation and review. Records can be analyzed in many ways. A first point to make, however, is that several samples collected over the year provide visible backup to any evaluation, no matter how the samples are analyzed. At a minimum, such records can be shared with parents to illustrate the child's progress and help parents understand the complexity of early reading. In one school, performance samples (reading, writing, drawing) collected at intervals over the year are an integral part of the child's cumulative folder, supplementing the teachers' narrative reports.

A second point to make is that the process of making notational records, regardless of how many are eventually obtained, pays dividends through its contribution to the teacher's sensitivity to children's reading in other contexts. Repeatedly, teachers commented on the value of giving sustained attention to a child's reading, both in the process of recording and in subsequent analysis. As a general rule, they recommended that it is better to focus on a few samples thoroughly than on many hurriedly.

In conclusion, performance samples — whether reading or writing — are not intended to be tests in disguise. A reading record is not meant to be a truer measure of a child's ability than the teacher's cumulative observations over time. Instead, the first purpose is descriptive rather than evaluative. The goal is to obtain concrete evidence of a child's reading behaviors at given points in the school year with given materials under certain conditions. Such samples can be throught of as staged observations; they represent occasions when teachers attend closely to behaviors that may be encountered daily, but otherwise remain undocumented.

The relationship between observation and performance sample is well stated by a kindergarten/first grade teacher.

> With beginners you can't assess comprehension directly. The stories they read are too thin. You won't get much if you ask them, "What did the story say?" Besides, they'll think it's a stupid question since you already know the answer. Instead, I notice their spontaneous comments and the kinds of errors they make, like, do they make sense?
>
> Oral reading tells me something about their skills at this point, but I need to look in other places for evidence that books actually mean something to them. I look at their reactions when I read them a story, or I notice that they later get the book and look at it.

Concluding Comments about Documentation

Throughout this paper, we have stressed the descriptive over the evaluative purposes of documentation because that is the focus most needed in assessing young children's learning. In other words, we do not need better tests to estimate children's relative status; instead we need assessment programs that bring out the links between emerging skill and the foundations of literacy. Teachers know which children read well in the conventional sense, which ones are wobbly, and which ones haven't begun. Tests are redundant. Methods of assessment that amplify rather than reduce are more helpful.

In planning a program of documentation, it is useful to distinguish *documentation* from *record keeping* and *testing*. With respect to its procedures, documentation falls somewhere between the highly standardized formats of tests and the idiosyncratic quality of teachers' own record keeping practices. Unlike record keeping, outcomes of documentation are meant to be shared and open to review and interpretation by others. Also, whereas record keeping meets immediate and practical instructional concerns, documentation is meant to support a more reflective posture. It offers opportunity for teachers to review and think about the evidence of learning.

A plan for documentation need not be elaborate, but it does entail institutional support for teachers' involvement in data collection and review. An important component consists of regular occasions for teachers to meet to discuss observations and performance samples.

In planning a program, it is especially important to bridge the kindergarten and primary levels if documentation is to bring out the connections between children's early literacy experiences and their

Figure 4
Two Reading Records from a Child's Folder

TA = Teacher Assistance
|| = Pause

Child's name ___M___
Teacher ___M.J.___ Grade ___I___
Date ___5/11/87___

Teacher Read Title

1st Reading

FLY WITH ME

Fly <u>with</u> me.   isolated w
   W   TA

Fly with me||up||<u>and</u> up.
            TA

Fly with me down||<u>and</u> down.

looked back to page 2
Re-read sentence on page 2 several times
then read "and"

Fly with me into the||clouds   Looked at picture

<u>and</u> <u>around</u> and <u>around</u>.   Looked back to page 2 but this time
 TA   TA   TA   couldn't remember "and"

Long
Pause

||Let's go fly over
<u>Look</u> <u>out</u> <u>for</u> the hill.   added "over"

let's go fly over a river.
<u>Look</u> <u>out</u> <u>for</u> <u>the</u> <u>bridge</u>.   "added over"

Let's not fly ⌃omit again
<u>Look</u> <u>out</u> <u>for</u> the ground!

(40 words)

text	substitution
with	"w"
and	—
around	—
look	let's
out	go
for	fly

text	substitution
the	a
bridge	river
ground	again

Figure 4 (continued)
Two Reading Records from a Child's Folder

Child's name ___M___

Teacher ___M.J.___ Grade ___I___

Date ___5│12│87___

2nd Reading
_____
Next Day

FLY WITH ME

Fly with me.

Fly with me up and up.

Fly with me down and down.

       through
Fly with me <u>into</u> the clouds

fly with me
   omit
<u>and</u> around and around.

  TA
‖ <u>Look</u> out for the hill. isolated "L", then said "look"

Look out for the bridge.

            TA
Look out for the ‖<u>ground</u>! isolated "g"
                used picture

                       (40 words)

text	substitution
into	through
and	fly with me

Later I isolated words in
text, she was able to
read all of them.
    look
    flying
    me
    and
    up

eventual competence and interest as readers. It is better to start with a modest plan that can be actually implemented and evaluated than with an overly ambitious effort. With regard to initiating a program of documentation, experience with the schools suggests something along the following lines.

Step 1. Give teachers the opportunity to use selected procedures with a cross section of five or six children in each classroom. The pace at which the teachers try out the methods should be reflective and investigative. The procedures and the ramifications of the data should be explored, thought about, and evaluated. Obviously, teachers will learn much about the children involved, but the real purpose is to explore the potential value of the methods.

Step 2. Teachers and support staff begin to modify and extend the methods used in Step 1. Selected procedures should be used with most of the students in a classroom. A documentation folder for each child could be developed as tangible support of the process. This should not be a catch all cumulative folder, but something that has an agreed upon organization and contents. The nature of such a folder and its connection to other forms of record keeping and reporting need to be determined.

Step 3. Ideally, an assessment program always should have an investigative flavor, responding to different questions that arise out of instructional or administrative concerns. Thus, perhaps there could be a special focus upon invented spelling, the emergence of phonic skills, or patterns of children's interests in books. Over time, the focus could shift but a core set of practices and procedures would remain intact.

Summary

An assessment program of the sort proposed is aimed at several objectives. First, such a program should promote teachers' competence in evaluating student progress. At a practical level, it should help teachers become more proficient at keeping track and at planning appropriate instruction. At a theoretical level, it should enhance teachers' understanding of the nature of reading acquisition itself. Second, an alternative assessment program can yield documents of pupil learning that begin to replace test scores as accepted forms of evidence. Third, the program should foster communication among teachers, administrators, and parents.

References

Allington, R. Oral reading. In P.D. Pearson (Ed.), *Handbook of reading research*. New York: Longman, 1984.

Anderson, S.B. et al. *Encyclopedia of educational evaluation*. San Francisco, CA: Jossey-Bass, 1975.

Bussis, A., Chittenden, E., Amarel, M., and Klausner, E. *Inquiry into meaning: An investigation of learning to read*. Hillsdale, NJ: Erlbaum, 1985.

Clay, M. *Reading: The patterning of complex behavior*. Portsmouth, NH: Heinemann, 1978.

Henderson, E. *Learning to read and spell*. DeKalb, IL: Northern Illinois University Press, 1981.

National Association of Educators of Young Children. NAEYC position statement on standardized testing of young children 3 through 8 years of age. *Young Children*, 1988, *43*, 42-47.

Shepard, L., and Smith, M. Synthesis of research on school readiness and kindergarten retention. *Educational Leadership*, 1986, *44*, 78-86.

Valencia, S., and Pearson, P.D. Reading assessment: Time for a change. *The Reading Teacher*, 1987, *40*, 726-733.

CHAPTER TEN

Designing the Classroom to Promote Literacy Development

Lesley Mandel Morrow

My purpose is to describe a physical environment that supports optimum literacy development in classrooms for children from preschool through the early childhood grades. Discussion of spaces and materials will concentrate specifically on instruction in reading, writing, and oral language. Classroom areas devoted to music, art, dramatic play, block play, science, math, and social studies will be described to illustrate how they can be designed to promote literacy throughout the school day.

Plato said, "What is honored in a country will be cultivated there." Teachers who honor literacy provide special spaces and materials in their classrooms to promote literacy development as an integral part of the total school curriculum.

Peter was the mail carrier today at school. That meant he got to deliver to his classmates letters that arrived from their pen pals from a kindergarten class in another school district. They wrote to one another once a week. Peter had on his mail carrier's hat, and he hung his mailbag on his shoulder. He had gone to the school office to pick up the letters and had placed them in the cubbies of the children to whom they were addressed. He was able to do this since each cubby was labeled with the name of a student.

Later in the day, the children opened their letters and shared them with great enthusiasm. Some letters had pictures, some had scribble writing, and some were written using invented spelling. Peter's pen pal, Jay, used a combination of real cursive writing and letter like forms. Peter was delighted to receive his mail. During center time he went to the writing area, took a piece of paper, and wrote a letter to Jay. Although most of Peter's writing at this time was a series of random letters in manuscript, his letter to Jay seemed to model the cursive writing his friend had used. Proud of his work, he showed his teacher, folded the letter, and placed it in an envelope. He copied Jay's name and address from a card he had especially for his pen pal, pasted on a sticker stamp, and dropped the letter in the outgoing mailbox in the writing center (see Figures 1 and 2).

Figure 1
Jay's Letter to Peter

Figure 2
Peter's Letter to Jay

In this example, we see children participating in functional literacy activities. The classroom had a writing center with paper, pencils, envelopes, stamps, and a mailbox for a pen pal program, as well as props to help a student act as a mail carrier. The classroom environment was prepared with materials and space that stimulated literacy behaviors.

This chapter describes a physical environment that supports optimum literacy development in an early childhood classroom. Discussion of spaces and materials will concentrate specifically on instruction in reading, writing, and oral language. Classroom areas devoted to music, art, dramatic play, block play, science, math, and social studies will be described to illustrate how they can be designed to promote literacy. The overall physical plan is designed around the concept of promoting literacy as an interdisciplinary pursuit integrated throughout the school day. The suggested plan will accommodate whole class, small group, and individualized learning, all of which are necessary in promoting literacy. The classroom features discussed here will be appropriate for preschool through the early childhood grades.

The Need for a Rich Literacy Environment

Careful attention to a classroom's physical design contributes to the success of an instructional program. Preparing a classroom's physical environment is often overlooked in instructional planning. Teachers and curriculum developers tend to concentrate on pedagogical and interpersonal factors, but give little consideration to the spatial context in which teaching and learning occur. They direct their energies toward varying teaching strategies while the classroom setting remains relatively unchanged. When program and environment are not coordinated, "Setting Deprivation" often results, a situation in which the physical environment fails to support the activities and needs of students (Spivak, 1973).

While the learning environment is often viewed as merely background or scenery for teaching and learning, there is another way to view the physical environment and the teacher's role in creating it. This view recognizes that in arranging the environment purposefully, teachers acknowledge the physical setting as an active and pervasive influence on their own activities and attitudes, as well as those of the children in their classrooms. Appropriate physical arrangement of furniture, material selection, and the aesthetic quality of a room provide a setting that contributes to teaching and learning (Phyfe-Perkins, 1979; Sutfin, 1980). Careful attention to physical classroom design is essential to the success of instructional programs (Weinstein, 1977).

Observations of homes where children learned to read without direct instruction before coming to school have taught us much about rich literacy environments. Initially, children who entered school already reading were described as having learned to read "naturally." The phrase "learning to read naturally" is somewhat misleading. It sounds as if the child learned to read without the support of an adult, other children, or the environment. Although most of these youngsters experienced no formal reading instruction such as that typically provided in school, they usually have supportive parents and an environment rich with the materials of literacy. The adults respond to children's literacy based questions and comments and provide experiences that help them learn to read.

More specifically, early readers tend to come from homes where parents read to them, help them write and read, and often read themselves. Such parents read a wide variety of materials, including novels, magazines, newspapers, and work related information. They keep reading materials in all rooms of their homes—especially in the children's rooms. They take their children to libraries and bookstores often (Durkin, 1966; Morrow, 1983; Taylor, 1983; Teale, 1984). Their homes hold ample supplies of books and writing materials for themselves and for their children. They generally value reading as an important activity, associate books with pleasure, and reward activities relating to literacy. Those activities are often functional and related to real life situations, such as cooperative preparation of shopping lists by parents and children, reading and following recipes, and leaving personal notes as a form of communication. Literacy serves a purpose and is a part of normal home functioning.

From the results of investigations into homes, Holdaway (1979) developed a theory of literacy development, part of which maintains that the rich literacy environment that characterizes such homes is appropriate to school based literacy instruction as well. Classrooms are characterized by self regulated, individualized activities; frequent peer interaction; and an environment rich with literacy materials.

Historically, other theorists and philosophers have emphasized the importance of the physical environment in learning and literacy development. Pestalozzi (Rusk & Scotland, 1979) and Froebel (1974) described real life environments in which young children's learning could flourish. Both described the preparation of manipulative materials that would foster literacy development. Montessori (1965) described a carefully prepared classroom environment intended to promote independent learning and recommended that every material in the environment have its specific learning objective or role. The objectives and materials she recommended were more highly structured than those of Pestalozzi and Froebel, who allowed for more natural learning situations in which children explored and experimented with materials in their environment.

According to Piaget, children acquire knowledge by interacting with the world or the environment (Piaget & Inhelder, 1969). Those who interpret his theories into educational practice involve children in problem solving situations where they can assimilate new experiences into what they already know. Learning takes place as the child interacts with peers and adults in social settings and conducive environments (Vygotsky, 1978). Ideal settings are oriented to real life situations, and materials are chosen to provide opportunities for children to explore and experiment. Dewey (1966) probably would have agreed with the educational settings provided by Piagetians. But, in addition, Dewey believed that learning was best when it was interdisciplinary. In other words, learning takes place through the integration of content area. He believed that storing materials in subject area learning centers encouraged interest and learning.

Based on the discussion just outlined, any classroom designed to provide a rich literacy environment and optimum literacy development will offer an abundant supply of materials for reading, writing, and oral language. These materials will be housed in a literacy center. Literacy development will be integrated with content area teaching and reflected in materials provided in content area learning centers. Materials and settings throughout the classroom will be designed to emulate real life experiences and make literacy meaningful to children. They will be based on backgrounds and information children already possess, and will be functional so that children can see a need and purpose for using literacy skills.

This chapter is devoted to a discussion of the classroom physical environment. However, although we can describe the optimal environment, in practice we cannot separate the teacher from the environment. While instruction is supported by the environment, a successful classroom cannot function without a competent teacher. Good teachers are the single most important factor in a successful classroom environment.

Preparing a Rich Literacy Environment

The program that nourishes emergent literacy requires a literacy rich environment, an interdisciplinary approach, and recognition of individual differences and levels of development. Although there is no single way to effectively arrange a classroom, one plan is suggested here as a guide. Teachers are encouraged to arrange their rooms to suit their needs and personal preferences, as well as those of their children.

Classrooms can be arranged in centers with sections dedicated to particular activities or content areas, such as social studies, science, math, art, music, dramatic play, block play, and literacy. Centers contain general materials pertinent to the content area and materials specific to topics currently under study. Resources are devoted to the content area but are designed to develop literacy as well. The materials are usually manipulative and activity oriented, and are designed so children can use them independently or in small groups.

Centers are separated by furniture that houses their materials and serves as a partition. Center materials can be stored on tables, on shelves, or in boxes. Centers often include bulletin boards. Areas are accessible and labeled. Each piece of equipment in a center should have its own designated spot so that teachers can direct children to specific items, and children can find and return them easily. Early in a school year, a center need hold only a small number of items, with new materials added gradually as the year progresses. Before new items are placed in centers, they should be introduced by the teacher as to their purpose, use, and placement (Montessori, 1965).

The room is designed so that the teacher can hold large group instruction when the children are sitting at their desks or tables, or sitting on the floor in the Library Corner or the Music Center, both of which are likely to be large enough for the entire class to meet together. The Teacher Conference Table provides space for small group and individualized instruction, necessary especially for interaction guided by an adult and for skill development. The conference table is placed in a quiet area of the room to facilitate the instruction that occurs around it, but it is situated so the teacher can see the rest of the room where children are working independently. The various centers offer settings for independent self directed learning.

As you will note on the classroom floor plan, the centers have been positioned so that areas where quiet work is typical (Literacy Center, Math

Classroom Floor Plan

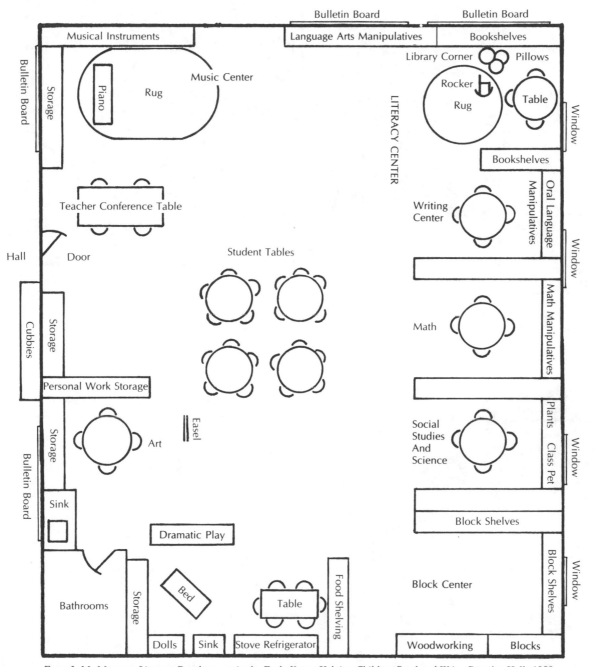

From L.M. Morrow, *Literacy Development in the Early Years: Helping Children Read and Write.* Prentice Hall, 1989. Used with permission.

From L.M. Morrow, *Literacy Development in the Early Years: Helping Children Read and Write.* Prentice Hall, 1989. Used with permission.

The library corner is a cozy place where children can relax and read, leaning on soft pillows, sitting on a rug, and hugging stuffed animals.

Center, Social Studies, Science) are away from typically noisy, more active centers (Dramatic Play, Blocks, Art).

The Literacy Center

The Literacy Center, which includes the library corner, writing area, oral language area, and additional language arts materials, is the focal point in the room (Stauffer, 1970). It occupies a portion of the classroom that is immediately visible upon entering. It is visually attractive and physically accessible (Morrow, 1983). Placement and size of materials, shelves, chairs, and tables are appropriate for young children, and all posters are at children's eye level. The effort of creating an inviting atmosphere for a classroom library corner or literacy center is rewarded by the increased interest of children in participating in the activities offered there (Huck, 1976). The literacy center can occupy about one-third of the wall space on one side of a room, thus dramatizing to the children that the use of reading, writing, and oral language is a valued and important part of the classroom. The materials range in difficulty to meet individual needs and different developmental levels. Each set of materials has its own place, is respected, and is designed for independent use.

The Library Corner represents and supports the notion that concepts about books and print are acquired when children are exposed to printed materials and given time to explore and experiment with them. A classroom library corner is essential if children are to enjoy immediate access to literature (Beckman, 1972). Bissett (1969) found that children in classrooms with their own collections of literature read and looked at books 50 percent more often than children whose classrooms housed no such collections.

It has been found that well designed classroom library corners significantly increased the number of children who chose to participate in literary activities during free choice times (Morrow, 1987; Morrow & Weinstein, 1982, 1986). Observations in nursery schools and kindergartens have identified specific design characteristics of library corners that correlated with children's use of those corners. Conversely, it has been found that during free choice periods, children did not use poorly designed library corners. The research evidence clearly shows that physical features of a classroom library corner are important if children are to be induced to use it voluntarily (Rosenthal, 1973; Shure, 1963).

While the library corner should be immediately visible and inviting to anyone entering the classroom, it also needs to afford privacy and physical definition for its users. It can be partitioned on two or three sides with bookshelves, file cabinets, or free standing bulletin boards. Its dimensions depend on the size of the classroom. Generally, it should be large enough to accommodate five or six children comfortably.

Well designed library corners provide two kinds of bookshelves. The first houses the bulk of the collection, and its books are shelved with spines facing outward. The second is open faced to display book covers, an important technique for calling attention and providing easy access to special books. Featured books are changed regularly. An alterna-

tive type of display shelving is the circular wire rack, commonly found in bookstores.

Books in the classroom collection should be shelved by category and color coded by type. The spines of all books on winter, for example, might be identified with blue circle stickers. The books might then be clustered on a shelf labeled *Winter*, with a blue sticker next to the label. Green stickers might distinguish books about plants. Color coding introduces children to the idea that books in libraries are organized by a system that makes them readily accessible.

Because much of the activity in a library corner takes place on the floor, it should be furnished with a throw rug and pillows or bean bag chairs, although it should also include a small table and chairs where children can use headsets to listen to taped stories or make their own books. A rocking chair allows comfortable reading, and a private "cozy" spot for reading can be made from an oversized carton that has been painted or covered with contact paper.

Attractive posters that encourage reading are available from both the Children's Book Council (67 Irving Place, New York, NY 10003) and the American Library Association (50 East Huron Street, Chicago, IL 60611). Stuffed animals also belong in a library corner, especially if they are related to available books. A stuffed teddy bear, for instance, might be placed next to a copy of *Bedtime for Francis* (Hoban, 1960) and other books in the Francis series, which tell about a family of bears. Children enjoy reading to stuffed animals or simply holding them as they look at books. A feltboard with story characters from favorite books is often heavily used in a library corner, as are roll movies. Viewing machines with story wheels are a source of literature for young children, and puppets help children act out stories. The corner should also include materials from which children can act out stories and can make their own books, felt stories, and roll movies.

Huck (1976) recommends five to eight books per child in a classroom library. Books are not difficult to accumulate. They can be purchased inexpensively at flea markets. In addition, many public libraries will lend teachers as many as twenty books a month. Parents sometimes donate books or sponsor fund raising events for book purchases. Children's paperback book clubs offer inexpensive books and free bonus books for bulk purchases. Especially if they are not current, children's magazines and newspapers are often available to schools from publishers and local distributors for the cost of mailing and shipping if they are indeed not donated.

Children should be involved in planning, designing, and managing a library corner. They can help develop rules for its use, keep it neat, and select a name for it, such as "Book Nook." To ensure continued interest in the library corner, new books and materials must be introduced periodically and others recirculated. Approximately twenty-five new books should be introduced every two weeks, replacing twenty-five that have been there for a while. With recirculation, "old" books are greeted as new friends a few months later.

Students should be encouraged to borrow books from the library corner to take home for a week. A simple checkout system should be used. At specified times during the school day, for instance, children might bring books they have selected to the teacher, who notes the date, borrower's name, and book title. With training, children as young as kindergarten age can learn to check out books themselves by copying titles and recording dates on cards filed under their own names. Youngsters also can record on $3'' \times 5''$ cards titles and dates for books they read. The cards can be secured by loose leaf rings hung on curtain rod hooks mounted on a bulletin board, one ring per child.

Books and materials selected for the library corner should appeal to a variety of interests and represent a range in grade levels, ideally with multiple copies of the more popular books. Children often like to read a particular book at the same time or because friends are reading it. Several types of children's literature should be represented at each reading level, including picture concept books, fairy tales, nursery rhymes, picture storybooks, realistic literature, easy to read books, fables, folktales, informational books, biographies, newspapers, magazines, and poetry (Cullinan, this volume; Morrow, 1985).

The Writing Center, also part of the Literacy Center, should include a table and chairs, as well as colored felt tipped marking pens, crayons, pencils (both regular and colored), paper, chalk, and a chalkboard. While various sizes and types of paper should be available, most should be unlined white paper or newsprint ranging in size from $8\frac{1}{2}'' \times 11''$ to $24'' \times 36''$. Index cards, used to record children's Very Own Words, should be available in the writing area, and the children's collections of Very Own Words should be stored there. Writing folders, one for each child, are used to collect writing output over the course of the school year. If available, a typewriter adds to the center's usefulness, as does a word processor.

Materials for making books are a must, including paper, hole punch, stapler, and construction paper for covers. Blank books prepared by the teacher, especially ones keyed to special occasions, invite children to fill in written messages and stories. A regular inventory of pictures, posters, magazines, and newspapers can stimulate and provide decoration and illustration of children's writing. Children's literature in the classroom collection also can stimulate writing activities and ideas. If the teacher is not immediately available to take dictation from those children who choose to dictate stories, a tape recorder serves as an excellent tool. The dictated story can be transcribed later.

Displaying children's writing requires a bulletin board, but equally valuable are Message or Notice Boards used to exchange messages among members of the class and with the teacher. Teachers find the Message Board helpful in sending messages to individual children as well as in posting important information for the entire class. Mailboxes, stationery, envelopes, and stamps for youngsters' incoming and outgoing mail may be placed in the writing center if a pen pal program is underway (Morrow, 1989).

Oral Language activities also are encouraged and supported by materials within the Literacy Center. Puppets, flannel boards, pictures, children's literature, and a tape recorder all stimulate the use of oral language. Children use these materials to retell stories or create new stories (Morrow, 1981). Stimulated by activities and units of study in the content areas, children can orally share home or school experiences with the entire class or, during free choice time, with individual friends or small

Puppets will encourage children to tell stories and create their own.

From L.M. Morrow, *Literacy Development in the Early Years: Helping Children Read and Write.* Prentice Hall, 1989. Used with permission.

groups in dramatic play areas, block corners, and outdoors. These activities aid vocabulary development as well as oral language skills.

Other materials should be available in the Literacy Center to help youngsters develop additional language arts skills. An alphabet chart in easy view helps children identify and shape letters they may need while writing. Tactile plastic, magnetic, wooden, and felt letters are useful language arts manipulatives that help children develop motor dexterity for the act of writing and aid them in letter recognition and formation. Other manipulative materials teach rhyme and sound-symbol associations for consonants, vowels, and digraphs. Real life objects also should be included—materials that use the senses and represent letters of the alphabet and the sounds of consonants, vowels, and digraphs. For example, a box supporting the letter *P* might include a *p*eanut to taste, *p*erfume to smell, a *p*ow-

der *p*uff to touch, a *p*icture to look at, and a tiny toy *p*iano to play.

Time should be set aside for children to use the literacy center during the school day. The teacher must introduce the materials by featuring them in lessons and then gradually adding them to the center. In one observation during a recreational reading period when children were using the center materials, there were children reading as they relaxed on soft pillows, some with stuffed animals clutched under their arms. One child read to another snuggled in the box called the "private spot." Two children used a felt board to tell a story—one manipulated the felt characters as the other read the book. A group listened to a taped story of *The Little Red Hen* (Galdone, 1975) on headsets. They followed the words in the book as they listened. Since the tape was audible only to the children with the headsets, it was amusing to suddenly hear them chanting along at the part in the story when the animals say, "Not I."

Two other children were writing letters to their pen pals, a few were checking out books to take home, and others were comparing the number of books they had read. One youngster was pretending to be the teacher and read a story to a group. Another child asked to have a turn at being the teacher.

At the beginning of the period, the teacher made sure the children were involved. First she read to a small group of children who asked to hear a story. Then she observed a few youngsters acting out *The Little Red Hen* with finger puppets. After that, she sat down with a novel and read, modeling her own interest in books. The room was generally quiet, but one could hear the buzz of activity. The children were learning in an environment rich with literacy materials.

Creating Classroom Environmental Print to Promote Literacy

Goodman (1984) found in a study of preschoolers that they already knew many of the things needed in order to read. They knew the difference between letters and pictures in books and were aware of environmental print in familiar contexts. They were able to read road signs, fast food restaurant names, and familiar labels on food cans and boxes. This finding suggests that first words can be read quite naturally if the environment is filled with print that is used regularly for functional purposes.

The classroom can be given its own environmental print to encourage and create a usefulness for reading and writing. Objects can be labeled, such as content area centers and children's cubbies. Labels and printed signs also can communicate what is expected of children in carrying out classroom tasks—charts that list daily routines, helper charts to indicate job responsibilities, daily attendance charts, center charts indicating which children are to use which centers and when, written assignments on a board for independent work, and a special news bulletin board to cover exciting events in the classroom, in the lives of individual children, or in the world. A calendar and a thermometer for the room also require reading.

New words generated in units of instruction should be listed on experience charts that are then hung for reading or copying. Similar treatment can be given to experience chart stories created by the class, whether the experience is performing an experiment in the science center or using a recipe in a cooking lesson. Include illustrations next to words whenever possible to help children not yet able to read. The routine of using environmental print in the classroom eventually enables children to read some of it.

Integrating Literacy into the Content Areas

Reading, writing, and oral language materials and activities are easily incorporated into subject area teaching, enabling the content areas also to provide a source for literacy learning. The creator of environmental designs for the classroom must be aware of the importance of integrating literacy into these content areas. Literacy becomes purposeful and takes on additional importance when it is integrated with other subjects rather than separately as a content area unto itself (Dewey, 1966).

The Literacy Center just outlined incorporates materials that stimulate writing, reading, and oral language. Materials also can be selected to create the same effect in the other content area centers throughout the classroom. Each new unit of study can bring new materials into all centers to enhance literacy development. For instance, assume that the topic of study is *Animals,* including those found in zoos, jungles, forests, farms, and as pets. The teacher adds the following items to existing centers.

Science Center. During the study of Animals, one teacher borrowed a setting hen whose eggs were ready to hatch. The class discussed the care of the hen. They started an experience chart when the hen arrived and added to it daily, recording the hen's behavior and the hatching of the eggs. They listed new vocabulary words on a wall chart and placed books about hens in the science area. Children kept diaries of events surrounding the hen. There were cards in the center for children to record new Very Own Words relating to the hen.

Social Studies Center. Children can learn

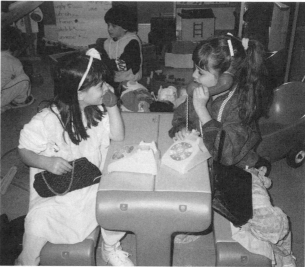

Experiences with science materials lead to new discoveries and provide the opportunity to learn new words.

From L.M. Morrow, *Literacy Development in the Early Years: Helping Children Read and Write.* Prentice Hall, 1989. Used with permission.

The opportunity to participate in dramatic play will stimulate language from real life.

From L.M. Morrow, *Literacy Development in the Early Years: Helping Children Read and Write.* Prentice Hall, 1989. Used with permission.

about animals specific to particular countries, such as the panda bear in China and the kangaroo in Australia. Pictures of these animals are placed in the center and labeled with names and countries. A map highlighting the appropriate part of the world is placed near each animal's picture. Books about the specific animals are available in the center, as are paper and writing tools children can use to make books about animals from other lands.

Art Center. Given the topic of Animals, children can first make dough by following a printed recipe on an experience chart. Then each child can use the dough to create a real or imaginary animal for a pretend zoo, which is set up in the block area. Each piece of work is labeled to identify the animal by type and name, and to identify the child who created it.

Music Center. During the Animal unit, the teacher uses songs about animals. To promote literacy, the words to new songs are written on chart paper and displayed in the area, encouraging children to read or copy the words. The teacher also can place animal song books or song sheets in the center.

Math Center. During the Animal unit, place in the center counting books that feature animals, such as *One, Two Three: An Animal Counting Book* (Brown, 1976) or *One, Two, Three to the Zoo* (Carle, 1968). Include magazines containing animal pictures so children can create their own number books using pictures of animals as the counting items for each numeral.

Dramatic Play. During the Animal unit, one teacher set up her dramatic play area as a veterinarian's office. There was a waiting room supplied with books and magazines about animals, as well as pamphlets about pet care and pet posters labeled with animals' names hanging on the walls. Other materials included an appointment book and appointment cards for pets and their owners. Signs included "No Smoking" and "Doctor's Hours." Patient information forms are filed in individual's patients' folders. There was a prescription pad, and stuffed animals served as patients. White jackets and toy medical equipment were available for doctors and nurses.

Blocks. As with the dramatic play center, the block center can change in character with each unit of study. For the Animal unit, the block area can become a zoo, housing animal figures, stuffed animals, and animals created by children in the art center. Children can build block cages and make labels for each animal and section of the zoo. Signs can include "Petting Zoo," "Bird House," "Pony Rides," "Don't Feed the Animals," and "Don't Touch Us, We Bite." There are admissions tickets and play money to purchase tickets, souvenirs, and animal food. The block area can include books and posters about zoo animals.

Conclusions

Teachers who have experienced school settings that include Literacy Centers with carefully designed Library Corners and Writing Centers support the value of a rich literacy environment through their reactions and comments.

"I never thought I would have enough space in my classroom for the Literacy Center, I was surprised that so many materials could fit into such a small area."

"The library corner and writing center became a place where children of all reading and writing abilities mingled....This social context seemed to provide an atmosphere for cooperative learning. The children looked forward to their time there each day."

"Children participated in the Literacy Center quite naturally and with enthusiasm. Children read more, wrote more, and took more books home from school than any group of youngsters I had in my classroom before. I think it's because the materials were so attractive and accessible. It suddenly dawned on me that while children had the opportunity to use the centers, they were practicing skills I'd been teaching them during direct instruction" (Morrow, 1987).

These next comments are those of children who have used Literacy Centers.

"Library Corners are nice in your classroom with pillows and lots of good books; it's cozy there, too. You get to read a lot when there is a library in your classroom. I'm reading so much that I get to practice reading, which will make me get better at it."

"You can choose the books you want to read. You can read short books if you want. You also get to read with your friends and you get to take books home. The things in the literacy center are fun. It makes you want to read and write and like to read, too" (Morrow, 1987).

The classrooms that generated those comments were rich in their literacy environment; literacy was honored, was cultivated, and thrived in them.

Studies and theoretical implications for classroom practice indicate that preparing a classroom for optimum literacy development should include concerted attention to environmental planning—allocation and design of space, selection of materials, and placement of those materials. Teachers no longer can think of themselves as just planners of strategies for instruction. Like an architect, the teacher must design a learning environment that supports specific instructional strategies (Loughlin, 1977).

The rich literacy environment described here allows for adult guidance and social interaction with peers. The facility underscores the concurrent, integrated nature of learning and using oral language, reading, and writing. The room is designed to promote functional literacy through real life experiences that are meaningful and interesting to the child. It provides for the integration of literacy and content areas to add enthusiasm, motivation, and meaning. It provides space for personal growth through direct instruction in small group and individual learning settings. It also provides ample space for children to learn independently and with peers through manipulation, exploration, and play.

The room is designed to help children associate literacy with enjoyment. With its appealing physical design, interesting activities, and the guidance of a competent teacher, the school environment described will help children develop literacy through pleasurable, positive, and successful experiences, thus ensuring a lifelong desire to refine and use literacy skills.

Creating an Art Gallery to Promote Literacy

1. Collect and hang prints of paintings by famous artists. Label the paintings with the name of the artist and the title of the work. Be sure to hang the prints at the children's eye level.

2. Discuss the artists and their work. Then read the titles of their paintings and their names. Include in the center books of artwork from these and other artists.

3. Provide artists' materials such as a palette, smock, easel, paints, chalk, crayons, magic markers, glue, and construction paper. Label each item and store each in its own container. Encourage children to do artwork, to title it, and to sign it. Provide a place in the gallery to display their creations.

4. Provide tags for the young artists to price their work, and provide order forms, receipts, and a cash register for them to sell their work.

5. Post a sign listing the name of the gallery (chosen by the children) and the gallery hours.

6. Provide 3″ x 5″ cards for Very Own Words when children want to copy new words relating to the art gallery, such as palette, easel, artist, and collage.

Cynthia Peters
Kindergarten Teacher
Belleville, New Jersey

Creating a Bakery to Promote Literacy

A bakery is set up in the Dramatic Play area in coordination with a unit on Community Helpers.

1. Materials included are a baker's hat, an apron, cookie cutters, a rolling pin, mixing bowls, measuring cups, spoons, trays, and boxes with labels for baked goods such as cookies, cakes, pies, and rolls.

2. Some classroom recipes that already have been made are hung in the center, and a file box with old recipes and blank cards for new recipes is available, along with pens and pencils. Cookbooks with recipes for baking also will be stored in the area.

3. For the purpose of buying and selling baked goods, there is an order pad, a cash register, receipts for purchases, number tickets for standing in line to be waited on, and name tags for the baker and salespersons.

4. Post a sign listing the name of the bakery (chosen by the students) and store hours.

5. Blank word cards are available for children to copy words they might like to have for their Very Own Word collection that relate to the bakery, such as cookies, cakes, pies, and rolls.

6. Baked goods actually will be made and sold in the classroom.

Joyce Caponigro
Kindergarten Teacher
Livingston, New Jersey

References

Beckman, R. Interior space: The things of education. *National Principal,* 1972, *52,* 45-49.

Bissett, D. *The amount and effect of recreational reading in selected fifth grade classes.* Unpublished doctoral dissertation, Syracuse University, 1969.

Brown, M. *One, two, three: An animal counting book.* Boston: Little, Brown, 1976.

Carle, E. *One, two, three to the zoo.* New York: Collins World, 1968.

Dewey, J. *Democracy and education.* New York: The Free Press, 1966.

Durkin, D. *Children who read early: Two longitudinal studies.* New York: Teachers College Press, 1966.

Froebel, F. *The education of man.* Clifton, NJ: Augustus M. Kelly, 1974.

Galdone, P. *The little red hen.* New York: Scholastic, 1975.

Goodman, Y. The development of initial literacy. In H. Goelman, A. Oberg, and F. Smith (Eds.), *Awakening to literacy.* Portsmouth, NH: Heinemann Educational Books, 1984.

Hoban, R. *Bedtime for Francis.* New York: Harper & Row, 1960.

Holdaway, D. *The foundations of literacy.* New York: Ashton Scholastic, 1979.

Huck, C. *Children's literature in the elementary school,* third edition. New York: Holt, Rinehart & Winston, 1976.

Loughlin, C.E. Understanding the learning environment. *Elementary School Journal,* 1977, *78,* 125-131.

Montessori, M. *Spontaneous activity in education.* New York: Schocken Books, 1965.

Morrow, L.M. Home and school correlates of early interest in literature. *Journal of Educational Research,* 1983, *76,* 221-230.

Morrow, L.M. *Literacy development in the early years: Helping children read and write.* Englewood Cliffs, NJ: Prentice Hall, 1989.

Morrow, L.M. Promoting innercity children's recreational reading. *The Reading Teacher,* 1987, *41,* 266-274.

Morrow, L.M. *Promoting voluntary reading in school and home.* Bloomington, IN: Phi Delta Kappa Educational Foundation, 1985.

Morrow, L.M. *Supertips for storytelling.* New York: Harcourt Brace Jovanovich, 1981.

Morrow, L.M., and Weinstein, C.S. Encouraging voluntary reading: The impact of a literature program on children's use of library centers. *Reading Research Quarterly,* 1986, *21,* 330-346.

Morrow, L.M., and Weinstein, C.S. Increasing children's use of literature through programs and physical design changes. *Elementary School Journal,* 1982, *83,* 131-137.

Phyfe-Perkins, E. *Application of the behavior-person-environment paradigm to the analysis and evaluation of early childhood education.* Unpublished doctoral dissertation, University of Massachusetts, 1979.

Piaget, J., and Inhelder, B. *The psychology of the child.* New York: Basic Books, 1969.

Rosenthal, B.A. *An ecological study of free play in the nursery school.* Unpublished doctoral dissertation, Wayne State University, Detroit, 1973.

Rusk, R., and Scotland, J. *Doctrines of the great educators.* New York: St. Martin's Press, 1979.

Shure, M. Psychological ecology of a nursery school. *Child Development,* 1963, *34,* 979-992.

Spivak, M. Archetypal place. *Architectural Forum,* 1973, *140,* 44-49.

Stauffer, R.G. A reading teacher's dream come true. *Wilson Library Bulletin,* 1970, *45,* 282-292.

Sutfin, H. *The effects on children's behavior of a change in physical design of a kindergarten classroom.* Unpublished doctoral dissertation, Boston University, 1980.

Taylor, D. *Family literacy: Young children learning to read and write.* Exeter, NH: Heinemann Educational Books, 1983.

Teale, W. Reading to young children: Its significance for literacy development. In H. Goelman, A.A. Oberg, and F. Smith (Eds.), *Awakening to literacy.* London: Heinemann Educational Books, 1984.

Vygotsky, L.S. *Mind in society: The development of psychological processes.* Cambridge, MA: Harvard University Press, 1978.

Weinstein, C.S. Modifying student behavior in an open classroom through changes in the physical design. *American Educational Research Journal,* 1977, *14,* 249-262.

CHAPTER ELEVEN

A Model for Change:
Framework for an
Emergent Literacy Curriculum

Dorothy S. Strickland

A curricular framework is presented for use in prekindergarten through early primary grades. The framework brings together and applies the research findings on young children's language and literacy in a manner that is manageable and efficient, yet flexible enough to be adapted to local needs.

"I really like what I've been hearing about the new emergent reading. I love it when the children write, too. I just can't seem to put it all together, though. I find planning for it hard. I need some kind of structure."

"My reading supervisor says it's all right to do these emergent literacy things, as long as I meet the district objectives. In other words, it's fine to give the kids a holistic program, but I have to show what skills I'm developing. I need some help with this."

"I'm afraid that my story time has been neglected. There's simply not enough time to do that and teach reading, too."

The preceding comments probably will sound familiar to anyone teaching or working with teachers implementing early literacy programs. It was comments such as these that led to the Core Experience Curriculum presented here.

This chapter describes a curriculum model that grew out of a study designed to bring current research and theoretical perspectives together with what kindergarten teachers believe to be essential to an effective early childhood literacy program. We were interested in how kindergarten teachers were meeting current demands for more formalized academic programs. What we learned from the teachers and their classrooms was analyzed in terms of the related research and literature on teaching and learning in early childhood settings. Particular attention was given to work reflecting an

135

emergent literacy perspective. Our purpose was to mesh the wisdom of good practice with that of respected theorists and researchers in order to determine what an optimum kindergarten program, focusing on language and literacy development, should be.

Phase one of the research consisted of an intensive investigation into the classrooms of kindergarten teachers across urban, suburban, and rural settings. Classroom observations were followed by extensive teacher interviews. In addition, many teachers were surveyed by questionnaires and through small focus group sessions to determine their ideas about reading and writing in the kindergarten. Phase two involved a curriculum research and development project in which some of the teachers involved in the initial investigation worked with the researchers to apply and refine curricular strategies based on what we had learned.

While the actual research is reported elsewhere (Strickland & Ogle, in press), the implications for practice and the resulting curriculum model are shared here. The model is not a commercially prepared program. Rather, it is a framework to be used by early childhood teachers and curriculum specialists to help them organize effective learning environments. Based on a set of core experiences, which are offered to children on a daily basis, it is presented as a structure for bringing together the many good ideas in this book. Meant to be used as a dynamic and malleable tool, it should be adjusted to suit the individual, ever-changing situations found in each community and classroom in which it is implemented.

Research Foundations

As stated, the curricular framework presented here is based on current research and theoretical perspectives on children's language and literacy development and on extensive collaborative work with many classroom teachers to determine what they think a good literacy program for young children should be. From these sources, the following principles emerged to guide our thinking. An effective early childhood literacy program will:

1. Reflect current research and theory on how children learn, how they learn language in particular, and what is known about effective teaching.

2. Capitalize on children's natural interests and curiosity by integrating the teaching of language processes (listening, speaking, reading, and writing) with instruction in content areas such as social studies and science.

3. Allow teachers to tie curricular experiences to district objectives, yet emphasize development of skill rather than specific skills.

4. Facilitate planning by providing a predictable framework within which varied content, grouping, and organizational patterns may fit easily.

5. Include methods for systematic, formative evaluation.

Philosophical Framework

The Core Experience Curriculum is a comprehensive curriculum of instruction that may be used in prekindergarten, kindergarten, and first grade. Its primary focus is on the development of language and thinking in conjunction with the social and physical sciences. The model is based on the belief that children, like adults, are driven to learn language, not for its own sake, but because of their natural curiosity about the world. They want to learn about their world and communicate about it. Therefore, children are helped to listen, speak, read, write, and think as they explore and increase their knowledge about content of interest and importance to them. The content serves as a unifying interest through which a series of shared events cohere the group into a community of learners not unlike the community of learners in the home (Strickland & Taylor, this volume).

The Core Experience Curriculum pays attention to the skills and objectives that early childhood teachers feel are important to language and literacy development; however, these objectives are not treated as discrete entities (Schickedanz, this volume). They are developed in an integrated, holistic manner through content themes identified as appropriate by the teachers using the model. The themes may be designated by the teacher, the district curriculum guide, or things that develop naturally out of everyday explorations of the group. Themes

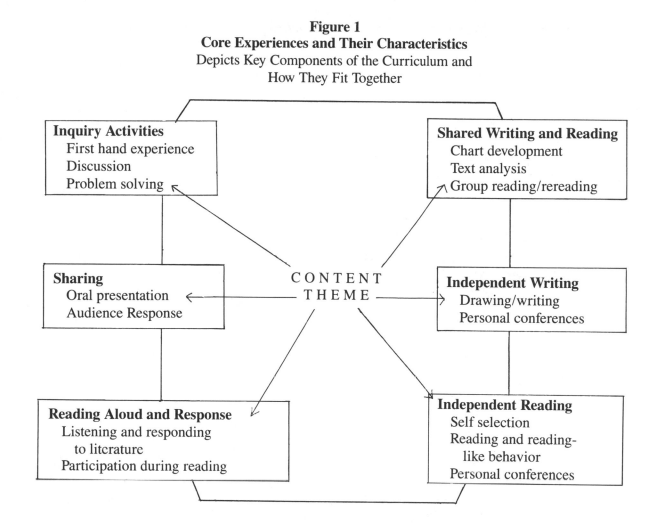

such as "The Five Senses," "My Community," and "Dinosaurs" act as the content through which listening, speaking, reading, writing, and thinking are developed.

A print rich classroom environment is fundamental to the successful implementation of the program (Morrow, this volume). Meaningful labels, signs, and captions that function as information to be used and responded to are required. The incidental learning that results from an environment that invites children to write, read, and talk is considered every bit as important and receives equal attention as the core experiences themselves. A strong literature base is another hallmark of the model (Cullinan, this volume). In addition to daily

read aloud periods in which children frequently act as participants during the reading and engage in varied modes of response, independent experiences with literature also are provided. Theme topics are explored through literature as well as through direct, hands on inquiry.

Figure 1 is a graphic representation of the key components of the curriculum and how they fit together. Each is described in greater detail.

The Core Experiences

This child centered curriculum model is based on a set of core experiences that are made available to every child every day. These core experiences include inquiry activities, shared reading and writing, independent reading, independent writing, listening and participating in read aloud sessions, and sharing.

Inquiry Activities

Inquiry activities allow children to explore concrete phenomena and ideas central to the content area theme. Children engage in thinking (particularly problem solving) and talking as they manipulate ideas and materials to develop understandings about the content being discussed.

Inquiry activities generally take place early in the day during circle time. Most often they involve the whole group. They range in time from fifteen to twenty minutes, depending on the developmental levels of the children. Although the content of inquiry is focused on the physical and social sciences, the methods of inquiry include an array of thinking operations. These include both basic concepts and higher order thinking associated with language and mathematics.

Good catalysts for inquiry include any one or any combination of the following:

1. Questioning, posing a problem to be solved. (We have been talking about the pretty flowers that are beginning to blossom in our neighborhood. What do we need to do to plant some flowers of our own?)

2. Displaying related objects. (Here are several leaves that I have gathered from the schoolyard. How can we learn more about them?)

3. Demonstrating. (Today, I'm going to show you what happens when certain colors are mixed together. Perhaps you can make a good guess.) At times, a picture book might be used in conjunction with these activities; however, emphasis is placed on active participation and talk.

Varied means are used to stimulate children to talk as the teacher models and encourages the use of vocabulary related to the theme. Varied uses of language are encouraged (Glazer, this volume). Children describe, label, and explain as they exchange language with others. Opportunities to develop thinking processes are capitalized upon whenever they emerge. Observing through all the senses, hypothesizing, making predictions, sequencing, interpreting, comparing and contrasting, classifying, determining cause and effect, and exploring concepts related to time, space, and quantity are some of the generic thinking processes that naturally evolve when children solve problems and explore ideas related to the topic under study.

Inquiry activities always end with an attempt by the teacher to help children summarize the ideas they have explored. This discussion may be stimulated by a simple question such as "What did we learn today?" In this way, children form the habit of reflecting on their own learning. Teachers also are encouraged to use this time reflectively, since it offers an opportunity to uncover problems and possibilities for further planning.

Shared Writing and Reading

During shared writing and reading, the medium of print is used to reformulate and extend ideas explored through the inquiry activities. Since shared writing and reading generally follow inquiry activities, they allow children to move directly from the concrete to the abstract. First they think, talk, and act on their ideas. Then they reformulate their ideas through print. Most often, the shared writing and reading center on a chart created by the teacher and group together; however, it may make use of some other enlarged text such as a big book or a related poem or chant prepared by the teacher in advance. The same texts may be used over several days in conjunction with a series of related inquiry activities. A chart may be augmented or changed, or it may simply be reread and enjoyed as a follow up to inquiry. Shared writing and reading activities range from ten to twenty minutes, depending upon the developmental levels of the group.

Chart production may take a variety of forms. Teachers may use "line a child" charts in which each child makes an individual contribution. In this case, the teacher writes down each contribution followed by the child's name. Some charts take a narrative form in which children may retell what they learned or describe an event. Sometimes lists of items may form a chart. One class studying animals decided to list those that were living and those that were not. Of course, Mickey Mouse and Jon's stuffed teddy bear appeared on the same list.

The teacher's role during chart production is that of facilitator and scribe. The children are encouraged to use ideas and language relevant to the theme topic and inquiry activities. Finally, the children are encouraged to join in as the completed chart is read aloud by the teacher.

A second feature of shared writing and reading is *text analysis*. Here, children move from participating in the construction and reading of a whole text to the analysis of its parts. They look for distinctive features such as letters and words they recognize, words and letters that are repeated, punctuation marks, and any other features that interest them. The teacher follows the children's lead as they point out features that interest them.

Every opportunity is used to help children make connections, see likenesses and differences, and draw conclusions about what they are discussing. For example, in one class a youngster named Pat was very pleased to point out that her name was included on the chart. When the teacher asked her to find it, she proudly pointed to the word "Put," which served as the beginning of one of the sentences. The teacher wisely praised the child for being such a good observer. She then wrote Pat's name on a card and helped her compare the two words. Pat's ability to discover the difference between the two was seen as even further evidence of her growing abilities in reading.

Every attempt by the children to scrutinize text and to talk about it is viewed as an important accomplishment in their growing awareness and understanding of print. The primary focus is on helping children discover and strengthen their personal understandings about the reading process. Teachers may introduce or reinforce concepts of their choice when appropriate, however, and may use this time to informally observe and monitor children's development of selected aspects of reading.

Shared writing and reading concludes with the group returning to reconsider the entire text as they follow the teacher's *rereading* once again. Thus, the children have moved from the whole to the parts and back to the whole.

Figure 2 shows a chart that was constructed in a kindergarten classroom involved in an exploration of the five senses. On the day the chart was made, the children popped popcorn. They discussed the various sounds associated with the pop-

Figure 2
Chart Generated During Unit on Five Senses

Popcorn, Popcorn
In the bag -- soft, slow sound.
On the fire -- hard, fast sound.
On the fire -- popping, popping sound.
In the mouth -- crunchy, crunchy sound.
Popcorn, Popcorn

corn—in the bag prior to popping, over the fire during the popping, and in their mouths after the popping. The resulting chart turned out to be a poetic retelling.

Later, during independent writing, several of the children decided to draw and write about what they had done. One child's piece included the table, the popcorn popper, the hot plate, and the teacher, whom she appropriately labeled MSTA YS (Mr. Weitz). It is notable that this occurred early in the year and that it was a first and very spontaneous attempt by this youngster to use writing with her drawing. The growing sense that she could communicate through writing is evidenced by her comment, "People need to know who that is."

Independent Writing

Each day, children are given opportunities to express themselves through drawing and writing as a communicative process. The writing may occur at a writing center set up with a variety of paper and writing utensils, or it may be handled as a whole class activity.

Teachers who use writing centers generally allow children to take turns in that center, just as they would in the block area or the dramatic play area. As much as possible, either the teacher, an aide, or a volunteer will be on hand to confer with the children about their writing. Although children are encouraged to use drawing and invented spelling (their own approximations of conventional spelling), some teachers combine this with dictation activities when children request it. Most often, however, dictation is used as the basis for reading activities.

The content of children's writing is varied. It frequently grows out of the morning's theme related activities. Thus, for many children, the inquiry activities serve as prewriting. At this level, drawing frequently precedes or is highly integrated with the writing. In addition to the drawing, children's texts will reflect a broad range of development — from scribbles and strings of letters that may be interpreted only by the student to labeling with initial consonants, words, and sentences used to extend and expand on the pictorial representation (see Sulzby, Teale, & Kamberelis, this volume).

When children have finished their writing, they are encouraged to complete the composing process by asking themselves questions such as "Is my drawing or writing just the way I want it to be? Do I need to change anything or do anything else? Am I satisfied with my work?" In this way, children are encouraged to develop the habit of looking back and reflecting on what they have done and to make their own decisions about any revisions and adjustments they feel are needed.

Other opportunities for independent writing are offered in a more informal and incidental manner. For example, some classrooms have mailboxes for every student so that children may write notes to one another. In one classroom, a logbook was located near the gerbils so children could record their feeding.

Independent Reading

One of the prerequisites of a Core Experience Curriculum is an attractive, well stocked classroom library. Children need daily access to an abundance of storybooks and informational books of all kinds. Having at least five books per child is a good goal. Time is set aside daily for children to browse through books of their choice. Children also may opt to use the classroom library during center time.

Books are displayed at eye level so they are easily accessible to the children. Carpeting and comfortable pillows provide an inviting atmosphere for children's browsing, page turning, discussion of pictures, and participation in oral recall of text previously read aloud by the teacher. Teachers circulate among the children as much as possible observing children's reading behaviors and briefly conferring with them about their reading.

In addition to the center based independent reading, teachers provide time for the entire group to select books for reading alone or sharing with a partner or small group. In one class, the daily read aloud session was followed by ten minutes in which children were allowed to select a book from the reading corner, find a comfortable place to sit alone or with a friend, and enjoy the book.

Although the children were often noisy and even exuberant during these sessions, they were decidedly on task. Youngsters could be overheard arguing over the correct name of a letter in an alphabet book or laughing uproariously over a funny picture from a book they had enjoyed earlier when the teacher read it aloud. Others might be found retelling a picture book story, employing a very serious tone and reflecting the style and mannerisms of the teacher. The teacher circulated among the children, noting the kind and quality of the reading and reading like behaviors among them.

Read Aloud and Response

Time is set aside each day for reading aloud to children and allowing them to respond to literature. A variety of books are selected, many of which may be related to the theme being studied. Quality fiction and nonfiction literature is used. Books with enlarged text (big books) and those with predictable language are especially valued.

Teachers structure the read aloud sessions in terms of what they might do before, during, and after the reading. The strategies they choose are determined by the developmental level of the group and the qualities of the particular book they are reading. Following are some examples of read aloud strategies that might be employed (see also Cullinan and Mason, Peterman, & Kerr, this volume).

Before the reading. The book is introduced or reintroduced to the children by giving the title and

Class Album

- Take photographs of pupils engaged in a variety of activities at school.
- Mount pictures on colored paper, two or three to a page, leaving space between the pictures to write captions and extra space on the left margin to punch holes.
- Under each picture, write brief sentences about what is depicted.
- Whenever possible, use repetitive language on a page, such as Sam rolls in the snow; Ginger jumps in the snow; we play in the snow.
- Laminate each page or cover with plastic.
- Put the pages in a binder and add to them during the year.
- Separate as a chapter a group of pictures depicting a particular activity.
- Give the book a title such as "Our Class Book" or "All About Us."
- Share the book for storytime, just as you would any storybook.
- Place the book in the library corner for children to read at their leisure.

Isabel Beaton
Prekindergarten Teacher
P.S. 62
New York, New York

---

author. Children may be asked to use this information to predict what the story may be about. If appropriate, a brief discussion may take place about relevant concepts to be encountered. Introductions are always kept brief.

During the reading. Teachers build positive attitudes about reading by showing their own personal pleasure and interest prior to and during the reading. They read in a lively manner, displaying interest in the story plot and the language. If big books are used, teachers may track the print with their hand, a ruler, or a pointer. At times, the teacher may pause and ask children what they think might happen next. Student questions are acknowledged and answered. Discussion during the reading is encouraged as long as it is focused and does not detract from the reading. Participation in the reading, particularly when stories have a repetitive line or refrain, also is encouraged.

After the reading. Students talk about the story in ways that personalize it for them. They are encouraged to ask questions of the teacher and of one another. An atmosphere of sharing prevails rather than one of the teacher questioning to test comprehension.

Responding to literature. Students respond to literature in a variety of ways. These include engaging in group discussion, pantomiming a story reread by the teacher, role playing scenes from a story, acting out an entire story, reenacting the story with puppets, retelling the story, and interpreting the story through art activities. Responding to literature is viewed as a means of reformulating or reexperiencing the story using a new modality. It is used as a means of strengthening children's understanding and appreciation of stories and helping them to internalize the structure of stories.

Sharing

Each day, children are given opportunities to share their ideas about the content being studied and to share relevant experiences that occur during

A Web of Activities

Inquiry Activities

Plant lima beans,
  observe growth,
  measure
Open seeds, examine,
  discuss
Plant garden outside
Plant seeds in plastic
  cups with moist towel
Plant seeds on sponge
Experiment to show how
  plants get food
Compare growth of
  different seeds

**Read Aloud and Response —
to Literature**

The Little Red Hen
  Discuss steps to make
  flour, dramatize
The Turnip, Janina,
*The Great Big Enormous
  Turnip,* A. Tolstoy
  Compare versions
  Cook a turnip
  Perform puppet show
Mushroom in the Rain
  Discuss how rain helps
  plants grow

Sharing

Independently written stories
Independent reading (best part,
  favorite page, picture)
Something I learned about seeds/plants
Planting experiences at home

**from
SEEDS
to
PLANTS**

Shared Writing/Reading

List what seeds need to
  grow
List steps in planting
  process
Chart plant growth and
  development
Recipe for vegetable
  soup
Poem "Maytime Magic,"
  M. Watts
List responses to
  The Carrot Seed,
  R. Krauss

Independent Writing

Draw/write stories about
  planting/growing things
Logs of lima bean growth
Use *Cherries and Cherry Pits,*
  V. Williams; share and discuss
  as example of child writer

Independent Reading

(Add to book collection)
The Seed the Squirrel Dropped, H. Hetie;
Jack and the Bean Tree, G. Haley; *Planting a Rainbow,* L. Ehlert; *Growing Vegetable Soup,* L. Ehlert; *Eat the Fruit, Plant
the Seed,* M. E. Selsam; *How a Seed
Grows,* H. Jordan.

Sample Web of Activities Based on Core Experience Curriculum

Dorothy E. Belin
Mindy Mandel-Werner
New York, New York

Strickland

the day. Independent reading, writing, and drawing make good content for sharing. Children's activities at the art, block, and dramatic play centers also make good material for sharing. Much of the sharing may actually occur at the centers before clean up time. Children may share in individual conversations with the teacher or in small or large group settings. When children share in group settings, attention should be paid to developing classroom guidelines for this activity. These should not be presented as a list of rules, but should evolve over time as children see the need for some established behavior. Teachers' own modeling of how to hold a book or piece of writing and talk about it and their demonstration of appropriate ways to respond as a member of the audience go a long way toward helping children understand their roles as presenters and members of the audience during sharing time. The teaching idea relating to seeds and plants shows a sample web of activities based on the core experiences.

Organizing the Day

Organization and management are key concerns for teachers who attempt to put a holistic literacy program in place. Their goal is to offer students a comprehensive program in which the learning objectives for listening, speaking, reading, writing, mathematics, the social and physical sciences, creative expression, and thinking can be clearly identified and accounted for. Yet these curricular objectives must be presented to the students in an integrated and meaningful manner, not treated as specific skill objectives or organized around materials designed to teach a particular subject. The core experiences allow teachers to do this in a manner very consistent with young children's need for variability and diversity in their day.

Figure 3 shows how one kindergarten teacher scheduled the day around the core experiences. A look at the list of activities reveals that language, literacy, and the content theme (science and social studies) permeate the day. Less obvious, perhaps, is where some of the other curricular areas reside. For example, math is always a part of inquiry. A math center, established early in the year, serves to extend the ideas presented during inquiry. Here,

children manipulate materials for counting, measurement, and estimation. Charts for shared writing and reading may include graphs and geometric shapes as well as narrative discourse. Teachers in full day programs generally add lunch, rest time, and large muscle activities to the daily schedule. Read aloud, sharing, and center time may be either repeated or extended in full day programs.

Assessment

Assessment of children's oral and written language development is done primarily through observational procedures and the collection of performance samples. Teale, Hiebert, and Chittenden (1987) have identified seven aspects of children's literacy development upon which developmental data should be gathered. These are listed here along with suggestions for the core experiences upon which a teacher might focus attention to observe their development.

1. Concepts of the functions and conventions of written language—shared writing and reading, independent reading, independent writing, and read aloud time.
2. Text comprehension such as the ability to understand and recall books that are read to them—independent reading, read aloud time, and sharing.
3. Abilities to read print commonly found in their home and community environments—inquiry activities and sharing.
4. Emergent reading of storybooks (strategies children use to read books before they are able to read conventionally)—independent reading, read aloud time, and sharing.
5. Metalinguistic awareness (including word awareness and phonological awareness)—shared writing and independent reading.
6. Emergent writing strategies (including composing, spelling, and strategies for re-reading their own writing)—shared writing and reading, independent writing, and sharing.
7. Knowledge of letters, letter sounds, and the relationships between them—shared writing and reading, independent writing, and independent reading.

Figure 3
Sample Daily Schedule for a Half Day Kindergarten

Approximate Time Frame	Core Experience	Organizational Pattern	Curricular Focus
15 minutes	(Entry)	–	
20 minutes	*Inquiry Activities* | | | (lead to) | | ↓	Whole Group	Social and Physical Sciences, Oral Language, Problem Solving, Math
20 minutes	*Shared Writing and Reading*	Whole Group or Small Group	Reading, Writing
30 minutes	*(Snack, Large Muscle Activities, Music)*	Whole Group	Motor Development, Music
50 minutes (Includes all centers – art, math, etc.)	*Independent Writing* and *Independent Reading*	Center based: Small group or Individual	Reading, Writing and other centers (art, math, etc.)
15 minutes	*Read Aloud*	Whole Group or Small Group	Reading, Writing, Oral Language
15 minutes	*Sharing*		
15 minutes	(Dismissal)	–	

Strickland

Functional Uses of Print

Children need to be given frequent opportunities to use print and to see print being used functionally. Here are two examples from classrooms where teachers are providing these opportunities.

This sign up sheet was located on the door to Deborah Davis's second grade classroom. Her students became very adept at reading aloud, telling stories, and reciting poetry for other classes.

Please sign up if you would like a
    Poet
    Storyteller
    Book read aloud to your class			

Teacher's Name	Poet	Storyteller	Read Aloud
Mrs. Jason	✓		
Mr. Brownley			✓

The chart below was located on the wall of Annette Ayers's first grade classroom. Children were encouraged to enter their favorite titles whenever they wished.

Recommended Book List		
Title	Author	Reader

Deborah Davis and Annette Ayers
P. S. 220
New York, New York

Many inventories, scales, checklists, and documentation procedures for use in monitoring and analyzing children's literacy development have appeared in the literature (Chittenden, this volume; Clay, 1979; Heald-Taylor, 1987; Sulzby, 1985; Teale, Hiebert, & Chittenden, 1987; Watson, 1987).

In addition to the categories of literacy development listed, children's oral language must be assessed. The inquiry activities, shared writing and reading, sharing activities, and read aloud time (particularly response to literature involving oral language activities such as story retelling, dramatics, and discussion) provide excellent resources for collecting data about children's oral language development. See Genishi and Dyson (1984) for good ideas on assessing language development.

An important goal of the Core Experience Curriculum is to link assessment to instruction as closely as possible. Collecting data about children's development is an ongoing natural function of the day. The information collected is reflected upon and used as the basis for planning and intervention where needed. It also becomes the basis upon which children's progress is reported to parents and administrators.

The Core Experience Curriculum was developed in response to the questions and concerns of many teachers and curriculum coordinators, who are attempting to translate new theoretical perspectives on emergent literacy into effective practice in existing school structures. It makes use of what the research says about young children's literacy development and what teachers say they need in order to operate effectively. It is a framework that teachers recognize as manageable and efficient, yet it allows for movement toward a program that is more consistent with the new knowledge about how young children learn to read and write.

References

Clay, M.M. *The early detection of reading difficulties.* Portsmouth, NH: Heinemann, 1979.

Genishi, D., and Dyson, A.H. *Language assessment in the early years.* Norwood, NJ: Ablex, 1984.

Heald-Taylor, G. Predictable literature selections and activities for language arts instruction. *The Reading Teacher,* 1987, *41,* 6-9.

Strickland, D., and Ogle, D. Teachers coping with change: Assessing the early literacy curriculum. In L.M. Morrow and J. Smith (Eds.), *The role of assessment and measurement: Early literacy instruction.* Englewood Cliffs, NJ: Prentice Hall, in press.

Sulzby, E. Children's emergent reading of favorite storybooks: A developmental study. *Reading Research Quarterly,* 1985, *20,* 458-481.

Teale, W.H. Bringing testing and teaching together in the early childhood classroom: Developmentally appropriate assessment of reading and writing as a case in point. *Elementary School Journal,* in press.

Teale, W.H., Hiebert, E.H., Chittenden, E.A. Assessing young children's literacy development. *The Reading Teacher,* 1987, *40,* 772-777.

Watson, D. (Ed.). *Ideas and insights.* Champaign, IL: National Council of Teachers of English, 1987.

CHAPTER TWELVE

Fostering Needed Change in Early Literacy Programs

Jerome C. Harste

Virginia A. Woodward

In this chapter we review what researchers have found that young children know about language and literacy, we discuss concerns about existing school practices in light of these findings, and we conclude with a series of policy guidelines for changing early literacy programs.

Not long ago, it was believed that young children learned oral language naturally but that written language had to be formally taught. During this period, it was not uncommon to find the language curriculum in preschool and kindergarten organized around "Letter A Day," "Letter B Day," and so on. Often these programs were formal, asking children to *study* rather than *use* language. This instructional trend was primarily the result of misconceptions about how young children learn.

We know better now. Research has shown that long before preschool and kindergarten children encounter formal language programs they know much about oral and written language (Hall, 1987). Based on this research, language curricula for nursery school, kindergarten, and primary children must change.

We now know, for example, that literacy learning is ongoing from infancy and strongly influenced by children's social and cultural background (Heath, 1983; Taylor, 1983). Reading and writing experiences at school should permit children to build upon their existing knowledge of language and literacy to further the development of their communication skills. Learning should take place in a supportive environment where children can build a positive attitude toward themselves and their use of language. For optimal learning, teachers should provide experiences that involve children actively, highlighting oral and written language as well as other communication systems.

We believe that high quality programs of language and literacy should be available for all preschool and kindergarten children (see policy statement in appendix). The word *program* is meant to emphasize *curriculum* and the fact that both what is taught in the name of language and literacy and how it is taught are of concern. To clarify these concerns, we initially review what researchers have found that young children know about language and literacy prior to coming to school. In light of these findings, we discuss current educational practices and trends of concern to educators.

We conclude the chapter with a series of policy recommendations. Because these policies are intended for use by teachers, parents, school administrators, policymakers, and others who provide educational programs for preschool and kindergarten children, we illustrate each recommendation with examples of appropriate action.

What Young Children Know about Language and Literacy

Language is learned through use rather than through practice exercises on how to use language. The more frequently children experience a particular language setting, the more successful they will be in producing appropriate texts for this context. Through invitations to participate in language events, children learn language, learn about language, and learn through language simultaneously (Halliday, 1978).

Because the markings four year old children produce prior to formal schooling reflect the written language of their culture, we can no longer assume that children come to school without some knowledge of written language. In contrast to Najeeba's (from Saudi Arabia) and Ofer's (from Israel), Dawn's writing looks distinctly like English (see Figure 1).

Because the markings three year old children make when asked to draw a picture of themselves look quite different from the markings they make when asked to write their name, we can no longer dismiss these efforts as mere scribbling. By age six, children move freely between communication systems in producing a text (see Figure 2).

These data suggest that children have internalized many rules as well as conceptualized processes for learning and using language and other communication systems.

**Figure 1
Cross Cultural Writing Samples**

Dawn, a four year old from the United States, writes in unconventional script using a series of wavy lines. Each line is written from left to right. Dawn creates a page of such lines starting at the top of her  page and finishing at the bottom of her page.

Najeeba, a four year old from Saudi Arabia, writes in unconventional script using a series of very intricate curlicue formations with lots of dots over the script. When she completes her story she says, "Here, but  you can't read it 'cause I wrote it in Arabic and in Arabic we use a lot more dots than you do in English!"

Ofer, a four year old from Israel, prints first right to left, then left to right, using a series of rectangular and triangular shapes to create his story, which his grandmother says, "looks like Hebrew, but it's  not." Her concern because he sometimes writes "backwards" sounds like the concerns of many parents and teachers in the U.S., with the difference being that left to right is "backwards" in Hebrew, and right to left "backwards" in English.

Harste, Woodward, & Burke, 1984. Used by permission of senior author.

Harste and Woodward

By ages five and six, most children have sorted out how language varies by context of use and have begun to explore the graphophonemic system of language. Their phonetic writing has been called invented spelling and has been found to progress systematically and predictably (see Figure 3).

By age four, the texts that children produce when asked to write a story as opposed to a letter are beginning to be distinctive. Their stories sound like stories, look like stories, and function like stories. Their letters sound like letters, look like letters, and function like letters. By age six, these distinctions are well developed and much more marked (see Figure 4).

Most children as young as three can read "Stop" on a stop sign, "McDonald's" when shown the golden arches, and "Crest" when shown a Crest toothpaste carton. By six, all children can read these and other items of environmental print they frequently encounter. The findings mean that we do not have to teach young children to read but, rather, we need to support and expand their continued understanding of reading.

By age three, when asked to read or pretend to read a book, children start to vary their normal speech to sound like "book talk." By age six, children who have been read to frequently have internalized the structure of stories in their culture and can produce many fine stories of their own (see Figure 5). By six, most children associate books with reading.

Figure 2
Alison, Age Six
Uninterrupted Writing Sample
Created after Telephone Conversation

Notes on Transcription

Alison said that her picture showed that after church on Sunday Jennifer (J.T.) and she (A.H.) were going to get together to "play ballerina." Jennifer would bring her ballet slippers, leotards, and hair ribbons in a bag while Alison would get equivalent items from her dresser. (Particularly note Alison's use of math, art, and language to placehold her message.)

From M. Siegel, *Reading as signification,* unpublished doctoral dissertation, 1983.

Figure 3
Invented Spelling Patterns

- Spelling the way it sounds
  Example: Jress for Dress (Js and Ds are formed at the same spot in the mouth (point of articulation).

- Spelling the way it looks
  Example: Fro for For (O added because "it didn't look right" indicating visual memory was involved).

- Spelling the way it means
  Example: Wasapanataem for "Once upon a time." (As a story starts, this phrase tells the reader/listener to suspend reality. Rather than perceive this phrase as a series of individual words, it is logical that children should see it as a single unit of meaning.)

Learning proceeds from the known to the unknown. Comprehension and learning are now seen as a search for patterns that connect, and growth is seen as a search for ever wider patterns. Instruction needs to start where the children are in their learning and proceed from there. Children need to be given opportunities to make language their own by making connections with their current life and background information. In short, there is no other place to begin in language than in terms of the language user's current background experience.

Language learning is risky business. Children learn best in low risk environments where exploration is accepted and current efforts are socially supported and understood. Language is a social event. Most of what we know about language has been learned from being in the presence of others.

Figure 4
Robin, Age Six
Story and Letter

Transcriptions

Story: The World's Greatest Dog
My dog
Tina
and my friend's
dog Ruby
are very nice
dogs. One day
a little girl
fell in the
water. Ruby and
Tina saved her.
The end.

Letter: Dear Dad
I love you. Is the
cat okay? The puppies
already have their
eyes open. Tina
had 7 puppies. Grandma's
puppies are 1 month
old. Willy said
Hi. My mom painted
my room. We got
an apple tree.
Oops, it's a pear tree.
Marcie said Hi.
I went to see
Gulliver and The
Great Muppet
Caper. Love Robin.

Harste, Woodward, & Burke, 1984. Used by permission of senior author.

Figure 5
Jason, Age Six
The Little Elf Story

Transcription
(Page 1)
The
Little Elf
by Jacob

(Pages 2 and 3)
Once an
elf was
very silly
but he
wasn't silly
at art.

(Pages 4 and 5)
He was
very good
at art
and liked
it.

(Pages 6 and 7)
He was
a happy
elf.
The end.

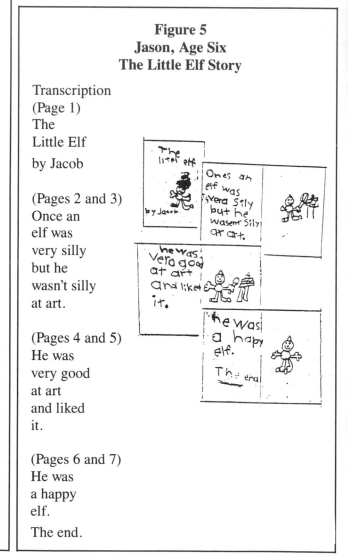

Harste and Woodward

New Potentials and Old Concerns

Although teaching reading and writing should not be the primary purpose of preschool and kindergarten, a well designed program can enhance children's already considerable language skills by providing ample opportunity for them to use reading and writing in their daily activities. The soundest preschool programs are based on the knowledge that children learn best from firsthand experience. In addition to clay, sand, water, and other materials to touch, pour, sift, mold, pound, and manipulate, there should be lots of printed materials around to provide opportunities for the same kind of experimentation with language.

Preschool and kindergarten programs that highlight literacy are places where storytime and books play a prominent role; where children are encouraged to draw and write independently or with their teachers and peers; where signs made by teachers and students are posted; and where mailboxes, charts, schedules, and sign in activities serve a functional purpose. Centers such as housekeeping, music, art, dramatic play, blocks, math, and manipulatives contain appropriate materials. General materials such as magazines, menus, message pads, typewriters, and blank paper also are provided. The centers serve as open invitations for children to use language and other sign systems in their play.

Visitors and planned excursions are provided to widen young children's view of the world. Children are encouraged and helped to use language to express their ideas, feelings, and frustrations. There are opportunities to choose individual activities or to play with others.

Concerns Raised by Inappropriate Curricula

In light of curricular possibilities such as these, certain trends in education are viewed with concern by early childhood educators. Many pre-first grade children, for example, are being subjected to rigid, academic prereading programs. These programs emphasize academic skill development and paper and pencil activities that fail to take into account how oral and written language are learned naturally.

In the curriculum, too much attention is focused upon isolated skill development or abstract parts of the reading and writing process, rather than upon the integration of oral language, writing, and listening. Too little attention is placed upon reading for pleasure and using reading and writing as tools for learning and exploration.

Inappropriate methods of instruction result in curricula that promote passivity instead of activity, creative expression, and critical thinking. Programs are judged on the basis of how quiet children are, how much seatwork is required, and the number of workbook pages completed. In short, production takes precedence over exploration.

Concerns Raised by Accelerated Programs

Other concerns are raised when decisions related to the curriculum are made based upon political and economic expediency rather than knowledge of how young children learn. In many cases, concerned adults who want children to succeed apply adult educational standards to the curriculum for young children and pressure early childhood programs to demonstrate that children really are learning. The pressures of accelerated programs do not allow children to be risk takers as they experiment with language and internalize concepts about how language operates. Too little attention is given to background experience and individual development.

Concerns Raised by Standardized Testing

The pressure to achieve high scores on standardized tests has resulted in wide scale retention of students, questionable remediation programs and practices, and a further narrowing of the language curriculum. Staff pressures have resulted in individuals who have had little or no early childhood training being assigned to teach young children.

The following recommendations grow out of concerns such as these. Rather than dwell on the negative, these recommendations accent the positive, given what we currrently know about the relationships among teaching and learning, curriculum, young children, and the evolution of literacy.

Recommendations

A literacy curriculum needs to support the success of each learner. All children come to school with a background of experience. Because "community" and "connectedness" are the hallmarks of learning, educators cannot afford to assume that the children they work with have no experience.

Similarly, although children differ in terms of their knowledge of oral and written language, research has shown that all children know something about written language. Learning begins with the known. Even if the children can read only "Stop" on a stop sign and "McDonald's" when they see the golden arches, this is a place to begin. Some teachers begin with an environmental print walk. Others ask children to bring labels from jars and boxes they can read at home. With these materials, teachers make books and support children in their efforts to write what they know about these products.

I · D · E · A · S
You Can Use

Use Open Ended Activities

Open ended activities invite children to explore a topic on their own terms. Unlike worksheets, there is no limit to what children can do or where they can begin. Children can pursue a topic in terms of their own particular interest, background experience, and hypotheses they are currently interested in testing.

In one early childhood program, children are given the opportunity to explore art through open ended activities. Building upon what we have learned about language, children are initially invited to create their own art from clay as well as explore pieces of fine art displayed in the classroom. Children are given journals to record the observations they make. During discussion time, children share their observations and discuss what they think the artist was trying to say.

During his involvement in this program, five year old Victor made a bull. When he was done, he took it over and sat it next to Picasso's bull. With his hand on his chin, he pensively announced, "Boy, Picasso didn't know much about bulls, did he?"

At another point in the program, fine art postcards were given to children. Victor selected a Modigliani portrait of a woman. In his journal, he recorded his observations in invented spelling: "She has a long neck. She has skneey eyebrows." At discussion time, the group discussed Victor's interest in lines and what the artist was trying to say in using them. Maggie, another five year old, selected a postcard of a little Victorian girl. Her observations related to her interpretation of the picture, "A little girl who lived in a castle with a King and a Queen."

Because the activities in this program were open ended, children were free to explore what they were currently interested in and, through discussion, have these interests expanded and extended.

Adapted from an idea by Laura Westberg
Former Director of the Campus Children's Center
Bloomington, Indiana

Harste and Woodward

Children should have many opportunities for writing.

Invitations to read and write must be open ended (Harste, Short, & Burke, 1988). Open ended activities allow children to enter and exit at their own level of interest and involvement. Even though teachers may specifically plan activities for the purpose of highlighting particular features or processes of literacy, children must be given the choice to focus on those demonstrations they find interesting. Teachers must not only accept the rights of children to attend to things they find interesting, but also must realize that it is through this process of relating current demonstrations to exisitng hypotheses that learning occurs.

Books and pencils should be in children's hands from their first day in school. Children's readiness is never an issue with open ended activities. The real issue is whether we, as teachers, can accept and value varying responses.

All educators need to appreciate and understand the role language plays in a system of knowing. Language is a process of symbolization. Language is the vehicle by which we make intuition public and communicable. This basic process is what education is all about. A theory of language learning is both a theory of learning and a theory of education.

All children come to school already involved in this process. Rather than denying the validity of children's involvement, the role of the early childhood educator is best seen as supporting their continued involvement by supporting authorship and ownership of the process of literacy learning.

Children need to have what they know confirmed and accepted so that no matter what the culture, the background experience, or the language facility, they feel good about themselves and see themselves as readers and writers. If what learners know is not valued, that knowledge will atrophy. Good instructional programs build upon and extend the experiential background of all children in terms of their knowledge of language and the world.

A literacy curriculum needs to be focused on learning. Classrooms in which literacy is highlighted are characterized as "communities of learners." Reading and writing are used functionally and presented as tools and toys for learning.

Language is learned through use. The only way to learn a process is by engaging in that process. Children need to be given daily opportunities to use reading and writing for functional purposes. Sign In sheets allow children to take their own attendance, generate lunch counts, and see who is or isn't present. Written conversations and mailboxes allow children to communicate with one another without disturbing classmates. Class composed books provide the opportunity for all children to write and make their contributions as part of a group.

Programs that are focused on learning involve risk and exploration. Classroom environments that are best for language learning are those that assume rather than eradicate mistakes. Mistakes are not so much failures on the part of teachers as they are opportunities for self correction and growth on the part of learners. Without mistakes, there is no evidence of learning.

Invitations to talk about reading and writing experiences can help children see reading and writing as tools for learning: "How are you different now from who you were before? What do you know now that you didn't know before?" Literature should be seen as a way for children to view their world through new eyes, rather than as a vehicle for teaching reading per se.

In the final analysis, our interest in reading and writing is an interest in learning. Reading is not so much taking meaning from texts as it is sharing meaning about texts. Writing is not simply a process of recording on paper already perfected ideas, but also a vehicle for organizing thought.

A literacy curriculum needs to let learners explore language in all its complexity. Children are capable of monitoring and directing their own literacy learning when they have many opportunities to encounter oral and written language in familiar situations. In too many classrooms, children are not given opportunities to talk their way through problems despite the fact that most of what they will learn throughout life will come as a function of speech. Unfortunately, children will encounter more words on worksheets than they will in books. While keeping things quiet and simple may help children master a particular rule quickly, this type of instruction does little to help children understand and use communication systems in the complex, interactive contexts they encounter outside of school. The complexity of literacy events actually supports learning.

Reading and writing are multimodal events. This means that there is no pure instance of just reading or writing. Writers read their work, sketch, talk to others, and do any number of things during writing. Readers compose, ask for clarifications, talk, and sometimes draw pictures in order to clarify what they are reading. The multimodal nature of literacy provides multiple entry points for understanding messages and for learning about literacy.

When children have opportunities to experience natural communication, they are able to form hypotheses that reflect the irregularities of communication as well as the ways in which it is systematic. To be strategic, readers and writers must vary their cognitive processes by content and context. Literacy is context specific. Different strategies are brought to the foreground when reading and interpreting a poem than when reading a content area selection. Too often, what children do in school bears no relationship to what real readers and writers do outside of school. Rather than learning to read and write, the real trick in school often is learning how to learn how to read and write. This is not how it should be. Children need opportunities to vary the processes they use in terms of content and context as they would occur in nonschool settings.

Classrooms must be places where children can see others using language for real purposes. Language is a social event. We have learned most of what we know about language from being in the presence of others. Natural language settings provide multiple demonstrations. Children learn by attending to these demonstrations and by orches-

Teacher as Learner

Directly after lunch, many teachers read a book chapter to their students. To demonstrate herself as a learner, one teacher instructs her students to "go ahead and discuss the chapter" as she steps outside the group and, with pad in hand, records their responses.

After collecting data of this sort, she begins to classify responses and seek articles by others who have studied student responses to literature. Later in the year, she shares with students her data as well as her initial observations and what other authors have had to say on the subject. Students give suggestions for her analysis and and discuss why and how her data differ from others. In this way, she actively demonstrates for her students ways of using reading and writing to learn.

As observed in Karen Smith's classroom
Herrera Elementary School
Phoenix, Arizona

trating new ones with those they have already sorted out. Children in environments where music, drama, art, math, and language are used for real purposes have access to demonstrations of the potential uses of these media for communication. Attention to demonstrations is generative. It is a means of learning how something might be done rather than how it must be done.

Although children may see their parents read, rarely does a parent discuss with the child his or her difficulty in understanding something or what strategies were used to resolve reading and writing problems. Similarly, children rarely see parents using reading and writing as a tool for outgrowing their current selves. This means that if we want to give children a notion of what it truly means to be literate, teachers and other adults should engage in the same communicative activities in which they ask children to engage. In such classroom environments, children learn from the teacher and from one another.

It is important that children be put in situations where they can see the strategies of successful writ-

ten language use and learning demonstrated. Teachers should invite parents, administrators, professional writers, and others into the classroom on a regular basis. While many educators believe that what people can do individually was first done socially, it is important to understand that learning how to use the social group as a vehicle to support learning may be the most important strategy acquired in a good literacy curriculum.

A literacy curriculum should help children expand their communication potential through the use of language as well as art, music, and other sign systems. There are many forms of authorship. The alternate sign systems of art, music, drama, math, language, and dance provide learners with different modes of representation by which to conceptualize their world and make their ideas public. Young children learn the form and function of each of these sign systems through use and experience. Learning in one sign system supports learning in another.

Students should be encouraged to use various forms of communication to express themselves in all subject areas. The choice of alternate communication systems should be respected, as should the more traditional choice of language as a mode of expression.

Organizationally, classrooms should have areas for art, music, math, cooking, blocks, and drama, as well as reading and writing. Beginning literacy instruction should provide opportunities to interact with print in all of these contexts using a multitude of expressive forms: listening to stories, sharing and talking about books, writing and illustrating stories, composing stories in block play, enacting stories through drama, interpreting stories in art and music, reading and writing recipes for cooking, interpreting music through dance, composing and writing music, writing math problems, reading poetry, and reading and writing predictable books.

No longer can we omit art, music, dance, and drama from the curriculum because they are frills. Nor should they be taught as separate skill classes. Students are unlikely to be fooled into believing that alternate literacies are valuable if the school confines them to a brief period a week.

Curriculum and curriculum development must be placed in the hands of the classroom teacher. The function of the curriculum is to provide perspective. A good curriculum sets directions and provides examples of the kinds of settings believed to permit children to take the mental trips we associate with successful language use and learning.

Professional educators have a responsibility to plan a tailor made curriculum for the children in their classrooms, using all available resources. These resources include observations of children, textbook series, curricular guides, and ideas from peers. In addition, this "paper curriculum" should reflect what is currently known about language and literacy, schooling, successful language use and learning, child growth and development, the relationship between teaching and learning, and more.

However, the "real curriculum" happens in the heads of the children. When children do not take the mental trips teachers envision them taking, new activities must be designed. This process is called curriculum development. Curriculum and curriculum development are dynamic and involve change based on a reflective look at the relationship between teaching and learning in specific classroom contexts.

For too long, administrators, state departments, and publishing houses have set the curricular agendas in schools. The underlying assumption has been that since so many teachers are incapable of planning their own curricula, these curricula must be imposed from outside.

For curricula to be dynamic, children need to be our curricular informants. To be effective, curricula must be negotiated at the point of utterance among teachers and children. In light of what we now know about good teaching, we no longer can afford to ask whether teachers can plan their own curricula but we need to assume that as professionals they are doing it implicitly. Since our assumption is that curriculum development is what teaching is all about, the role of the principal changes to that of helping teachers become more explicit about what they are doing in this critical process.

Administrators must support teachers in reclaiming their classrooms. Trying new ideas is risky. But just as children take risks as they explore language, teachers need to be free to take risks as they explore literacy instruction.

Teacher support groups have proven to be an effective vehicle for supporting teachers as they develop a collective voice. Peers help teachers question whether their practices are theoretically sound as well as articulate a practical theory of literacy instruction.

Administrators have an important role in supporting teachers as they learn collaboratively and work toward improving literacy instruction. It is their role to encourage and support professional development by holding inservice programs, encouraging teachers to attend and to present at professional meetings, and establishing teacher support groups focusing on curriculum development and evaluation.

If individual school principals must support their teachers in developing sound literacy curricula, then principals must be given autonomy for their schools. Principals and teachers should be given freedom in deciding on instructional materials, instructional strategies, and evaluation measures.

Storying

One researcher reports that he begins collaborative projects by sitting down with the teacher to view a particular teaching event. Instead of discussing specific things, both he and the teacher write narratives in which they try to capture what they perceived as being the most salient features of what they saw. By comparing these narratives, they begin to identify what and why certain tensions exist between the two accounts. This activity helps them to identify unstated assumptions and beliefs and leads them to new ways of thinking and change.

If knowledge develops socially through the stories we tell, this strategy would seem to be useful for improving communication and understanding among the adults responsible for children's educational welfare. Teachers, parents, and administrators might try viewing the same activity (perhaps videotaped), writing their perceptions in narrative style, and then sharing them with one another. Through discussion, participants will learn what ideas others think are important, as well as grow in their understanding of effective early childhood curricula.

Adapted from the work of Fred Ericksen, University of Pennsylvania
Gordon Wells, Ontario Institute for Studies in Education
Harold Rose, University of London

Principals and teachers must be willing to speak out against practices that violate what we know about language and learning. Recent examples include issues relating to textbook adoption, assertive discipline, time on task legislation, effective teaching, and more. When policies limit what becomes possible in the curriculum or stymie teachers in their efforts to continue to develop as professionals, administrators must support teachers in developing a collective voice on behalf of children.

A literacy curriculum sees culture and parents as participants and partners in learning. We often treat culture as if it were something children could leave at the schoolhouse steps. Culture is not an entity, but rather part of how you make sense of the world. Operationally, it is when you find yourself sounding like your mother despite the fact that you promised yourself never to sound that way.

In most public schools, the curriculum educates learners to the goals, values, and attitudes of the dominant culture. In a pluralistic society like ours, this practice can cause learners to perceive schooling as strange and to become alienated from their own family culture. If education is to help children move ahead from where they are in their experiential background and their knowledge base, it is critical that teachers become culturally sensitive and learn to respect the family cultures of their pupils.

Administrators and teachers need to involve parents in their children's formal education in a meaningful way. Parent education programs can explain how literacy is learned, why open ended instructional activities are used, why process approaches to reading and writing theoretically support literacy learning, and how learning will be evaluated. These programs need to consider the many ways in which the family and community can become part of the content of instruction. This involvement should go well beyond food fairs and special holidays to the actual study of what literacy means in the community and what forms of literacy are highlighted in the culture.

Parents are their children's first teachers, and this role should not be taken away. Research tells us that children who are successful readers and writers are children who come from homes where parents have been involved in their learning.

School involvement should be more than just parent meetings. It should include opportunities for parents to participate in classroom activities. When parents feel a part of the school, they are more apt to extend their participation to more meaningful literacy events at home. Parents need to be given choices as to how they might participate in classrooms, just as young learners select from alternative options for learning. Encourage parents to get involved in reading with students, sharing in content area learning, making blank books, typing manuscripts, helping children make films and compose music, and going on class excursions.

Effective programs of evaluation engage administrators, board members, parents, teachers, and pupils in the twin processes of reflection and growth. The chief purpose of evaluation is to improve instructional decision making. From an instructional perspective, the key question is "In light of what is known about language and literacy and how these students are performing, what instruction should be provided?" This question places evaluation at the heart of the educational process.

Administrators should work with teachers in establishing the criteria they will use to document that their literacy program is working. Such collaborative projects will result in the development of more appropriate criteria, consideration of alternate evaluation techniques, and growth and learning on the part of each of the participants involved.

The functions of all evaluation are growth and learning. Testing programs that label schools, administrators, and children as being successes or failures violate what we know about how people learn. Research shows us that failure and retention only breed failure and retention. This is true for school staffs as well as for children.

Given the problems in standardized testing, responsible educators no longer can assume that tests are valid and programs invalid. If the program implemented reflects what we know about supportive environments for language learning, educators might begin by assuming that their program is valid and the test invalid. Given this new assumption, the task becomes one of finding measures that support what is known. Cambourne and Turbill (1987) have identified a set of seven characteristics for judging supportive language environments in classrooms and are in the process of identifying a battery of instruments teachers might use in assessing the quality of their current instructional programs.

Similarly, pupils need to be helped to ask themselves, "What have I learned?" and "If I were to study this topic again, what would I do differently?" Toward this end, many teachers now use Learning Logs in which children daily record what they learned. In one school, each child is given a three ring notebook. Each year the teacher, parents, and child select three pieces of writing for inclusion in this permanent record. At the end of elementary school, the child and his or her family receive the notebook as a graduation present and as a record of the growth that has occurred. Just as good instances of instruction are generative, good programs of evaluation are not mired in the present, but set directions for how to proceed in the future.

Administrators need to assess not only how they are doing currently, but what else they might do to support teachers in their personal professional development and curriculum development. Similarly, board members need to assess their own functioning in terms of providing support for improving instruction, rather than envisioning themselves as public gatekeepers of standards. Everyone involved in policy decisions in education must take personal responsibility for what they know as well as what they don't know. To insist that educators return to the way board members were taught, often cloaked as a return to the basics, would be equivalent to insisting that doctors abandon modern medicine and return to bloodletting.

Good evaluation provides opportunities for all participants in the educational enterprise to reflect upon where they are and where they wish to go. In this way, the focus of evaluation is upon self evaluation and the result is growth and learning.

In short, evaluation is everybody's business. It is learning to use ourselves and others as instruments for our own growth that separates good evaluation programs from those only pretending to be supportive of schools and learning.

Conclusion

In the final analysis, educational institutions are arrangements of people. As social policy, educational policies are not innocent. Current practices and policies in literacy and early childhood education perpetuate certain social arrangements while they make other options invisible.

To do nothing is to maintain the status quo. Given what we currently know, the status quo is a disadvantage to certain children and an advantage to others. To do nothing, then, is to do something.

To make educational change is to change the existing set of social arrangements. We now know how to empower children who previously have failed in educational settings. Given this knowledge base and the principles of a democratic society, it is time to develop policies that foster change and continued learning on the part of all participants.

The literacy policies we recommend for early childhood education are rooted in what is currently known. Because it is only by testing what we currently know that the profession can grow, these policies call for parents, children, and all educators to become a collaborative profession of language learners. We believe that the continued development of a practical theory of literacy learning rests upon this learning cycle of action, reflection, and change. Our hope is that these policy recommendations empower teachers and others concerned with quality literacy programs in their communities to take needed action.

References

Bean, W., and Bouffler, C. *Spell by writing.* Portsmouth, NH: Heinemann, 1987.

Cambourne, B., and Turbill, J. *Coping with chaos.* Portsmouth, NH: Heinemann, 1987.

Hall, N. *The emergence of literacy.* Portsmouth, NH: Heinemann, 1987.

Halliday, M.A.K. Meaning and the construction of reality in early childhood. In H.L. Pick, Jr., and E. Saltzman (Eds.), *Models of perceiving and processing information.* Hillsdale, NJ: Erlbaum, 1978.

Harste, J.C., Short, K.G., and Burke, C.L. *Creating classrooms for authors: The reading-writing connection.* Portsmouth, NH: Heinemann, 1988.

Harste, J.C., Woodward, V.A., and Burke, C.L. *Language stories and literacy lessons.* Portsmouth, NH: Heinemann, 1984.

Heath, S.B. *Ways with words: Language, life, and work in communities and classrooms.* Cambridge, England: Cambridge University Press, 1983.

International Reading Association. *A policy statement concerning literacy development and prefirst grade* (mimeographed). Newark, DE: Early Literacy Committee, International Reading Association, 1986.

National Association for the Education of Young Children. Position statement on developmentally appropriate practice in programs for four and five year olds. *Young Children,* 1985, *86,* 20-29.

Siegel, M. *Reading as signification.* Unpublished doctoral dissertation, Indiana University, 1983.

Taylor, D. *Family literacy.* Portsmouth, NH: Heinemann, 1983.

Literacy Development and Prefirst Grade

A Joint Statement of Concerns about Present Practices in Prefirst Grade Reading Instruction and Recommendations for Improvement

- Association for Childhood Education International
- Association for Supervision and Curriculum Development
- International Reading Association
- National Association for the Education of Young Children
- National Association of Elementary School Principals
- National Council of Teachers of English

Prepared by the Early Childhood and Literacy Development Committee of the International Reading Association.

Literacy learning begins in infancy. Children have many experiences with oral and written language before they come to school.

- Children have had many experiences from which they build ideas about the functions and uses of oral and written language.
- Children have a command of language and of processes for learning and using language.
- Many children can differentiate between drawing and writing.
- Many children are reading environmental print, such as road signs, grocery labels, and fast food signs.
- Many children associate books with reading.
- Children's knowledge about language and communication is influenced by their social and cultural backgrounds.
- Many children expect that reading and writing will be sense-making activities.

Basic premises of a sound prefirst grade reading program

- Reading and writing at school should permit children to build upon their already existing knowledge of oral and written language.
- Learning should take place in a supportive environment where children can build a positive attitude toward themselves and toward language and literacy.
- For optimal learning, teachers should involve children actively in many meaningful, functional language experiences, including *speaking, listening, writing* and *reading.*
- Teachers of young children should be prepared in ways that acknowledge differences in language and cultural backgrounds, and should emphasize reading as an integral part of the language arts as well as of the total curriculum.

Concerns

- Many prefirst grade children are subjected to rigid, formal prereading programs with inappropriate expectations and experiences for their levels of development.
- Little attention is given to individual development or individual learning styles.
- The pressures of accelerated programs do not allow children to be risk takers as they experiment with written language.
- Too much attention is focused upon isolated skill development and abstract parts of the reading process, rather than on the integration of talking, writing and listening with reading.
- Too little attention is placed on reading for pleasure; therefore, children do not associate reading with enjoyment.
- Decisions related to reading programs are often based on political and economic considerations rather than on knowledge of how young children learn.
- The pressure to achieve high scores on tests inappropriate for the kindergarten child has led to undesirable changes in the content of programs. Activities that deny curiosity, critical thinking and creative expression are all too frequent, and can foster negative attitudes toward language communication.
- As a result of declining enrollment and reduction in staff, individuals with little or no knowledge of early childhood education are sometimes assigned to teach young children. Such teachers often select inappropriate methods.
- Teachers who are conducting prefirst grade programs without depending on commercial readers and workbooks sometimes fail to articulate for parents and other members of the public what they are doing and why.

Recommendations

1. Build instruction on what the child already knows about oral language, reading and writing. Focus on meaningful experiences and meaningful language rather than on isolated skill development.
2. Respect the language the child brings to school, and use it as a base for language and literacy activities.
3. Ensure feelings of success for all children, helping them to see themselves as people who enjoy exploring both oral and written language.
4. Provide reading experiences as an integrated part of the communication process, which includes speaking, listening and writing, as well as art, math and music.
5. Encourage children's first attempts at writing, without concern for the proper formation of letters or correct conventional spelling.
6. Encourage risk taking in first attempts at reading and writing, and accept what appear to be errors as part of children's natural growth and development.
7. Use reading materials that are familiar or predictable, such as well known stories, as they provide children with a sense of control and confidence in their ability to learn.
8. Present a model for children to emulate. In the classroom, teachers should use language appropriately, listen and respond to children's talk, and engage in their own reading and writing.
9. Take time regularly to read to children from a wide variety of poetry, fiction and nonfiction.
10. Provide time regularly for children's independent reading and writing.
11. Foster children's affective and cognitive development by providing them with opportunities to communicate what they know, think and feel.
12. Use developmentally and culturally appropriate procedures for evaluation, ones that are based on the objectives of the program and that consider each child's total development.
13. Make parents aware of the reasons for a broader language program at school and provide them with ideas for activities to carry out at home.
14. Alert parents to the limitations of formal assessments and standardized tests of prefirst graders' reading and writing skills.
15. Encourage children to be active participants in the learning process rather than passive recipients, by using activities that allow for experimentation with talking, listening, writing and reading.